# Kid Power, Inequalities and Intergenerational Relations

# Kid Power, Inequalities and Intergenerational Relations

Clara Rübner Jørgensen
Michael Wyness

A

ANTHEM PRESS

Anthem Press
An imprint of Wimbledon Publishing Company
*www.anthempress.com*

This edition first published in UK and USA 2023
by ANTHEM PRESS
75–76 Blackfriars Road, London SE1 8HA, UK
or PO Box 9779, London SW19 7ZG, UK
and
244 Madison Ave #116, New York, NY 10016, USA

First published in the UK and USA by Anthem Press in 2021

*British Library Cataloguing-in-Publication Data*
A catalogue record for this book is available from the British Library.

Library of Congress Control Number: 2023936192

ISBN-13: 978-1-8399-8970-4 (Pbk)
ISBN-10: 1-83998-970-X (Pbk)

Cover image: Di PiXXart/Shutterstock.com

This title is also available as an e-book.

For the three generations in our lives: our children,
our parents, Beth and Erez

# CONTENTS

# ACKNOWLEDGEMENTS

We want to acknowledge the help and guidance from Megan Greiving and Jayashree at Anthem Press and the copy editor of the book. We also thank Loraine Blaxter, Kaare Rübner Jørgensen and the anonymous reviewers for their constructive commentary on earlier drafts. Much of this book was written under 'one-dimensional power conditions' – Covid-19 and the various lockdowns formed the backdrop to our analysis. We write about this in our conclusion, but we would like to thank our respective families during this period for their love, support and diversion: Beth, Alec and Henry for Wyness, and Erez, Naomi and Maya for Jørgensen.

# INTRODUCTION

The past 30 years have seen significant changes in the ways children are conceptualised within research, policy and practice. The UN Convention on the Rights of the Child (CRC) (UNICEF 1989) established children as individual holders of rights to survival and development, protection and participation. Particularly, participation rights have become associated with children's rights to have a voice and power over decisions of relevance to them (Montgomery, 2010). An increasing number of countries have incorporated children's rights into policies and practice, some by integrating children's participation rights into national constitutions, others by building them into child-specific legislations (European Commission, 2015), for example, education or welfare services (Heimer et al., 2018; Križ and Skivenes, 2017). Schools and other childhood settings and organisations often make reference to the rights of children to have a say over matters of importance to them, although this is interpreted across countries in significantly different ways. Within research, it is also generally acknowledged that children's experiences need to be included and studied in their own right (Christensen and James, 2008a; Kellett et al., 2004; O'Kane, 2008; Prout, 2005; Wyness, 2015) and that children must be considered as research subjects rather than as objects of research (Horgan, 2017; Kellett, 2005).

There is now a well-established body of literature on children's rights and agency (James, 2011; Oswell, 2013; Smith, 2007) which incorporates the idea that children have global entitlements and makes research-based assumptions about children's capacities and contributions. Within this literature, the rights of children to have a voice, exercise agency and participate in matters of importance to them is often associated, and at times conflated, with the idea that children have more power. Common sense and public commentary on childhood also tends to assume that children's power derives from the increase in legal and political arrangements that give children an opportunity to make a difference in their own lives and in the lives of those around them. This linkage between rights, agency, participation and power presents the basis for one model of what we in this book refer to as *kid power*.

The concept of 'power' is widely acknowledged as the capacity of an actor to get other actors to do something which they would not otherwise have done (Dahl, 1968; Weber, 1978). In the context of childhood, this capacity is mostly attributed to adults who, given their power, are able to control and shape the actions of children. However, kid power has also increasingly become a feature of a Northern conception of childhood where children's right to participate, combined with the idea that they have 'agency', has led to a multitude of claims with regards to their increased level of power. This is often associated with a decreased level of adult power, assuming a zero-sum conflictual notion of power and a dichotomous division between children and adults. For example, among those who advocate for children's participation in research, there is a tendency to focus on how unequal adult–child power relations shape the research encounter and how adults may 'hand over' power to children in the research process (Holland et al., 2010). Typologies of children's participation in research, such as Hart's (1997) adaptation of Arnstein's (1969) 'ladder of citizen participation', similarly tend to represent a simplified view of child versus adult power which marginalises relationships between them and assumes a zero-sum conception of power in adult–child interactions (Birch et al., 2017; Hinton, 2008).

Zero-sum and binary conceptions of power also seem to prevail in arguments against the promotion of children's rights and participation. For example, Howe and Covell (2005) discuss an election being organised by UNICEF Canada for school children in celebration of the tenth anniversary of the CRC, where the children were asked to debate and vote on the importance of children's rights in different areas of their lives. This initiative drew strong opposition from a number of organisations, who argued, among other things, that teaching children about their rights would undermine family and parental authority. However, as commented by Howe and Covell (2005: 4),

> the election was remarkable in the irony of the results. Many had expected that the students would become overly demanding and defiant and would give priority to their own personal freedoms. Contrary to these expectations, however, the results, announced by UNICEF, showed that the right held to be most important to children and youth was the right to grow up in a family.

Consumption is another example of an area where children's increasing 'power' over their parents has been interpreted in a predominantly zero-sum manner. Here the negative and derogatory concept of 'pester power' has been used to describe children's 'attempts to exert influence over parental purchases in a repetitive and sometimes confrontational way' (Nicholls and

Cullen, 2004: 77). Although there are also more positive ways of looking at child–parent purchase relations (Lawlor and Prothero, 2011), these examples illustrate a common perception of kid power as binary and conflictual, assuming that children and adults have fundamentally different agendas and that intergenerational encounters are shaped by negotiations or struggles over whose agenda should prevail.

In this book we wish to propose a different, wider and less binary framework for understanding kid power. Our framework is based on three main propositions. The first proposition is that kid power should be understood not only as zero-sum, with children gaining power at the expense of adults, but also as positive-sum (Haugaard, 2017), with children and adults jointly emerging as potentially more powerful. This interpretation involves a more consensual understanding of power in intergenerational relations, a fuller acknowledgement of interdependency and commonalities between adults and children (Percy-Smith, 2010) and a broader focus on dialogue and collaboration as 'arenas' for power, alongside potential conflicts.

The second proposition is that differences of power are not only intergenerational but also fundamentally intragenerational. To understand kid power, we thus need to incorporate and analyse the diverse responses of different kinds of adults (parents, teachers, policymakers, etc.) to children's actions and pay close attention to power inequalities between children within and across countries. Shier (2019) has discussed the diverse responses of adults to 'protagonismo' – children's 'autonomous' participation and organisation:

> On the one hand, adult supporters may be involved in facilitating, building capacity, mobilizing, and resourcing actions that children themselves organize and direct. On the other hand, adults also have power to control access to spaces and resources and can use this to manage and constrain children's mobilization and thus limit their autonomous actions' [...] sometimes adults in authority approve and praise it [protagonismo], recognizing it as a positive expression of active citizenship by students and reporting positive outcomes. On many occasions, however, for example, when students organize marches, protests, sit-ins, and other kinds of political actions, it is seen as cause for concern, a challenge to legitimate adult authority, and disruption of established power relations (Shier, 2019: 5).

This description bears many resemblances to the way different groups of adults have responded to other examples of children's activism, for example, the recent climate school strikes (Fridays for the Future) organised by children and young people across the world to protest against climate inaction. It illustrates the observation made by Taft (2015: 460) that 'in the context of children and adults' unequal social and political power, pursuing the ideals of collaboration, dialogue, and partnership is a highly complex and difficult endeavor'. Children may participate in a multitude of activities without adult help, support or awareness of their activities (Shier, 2019). However, as we will discuss throughout the book, they also often rely on adults to help them instigate and implement changes, or work with them to manage challenging situations. This further supports our first proposition – the need to examine kid power from a positive-sum perspective. It also emphasises the importance of exploring the position of different groups of children as mediators between their families and the surrounding society.

Finally, the third proposition presented in the book is that kid power is multidimensional and needs to be analysed as such. Discussions about the presumed increased levels of kid power, both among those who frame it as a 'positive' and those who see it as more 'negative', tend to predominantly focus on children participating in or making decisions, and exercising their power by 'having a voice'. Drawing on theories of power, this element, however, only represents one dimension or 'face' of power (Bachrach and Baratz, 1962; Lukes, 2005) and may obscure more covert dimensions of power. The emphasis on discursive manifestations of power furthermore limits understandings of other more material and practical aspects of kid power. A focus on overt decision-making and voice may thus both give the wrong impression about the 'real' level of kid power and look for it in the 'wrong' places. For example, in the United Kingdom, a common area for exploring children's power in schools has been their involvement in school councils. However, school councils are not always effective as a forum for children making decisions about their school, as the space they provide is highly structured by existing power relationships between children and their teachers (Percy-Smith, 2010). To understand the different dimensions of children's power, it is thus necessary to look beyond such structured opportunities for participation and explore other less obvious areas where children may have a greater chance of influencing the actions of others – or, alternatively, to look for spaces where children exercise their power with adults.

This book discusses these three propositions through an analysis of kid power within different areas of children's lives. The book draws on two key theoretical approaches to power: Lukes's (2005) radical view of power and Foucault's (1980, 1982, 1991) analyses of mechanisms of power and knowledges of truth. Lukes emphasises the importance of looking beyond patterns of decision-making and agenda-setting in areas of conflict and draws on Foucault to analyse the mechanisms that make actors avoid conflict in the first place. Both Lukes and Foucault furthermore propose the idea that the social knowledge of actors reproduces social structures and relations of domination (Haugaard, 2012). This is, as we will see, highly relevant in relation to kid power. Dominant narratives on the capacities of children and responsibilities of adults form a particular knowledge of truth and represent an important mechanism of power which potentially reproduces child–adult relations of domination. However, as both Lukes and Foucault also recognize, people always resist, negotiate and challenge power relations, and examples of this will become evident in our empirical chapters.

With a few exceptions (Devine, 2002, 2003; Gallagher, 2008a), the literature on children's rights, agency and participation seldom includes explicit reference to power theories and thus pays relatively little attention to the complexities of what power is and how it operates in generational terms (Hill et al., 2004). Children also play a relatively minor role within theories of power, where most analysis has centred on power differences between different groups of adults (e.g. men and women), communities or citizens in relation to the state. However, an analysis of power through the lens of childhood enables important and additional insights to emerge, for example, around the complexities of shifting and culturally diverse notions of protection and responsibility, and their interrelation with children's capacity to act and change the actions of others.

In her discussion of gender and power, Davis (1991) has outlined two main options for analysis: one which assumes that social relations can best be understood through gender and thus takes gender as its starting point in its attempt to generate a feminist theory of gender and power, and another which considers power as the key concept to understand social experience and raises a feminist critique of existing power theories. While Davis chooses the second option, our analysis offers a combination of the two in generational terms. Our starting point is a critical examination of the diverse ways in which children participate in activities of relevance to their lives, interact with the adults around them and can be understood to exert power in ways described in the theoretical framework adopted for our analysis. However, in the process of identifying patterns and processes of power, we also touch upon a number of areas in which an explicit focus on childhood may offer new and additional insights to power theories. For example, the dominant idea that children are vulnerable brings to the fore some important questions about how much power children can and should have in a world where they are also, at least to some extent, in need of protection. In many contexts, adult authority over children is considered legitimate, and this may in itself be interpreted as an important instrument of power. However, the particular relation between power, protection and authority may play out differently in different time periods and world regions (Wells, 2009). Different actors may, furthermore, have varying views on the extent and scope of adults' legitimate power over children, supporting our assertion that kid power needs to be explored intergenerationally, intragenerationally and multidimensionally.

Analysing power in this way points to the fact that the level of power of an individual or a group is not static but subject to constant negotiation. This is particularly evident among children, as their capacity for exercising power inevitably changes with age. Most people would agree that children should be given gradually more power as they grow older. However, societies differ significantly in their conceptions of appropriate ages and stages for different activities, for example, when children should begin to have responsibilities in their home, when they can responsibly be left alone at home and when they can be made legally responsible for criminal actions. These are debated locally and internationally and negotiated with different effects on the levels of power of children within given age groups, societies and communities.

In this book, we adopt the common acceptance of childhood as a category covering children from birth to 18 – often referred to as the 'straight 18' position (Rosen, 2007). We recognize that this broad definition includes a wide variety of children with different capabilities, allowances and responsibilities, and that this makes it difficult to discuss kid power in general terms. The terminology used to describe children from 0 to 18 varies and is significantly context-dependent. It includes terms such as 'children', 'young people', '(pre-)adolescents', 'teenagers', 'students', 'pupils' and 'kids', which have varying relevance within, for example, school, family or legal contexts. Throughout the book, we have as far as possible attempted to be specific about the particular age groups described and use the terms adopted by the authors we refer to or simply the general term 'children'. However, in the framing of our main thesis, we have chosen to use the word 'kid' and the term 'kid power' to signify a more informal and inclusive approach to children of all ages and contexts.

Age is only one line across which power operates. As increasingly acknowledged by childhood researchers, attention also needs to be paid to other characteristics, such as gender, ethnicity and social class and how they intersect in children's lives across different societies in the Global North and South[1] (Cook et al., 2018; Hanson et al., 2018; Spyrou et al., 2018). Much of the literature on children's lives, particularly among UK sociologists, centres

---

[1] The Global North and Global South are geopolitical categories which are increasingly used as less value-laden terms to describe groups of countries formerly classified as 'the first' and 'third world' or as 'developed' vs 'developing', and located geographically either in the northern or southern hemispheres. The distinction between the two, however, is not completely straightforward, as it involves various interpretations of income, uneven economic development and the impact of globalization and colonization (Clarke, 2018).

on class as a main differentiating factor, and consequently class forms a key dimension in our analysis of kid power. However, class as a concept does not have equal relevance in all countries. It combines a variety of factors, including wealth, social and cultural capital, and these may not always translate neatly across societies or be transferable, for example, in the case of migration. Class and wealth, furthermore, intersect in important ways with other characteristics, such as race/ethnicity and gender to consolidate or limit power. We have attempted to include considerations of such intersections in our analysis to illustrate diversity within child populations in relation to power. However, the book is also written in a time where standard sociological categories, such as gender, are increasingly contested and negotiated. It is beyond the scope of the book to fully address such complexities, but we acknowledge the importance of considering a range of constellations in relation to power and hope that the book will invite further discussion and debate around some of these.

By discussing children's lives in different contexts and regions of the world, the book draws attention to some of the many dimensions of power in children's lives and attempts to problematize common conceptions of kid power. Traditionally, childhood studies as a discipline has predominantly focused on children in the Global North. Children's rights and relationships with adults are also often seen within the context of Northern childhoods. Our analysis is not able to include a detailed account of all possible complexities of kid power as it plays out across the world. Some chapters will have an overweight of literature from the United Kingdom, where we are both based, and Europe in general. However, we have tried wherever possible to also include insights and literature from the Global South and hope that we, through this, begin to frame a more inclusive conceptualisation of kid power.

## Why This Book?

When discussing this book with her then 9-year-old daughter, Jørgensen was told, 'No child is ever going to read it. Can we stop talking about that boring book?' While this view (hopefully) would not be shared by all children, it raises two important questions: first, whether a book on kid power, which takes power theory as its starting point, is in itself an adult-centric project with little relevance to children and thus contradicts the idea that research should be done *with* children rather than *on* children, and second, related to this, whether childhood studies should pay particular attention to power, or rather focus on children's own concepts and interests.

The many notions and understandings of power put forward in social theory not only present an analytical problem but may also challenge the usefulness of the concept in general. As Lukes (2005: 12) puts it, in the face of unending disagreements about how to define it and study it, do we need the concept of power at all and, if we do, what [do] we need it for – what role [does] it play[s] in our lives?

He goes on to answer this question himself by saying,

I argue that these disagreements matter because how much power you see in the social world and where you locate it depends on how you conceive of it, and these disagreements are in part moral and political, and inescapably so.

With this book we similarly argue that it is important to analyse and discuss power in the context of childhood. First of all, a critical analysis of power may help challenge and filter out some of the many claims about kid power made without much theoretical or indeed empirical basis. Drawing on power theory to analyse empirical studies of children's lives helps us challenge dominant normative perspectives of child and adult power. In his critique of normative analyses of power, Dowding (2012: 126) notes that he is opposed to 'those who want to moralize concepts so that actions they consider justified are only described in a language with positive normative connotations'. Similarly, we believe that in the context of childhood, power will benefit from being discussed more 'non-normatively', avoiding easy conclusions about its either positive or negative effects.

Second, drawing on insights from theoretical approaches to power enables a more complex understanding of power relations between children and adults, which, as we have argued for above, takes into account not only conflicting agendas but also intergenerational relations, dialogues and collaboration. The explicit focus on theories of power furthermore helps illustrate some of the many complexities and levels upon which power may operate in the context of childhood. While children are generally considered less powerful than the adults around them, children and adults are complex categories whose power in relation to one another requires careful scrutinisation. It is thus entirely possible that *some* children may be more powerful than *some* adults, as, for example, in the relationship between a child in a wealthy family who employs an adult servant. Children and their parents may in addition be relatively powerless in relation to larger institutions, such as welfare agencies. As commented by Shier (2019: 6), power is not a 'monolithic force that is wielded in top-down hierarchies, it can be conceived as something much more fluid that is enacted within networks of people through their everyday actions'. The argument in this book is that such networks need to be more thoroughly analysed in their context, taking into consideration both inter- and intragenerational relations.

This leads to our third reason for critically and theoretically analysing kid power: approaching intragenerational relations between different groups and individual children through the lens of power enables a more in-depth analysis of the role of power in children's diverse lives and the way in which it plays out in different contexts, for example, in families, communities, on social media and in research. In her discussion of children's agency, Valentine (2011: 356) has argued that 'critical perspectives on agency seem necessary to ensure that privileged children are not recognised as agents and therefore entitled to participate, to the exclusion of less privileged children'. Similarly, in the context of power, we argue that a critical perspective on kid power is necessary to avoid drawing imprecise conclusions about children's levels of power based on the capacity of particular groups of children to impact the actions of others.

This book provides a framework for understanding and discussing kid power as an intergenerational, intragenerational and multidimensional concept. It adopts a critical theoretical approach to children's varied levels of participation, mediation and involvement in their families, communities, online and in research. Through this, the book aims to provide a nuanced view of children's levels of power and a critical examination of the power dynamics between children, and between children and adults in different contexts and areas of the world.

## Contents of the Book

The book is divided into two parts. Section 1 (Chapters 1–4) outlines the background for our developing framework of kid power. Chapter 1 discusses different theories of power, with a particular focus on Lukes's and Foucault's interpretations of power. The chapter outlines the three dimensions of power (Lukes, 2005) and relevant mechanisms for exercising them (Foucault, 1991). It furthermore discusses the two dominant views of power as zero-sum or positive-sum, and considers generational power as an area of particular importance to our analysis of kid power. In this chapter, we also briefly outline two power-related concepts – agency and empowerment – which both play a key role in the way power is conceptualised within childhood studies.

The next three chapters provide a discussion of what we see as existing and dominant ways of framing kid power, expressed through a focus on children's global rights, child-centredness and the notion of 'lost' adult power. Chapter 2 discusses children's rights in a global perspective, focusing particularly on children's participation rights and the idea that these lead to increased kid power. We look at different definitions of participation and argue that, although major changes have happened to the status of children as a result of the CRC, it remains questionable whether these changes can be interpreted as an increase in kid power. We argue that the CRC puts pressure on adults and institutions to support children and regulate their participation. On the one hand, this strengthens their capacities to shape children's lives. On the other, these responsibilities can also be understood as obligations, which have variable effects on institutions in different regions of the world.

Chapter 3 explores the concept of child-centredness as a pedagogical and educational approach and asks whether child-centredness can be seen to equate with more power for children. We trace some of the history of the concept and give examples of how it is used within education. It is clear that child-centredness presents a different model from more teacher-oriented classroom practices and, compared to these, gives children more of a say in their daily activities. However, we argue that child-centred approaches present teachers with new ways of regulating children from a distance, and perhaps also favour certain types of students. There is thus little sense that child-centredness on its own signifies increased kid power for the broad population of children.

Chapter 4 challenges the notion of zero-sum power in child–adult relationships. The starting point of this chapter is Postman's (1982) classic thesis on the disappearance of adulthood, which we unpick and challenge with the use of material on children's consumption and online participation. We go on to discuss the potential loss of parent power as the political and legal contexts have shifted from bipartite relationships between the state and the family towards tripartite relations where children themselves play a third party. The changed role of the state in relation to children and families illustrates the importance of acknowledging power dynamics between various adult actors and the variable effects on different classes of children and their families. This chapter also includes a section on children's own narratives around adult power, showing that children may challenge their parents for failing to take responsibility or action, but seldom challenge their power per se.

Section 2 of the book moves away from a zero-sum conception of power and presents an alternative framework for understanding kid power, which critically analyses its intra- and intergenerational aspects, as well as its multidimensional character. Whereas the first section discussed dominant conceptions of children and adults as primarily opposing categories, this section begins to address areas where children play a more mediating role with parents. In addition, it elaborates on some of the differentiating and intersecting characteristics which shape children's different levels of power vis-à-vis their peers. The section discusses four areas of children's lives, using the theoretical power framework set out in Chapter 1, to identify intra- and intergenerational complexities in relation to the various dimensions and mechanisms of power. Each chapter provides examples of children's engagement and participation in the lives around them and shows the potential of many different power scenarios depending on the particular context, the groups of children and adults involved and the particular setting of their interactions. The four chapters in the second section offer a discussion of different sites or contexts within which we can analyse intergenerational power relations, moving from the predominantly private realm of the family to the more ambivalent public/private domain of the Internet and ending in the public sphere, represented by children's community and research involvement.

Chapter 5 focuses on generational power within the context of family relations. In this chapter we break down the binary generational power relationship and introduce the idea of the bi-nuclear family. We argue that the latter emerges conceptually from the former. Our discussion focuses on children's material and practical participation within their families, with a specific focus on children's lives in the contexts of divorce, migration and child-headed households. The chapter challenges the 'bi-nuclear family' through the concept of *mediation* and describes how children mediate between different households (in the case of divorce), between their parents and the surrounding society (in the case of migration) and between their own household and relevant adults (in the case of child-headed households). By analysing the varied ways in which children contribute in a material and practical sense towards the integrity of their households, we argue that mediation may be seen as a form of intergenerational power that refines the zero-sum conception of power relations. Mediation permits children to navigate their lifeworlds *with* their parents or other relevant adults, rather than against them.

Chapter 6 discusses the increasing relevance of the Internet and social media in children's lives through the lens of kid power, and also uses the term 'mediation' to describe the way children and adults interact in relation to digital media. We examine the role of the Internet and social media for children's peer relations, political and community engagement and consumption. Through this, we outline some of the contradictions between children, on the one hand, being perceived as 'digital natives' and, on the other, as vulnerable in need of protection through increasing safeguarding measures. These contradictions are analysed in the context of power, arguing that the relationship between children's Internet and social media use and their power is highly diverse, multilayered and contextual, and that an intergenerational approach offers more promise than a zero-sum equivalent.

Chapter 7 analyses and explores the link between children's participation in their community and power. The chapter discusses three examples of children's active community involvement: school councils in the United Kingdom, the recent global climate strikes (Fridays for the Future) and working children's organisations in Latin America, Africa and Asia. We use these examples to illustrate and critically discuss different dimensions of power, and the many levels upon which power may operate within the context of children's community action. Within all three examples, children's potentially diverse experiences are analysed alongside different intergenerational dynamics, arguing for increased attention not only to power differentials between children and adults and between children themselves but also to potential convergence of interests and cross-generational alliances.

Chapter 8 focuses on children's participation in research, an area where three key discourses of power are prevalent. One is the primacy of adult/child power differences in research and the consequent lack of attention to power differences between children. The other is an understanding of power 'handed over' to children by adults within the field of childhood studies, which contradicts more theoretical understandings of power as relational and dynamic. Finally, children's involvement in research is often described as empowering for the children, emphasising an individual and process-oriented focus, rather than a more outcome-based and collective transformation. Drawing on power theories, we critically analyse these three discourses and argue for a more multidimensional, intragenerational and intergenerational understanding of children's involvement in research.

Through discussion of these four areas, we develop a model of kid power which allows for a more positive-sum intergenerational analysis of power than the one currently dominating discussions and debates. Rather than viewing kid power as a means of separating children from adults by focusing on children's rights as autonomous individuals, we demonstrate that power and agency are embedded in 'intricate family relations' and emerging connections made within peer cultures as children grow up (Bjerke 2011: 97).

This position is summed up in the conclusion, where we join together the analysis made in the main chapters around three main themes: firstly, mediation and representation; secondly, inequalities and material challenges to adult power; and thirdly, intergenerational dialogue. Within these three themes we draw links between the different chapters of the book to argue for a relational approach, which acknowledges kid power as embedded in both intergenerational and intragenerational relations, and as a potentially positive-sum force in the relationships between children and adults, alongside its more common conflictual interpretations.

While we were writing this book in 2020, large parts of the world were overtaken by the Covid-19 pandemic. At the time of writing, the full implications of the pandemic were not yet known, but it was clear that the pandemic was having a huge impact on children and adults alike, with many of the relationships and settings described in the book significantly affected. Having reflected on the best way to address this, the 2021 publication of the book included a Covid-19 postscript, which acknowledged the significance of these changes and some of their potential implications for kid power. This 2023 version of the book has retained the post-script, but included a few updates to reflect the current situation. The remainder of the book is presented in its original version.

# Section 1

# THE 'PROBLEM' OF KID POWER

# Chapter 1

# POWER AND CHILDREN

We speak and write about power, in innumerable situations, and we usually know, or think we know, perfectly well what we mean. In daily life and in scholarly works, we discuss its location and its extent, who has more and who has less, how to gain, resist, seize, harness, secure, tame, share, spread, distribute, equalize or maximize it, how to render it more effective and how to limit or avoid its effects. And yet, among those who have reflected on the matter there is no agreement about how to define it, how to conceive it, how to study it and, if it can be measured, how to measure it. There are endless debates about such questions, which show no sign of imminent resolution, and there is not even agreement about whether all this disagreement matters (Lukes, 2005: 61).

Acknowledging the diversity of power theories and concepts, Haugaard (2002: 61) has argued that 'we should not look for a single theory of power, but rather construct meso-level theories which we use as conceptual tools for specific tasks'. Adopting this argument, the purpose of this chapter is not to provide a comprehensive theoretical account of power or a summary of the many positions and debates in the field. Rather, it is an attempt to construct a theoretical framework for the specific task of analysing kid power as a multidimensional, intragenerational and intergenerational phenomenon. However, the way in which we think of power, and the particular theoretical framework we chose, is also to some extent a political decision, which may be controversial and have significant consequences (Lukes, 2005). The framework we have chosen to develop our analysis of kid power is therefore not neutral or objective, nor is it the only one which could possibly have been used for the task. Dowding (2012) has argued that discussions of power should be kept as non-normative as possible and not automatically assume either positive or negative elements. Throughout the book, we try as far as possible to draw on empirical material to discuss power as a concept rooted in children's realities, rather than presupposed ideas about its inherently positive or negative implications. In this chapter, we set out the theoretical basis for this endeavour.

The chapter begins with a discussion of the question of what power is. For this section, we draw on Lukes's now classic description of the three dimensions of power and some of his less referenced discussions of the distinction between 'power over' and 'power to'. *Power over* is most often equated with domination and *power to* with emancipation and empowerment, and where the former tends to centre on zero-sum notions of power, the latter is more open to the consensual potential of power. However, with Haugaard (2012) we explore the possibility that all dimensions of power may have both conflictual and consensual elements. Second, we discuss instruments or mechanisms of power, using Foucault's notions of knowledge and regimes of 'truth', which emphasise the ways in which power permeates all elements of daily interactions and leads to the self-governing of individuals (Foucault 1982; 1991). Following on from this, we extend the theory by providing an overview of current approaches to generational power. We argue that power is rarely used as a concept to describe everyday child–adult relations and that researchers have often drawn on class analysis and feminism, rather than age, to construct a meta-theoretical framework around generation. Finally, we discuss two concepts, both closely related to power and extensively applied in the literature on childhood—namely, agency and empowerment. We argue for the importance of not conflating them with power when writing about children's lives and engagement with the world around them.

## What Is 'Power'? The Three-Dimensional View

At its most fundamental level, power has commonly been described as the capacity of an actor to get other actors to do something which they would otherwise not have done (Dahl, 1957). However, as evidenced by the extensive literature and debates about power, this formula leaves open many questions as to how power is exercised, how compliance by those subjected to it is secured, whether it always is against the interests of those that have to comply and whether an exercise of power always involves conflict. These questions are addressed in Lukes's widely cited book *Power: A Radical View* (Lukes, 2005), in which he outlines three dimensions of power.

The first dimension is exemplified by what are often called 'pluralist models of power'. Such models see power as an intentional, observable act that can be measured by its exercise, namely *who* prevails in decision-making situations (Lukes, 2005). Decision-making power may be 'multi-pyramidical' – that is, people may have power in different contexts and domains, and relatively powerless groups may exercise resistance or seek to influence decision-making in particular areas (Dahl, 1968, 2005). In relation to children, such an approach acknowledges the importance of a 'spatial analysis' of children's different levels of involvement in decision-making within different areas of their lives (e.g. at home, in school and, in some cases, online) (Mannion, 2007). However, a one-dimensional or plural model of power does not enable analysis of the less visible ways in which systems may be biased against or in favour of certain groups (Lukes, 2005: 39). Pluralist models have thus been critiqued for being too narrow and ignoring what Bachrach and Baratz (1962; 1970) refer to as 'non-decision making' – 'the extent to which a person or a group – consciously or unconsciously creates or reinforces barriers to the public airing of policy conflicts, that person or group has the power' (Bachrach and Baratz, 1962: 949).

The second dimension of power considers who gets to go to a decision-making forum and who has the power to decide over the issues that are brought to the forum in the first place. This is of key importance in relation to kid power and, as we will see in Section 2 of the book, plays out in a number of ways in relation to children's participation in their families, communities and online interactions. The literature on children's participation in research has also highlighted other, more subtle ways of exclusion, which may be seen as an expression of the two-dimensional power of adults. Children have, for example, identified barriers to their participation and decision-making power in research, including that people speak too fast in meetings, that agendas are not sent out in advance, that the words used are too 'big', and that meetings are often scheduled straight after school when children are hungry and tired (Kellett, 2010; Kellett et al., 2010).

Bachrach and Baratz's two-dimensional interpretation of power begins to reveal the bias of systems. However, Lukes questions both the one-dimensional and the two-dimensional approaches for their focus on situations of 'observable conflict'. Instead, he argues that the main question in relation to power is how one secures consent and willing compliance and thus prevents conflict from arising in the first place. This question forms the basis for his notion of three-dimensional power – 'the power to prevent people, to whatever degree from having grievances by shaping their perceptions, cognition and preferences in such a way that they accept their role in the existing order of things' (Lukes, 2005: 11). Three-dimensional power is a necessary element of any analysis of power, although the way it is studied in practice carries some challenges, as it may involve inaction rather than action, be unconscious and furthermore be exercised by collectivities or institutions rather than individuals (p. 52). In this book we follow Lukes by attempting to unpack the different dimensions of kid power and analyse some of the ways 'the existing order of things' in relation to child–adult relations work to limit or shape child power. We also argue that common assumptions and dominant discourses around children as a group, separate from adults, have created an agenda of its own which seems to neglect the intragenerational power dynamics between children and constructs power predominantly as a zero-sum notion, assuming conflict rather than consensus. These discourses are discussed in further detail in Chapters 2–4.

Lukes discusses the distinction between conflictual and consensual notions of power through his analysis of 'interest', 'domination' and 'beneficent power'. He discusses these concepts in relation to two distinct understandings of power: 'power over' and 'power to'. The first is a common conception of power, which predominantly sees the power of one actor as an act against the interests of another. However, Lukes argues that 'there really is no reason for supposing that the powerful always threaten, rather than sometimes advance the interests of others' (p. 83). He also emphasises that 'you can be powerful by satisfying and advancing other's interests' (p. 12). *Power over* is thus a narrow interpretation of power, a sub-concept of the broader *power to*, which Lukes draws on Spinoza to describe as 'the power of things in nature, including persons, to exist and act' (Lukes, 2005: 73).

Haugaard (2012) similarly discusses two main approaches to power: the zero-sum approach, which implies that the gain of power of one actor automatically involves the loss of power of another, and the 'non-zero sum' or 'positive-sum', which does not involve one actor gaining at the expense of the other but may instead increase power for both (p. 35). *Power over* is often seen as a manifestation of the former approach and synonymous with domination, whereas *power to* is more commonly described as the latter approach and equivalent to empowerment (Pansardi, 2012). However, Haugaard argues that if power is conceived as positive-sum, in principle 'not all exercises of "power over" constitute domination' (Haugaard, 2012: 37). To illustrate this, he mentions the example of democratic elections, where generalized structures ensure the power of all and where no individual actor is a 'means to an end'. With regards to domination, Lukes (2005: 111–14) also notes that it is important not only to question how the powerful secure the compliance of those they dominate but also to consider the complexities around who might be dominated and on what basis. He suggests that the answer to this question is to consider domination as a situation where those subject to it are 'rendered less free'.

Lukes argues that being 'free' can be interpreted in a minimalist way, which considers people as free to the extent that no external force restricts or interferes in their life. However, another non-minimalist interpretation of being free includes also internal constraints – how 'adaptive preferences' are shaped and internalised (Lukes, 2005). The shaping and internalising of preferences is part of Lukes's three-dimensional power – 'the capacity to secure compliance to domination through the shaping of beliefs and desires, by imposing internal constraints under historically changing circumstances'

(Lukes, 2005: 144). He mentions critiques of this view of power for being condescending, pretending to know people's 'real interests' or treating them as 'cultural dopes' but briefly refutes these critiques by acknowledging that people will always resist and challenge power. Nevertheless, his theory leaves open some important questions about the mechanisms of power – how these beliefs and desires and adaptive preferences are shaped in the first place.

## Instruments and Mechanisms of Power

Lukes draws extensively on Foucault in his discussion of three-dimensional power. The similarities between their positions on power has been summarized by Haugaard as follows: 'The idea [is] that there is a direct mapping between the tacit social knowledge that actors use to reproduce social structure and the reproduction of relations of domination' (Haugaard 2012: 42). Power theorists generally agree that a certain number of options need to be available to the actor, who is subjected to influence from another actor, in order for their relation to be constituted by power. Foucault has thus argued that power is only exercised over 'free subjects' with a range of actions available to them and that power is the ability to govern these actions (Foucault, 1982). He contrasts earlier forms of sovereign power in the seventeenth and eighteenth centuries, which worked through prohibition and sanctions, with modern forms of disciplinary power, which 'inculcates the required action by making it the desired action within the inescapable framework of political rationalities and technologies of power' (Stewart, 2001: 19). Disciplinary power is less likely to be exercised in a top-down fashion by a central sovereign figure and does not form part of any public displays of power. It is therefore harder to observe (Foucault 1991). This form of power is related to the concept of 'governmentality', which describes the process by which human behaviour is directed, including the governing of the self. In his classic book *Discipline and Punish*, Foucault (1991) explores the nature of self-governance and power through his image of Bentham's panopticon. The panopticon is a physical structure inhabited solely by the teacher, the prison officer or factory supervisor who is in a position to constantly observe the activities of subordinates such as pupils, workers or prisoners without being seen by the latter. This generates uncertainty in the minds of those being surveilled: they can never know whether they are being observed at any one time and are therefore less likely to deviate or misbehave for fear of being observed doing so. Over time, this generates changes in behaviour among those being surveilled, forms of self-discipline which have the potential to bring them in line with the expectations of the teacher or jailer. The panopticon is thus a simple device that illustrates the hidden nature of power. However, individuals are also regulated, shaped and constructed in more complex ways and at a distance by institutions and organisations which induce in these individuals a capacity to make these changes themselves. Power in these terms thus becomes the regulation of behaviour and understanding through forms of governance that structure behaviour and mindsets, generating the conditions for individuals themselves to take on the responsibility for behavioural changes. This emphasises the importance of studying power at the level of people's everyday lives, what Foucault refers to as the 'microphysics of power', rather than just at the state level (1995: 26). Foucault (1995) also refers to power as 'capillary' – as ingrained forms of consciousness and practice leading to the self-governing of individuals.

For Foucault, power is essentially a strategy, which is exercised, rather than possessed. Power is thus not simply a matter of obligation or prohibition on those 'who do not have it':

> It invests them, is transmitted by them and through them; it exerts pressure on them, just as they themselves, in their struggle against it, resist the grip that it has on them. This means that these relations go right down into the depth of society. (Foucault, 1991: 27)

An important part of this process is the systems of knowledge and truth through which power operates. The ability to define what is considered 'truth' in a given time and place is closely linked to power but may also be resisted and changed over time. Power and knowledge are furthermore closely interlinked, as power produces knowledge, and knowledge both presupposes and constitutes power relations (Foucault, 1991: 27). In his essay 'The subject and power' (1982: 780), Foucault mentions a number of examples of recent opposition to existing power relations, for example, 'of men over women, of parents over children, of psychiatry over the mentally ill, of medicine over the population, of administration over the ways people live'. Without going into details of these particular relations, he outlines six commonalities for the struggles surrounding them: (1) they are transversal – not limited to one country; (2) they target power effects rather than the particular actors; (3) they look for the immediate, rather than the 'chief', enemy and they don't expect a solution in the near future; (4) they question the status of the individual; (5) they oppose the link between power, privilege and knowledge; and (6) they question 'who we are' and refuse scientific and administrative definitions of who one is (Foucault, 1982: 130).

The constitution of the 'new social studies of childhood' (Prout, 2005: 1) can usefully be understood in relation to these points. It challenges developmental models of childhood and children's age-specific capabilities as 'regimes of truth' and argues for a redistribution of power, mainly targeting the adults around the children rather than the 'chief enemies' in the form of more structural political or economic barriers to participation. However, persistent regimes of knowledge or 'truth' defining children, not only as vulnerable and in need of protection, but also as a universal group opposed to adults, at the same time challenge this very redistribution of power, as they affect both adult and child perceptions of what children can and should be doing.

## Generational Power

The assumed natural and universal status of generation in all societies represents a significant third dimension of power or, in Foucauldian terms, a 'regime of truth'. However, the generational dimension is rarely discussed in terms of power, social structure or inequality. The lack of attention to generation is evident in three main regards. First, power seldom features in the language used to talk about everyday kinds of relations adults have with children, for example, within families. Second, childhood theorists have generally drawn on one established approach to power, feminism, in constructing a generational theory of power. Third, there is a marked absence of theorising on generational relations within the social sciences and thus limited conceptual space to talk about generational power.

### *Generational power as abnormal*

The talk of adults exercising power over children is normally construed in a negative sense as an excess of power, most explicitly in situations where children are exploited and abused. This has created a distinction between 'powerful' adults who exploit and abuse children, and 'normal' adults who, on the other hand, are charged with 'educating', 'disciplining', 'controlling', 'regulating' and having responsibility towards children. The latter attributes of adults, particularly parents, are rarely couched in terms of the language of power and domination. For example, adults invoking 'children's best interests' involves them taking decisions on behalf of children, often without any consultation with the children, on the basis that the latter have limited moral and social capacities to take decisions for themselves. Archard (2015) refers to adults taking on a 'caretaker' role by structuring children's lives and speaking on their behalf. While there is a danger that the decisions that adults take in children's 'best interests' can be viewed as partial, the expectation is that adults will always act in favour of children in terms of what they think is best for the child, irrespective of their own interests and well-being. As children are considered too young and immature to know what is in their best interests, parents are charged with responsibility for defining these interests on behalf of their children. This is rarely spoken about in terms of parents or adults exercising power over children, nor is it usually questioned whether these actions constitute domination. Nevertheless, power is implicit in the assumed capacity of parents to expect children to adopt a particular course of action based on an assessment made by the parents rather than the children.

The complexities of generational power become evident through Lukes's (2005) three-dimensional analysis of power, in that the continual constraining of children by adults is generalised due to the expectation that adults are caring for children and acting in their best interests. From a Foucauldian perspective 'best interests', despite suggesting that there are 'other' interests available, can be conceptualised as a discourse that normalises and naturalises generational relations. It is less likely to be viewed as being constructed out of 'a whole range of institutions, economic requirements, and political issues of social regulation' (Foucault, 1980: 237).

### Generation and gender power

A theoretical approach that highlights the significance of 'generation' as a differentiating factor when analysing power and inequality is largely absent from social theory. The sociological status of children is generally understood as bearers of systems of stratification. Children are seen as inheriting their parents' class position within the social structure or internalising a gendered identity through the system of patriarchy (Wyness 2015). Their subordinate positions within the social structure are thus predominantly due to their parents' social characteristics rather than their status as children. For example, children lack power within the school system, not as children, but as proto members of social class and gender structures. This approach reflects Lukes's (2005) third dimension of power, as the constraints of adults on children are articulated in non-generational terms as instances of social class and gender.

Feminists have theorised power, in terms of the dominance of patriarchy, the political and cultural structure that locates power in terms of the subordination of women by men. At one level, children's subordination has limited purchase within feminist theory. Patriarchy incorporated women in terms of their 'natural' responsibilities for children, and male power was justified in terms of these maternal responsibilities. Beyond children being objectified as burdens, the generational dimension generally played little part in feminist thinking around power (Thorne, 1987). Nevertheless, feminists with an interest in conceptualising childhood have highlighted the way that children as well as women are largely a subordinated group within society.

Patriarchal structures interact with generation, for example, in identifying girls as historically and cross-culturally exploited in terms of their domestic labour (Blagbrough, 2008; Nieuwenhuys, 1994). Others have explored the way that political and economic power generate parallel and interconnected lines of disadvantage for women and children (De Grave, 2015; Oakley, 1994).

Feminist theory thus provides some potential for an analysis of generational power. Frye (1983: 103), for example, refers to male power in terms of 'asymmetrical access […] the creation and manipulation of power is constituted of the manipulation and control of access'. In this view, men have power over women because they have access to all areas of women's lives, whereas women only have limited access to men's lives. Similarly, adults can be argued to have power over children through 'asymmetrical access'. Whereas children have limited access to adults, adults have full access to children at a number of levels: they have access to all aspects of children's lives and are in a position to exclude children from various actions and areas, thus denying them access. This control of access may take various forms, including physical and embodied forms. In the first case, adults dominate children by limiting their access to public spaces. For example, children wandering into shopping malls during school time is viewed as deviance, invoking localised punitive responses from communities and the state (Corsaro, 2017). Adults also restrict children's use of time and have power over their daily timetables. The school offers a compelling illustration of the ways in which children's access to physical spaces within and outside school is heavily regulated in temporal terms through timetables. As James et al. (1998: 75) note,

> schooling imposes complex temporal schedules which, through their intersection, structure daily, weekly and yearly cycles and create, for children, different spatial and temporal constraints and possibilities in relation to their school work which must be negotiated with parents and teachers.

The timetable dominates children's school lives, compelling them to be in certain physical spaces within certain time periods, clearly differentiating when, where, how often and with whom they can spend formal and informal time (Wyness, 2019). The timetable is thus a way of mapping out and distributing children's bodies in time and space. In 'panoptical' terms, the timetable creates a heavily restricted space within which children learn to discipline their physical movements. It becomes a form of time discipline, with children learning about the structuring of time and its functions within the school and beyond. As we will discuss in Chapter 6, children's attempts to break some of these regulations, for example, by striking from school, are met with mixed responses.

Foucault (1991) also refers to power in terms of the disciplining of the body. Adults can be seen as having asymmetrical access to children's bodies, as exemplified by Hood-Williams (1990), who discusses adults' bodily power over children. This can be conceptualised as a form of *corporal power*, the capacity that adults have to caress, cuddle and physically chastise children and the difficulties that children might have reciprocating without any adult prompting. Given the dominance of the safeguarding agenda, for example, in many English-speaking countries, adults in general are more reticent now to have physical contact with children. Nevertheless, there is still an expectation that parents stroke, caress and wipe children's bodies. Reciprocal touching from children, on the other hand, is likely to be viewed by adults as an infringement of their physical integrity.

Hood-Williams (1990) views adult power over children as part of patriarchal power. While patriarchy emphasises the power of men, the origins of generational power stem from what he refers to as family patriarchy, where men have control over women and children within their families. Drawing on a Weberian theory of traditional authority, men have domination over the family household, which includes women and children (Weber, 1978). However, the nuclear family structure works around two axes of power: gender and generation. As we have argued, gender is a well-established field of power; generation, on the other hand, needs to be denaturalised and reframed in terms of power.

### Generation as a meta-theory

The emphasis on a meta-theory of generation permits children an ontological status: children are of the social world rather than languishing on the periphery as semi-social actors, often referred to as 'human becomings' (Qvortrup, 1994). As Alderson (2008: 23) argues, 'children are not simply learning and practicing, they are living and accomplishing'. If there are any impediments to the latter, then it is partly down to their subordinate position within a generational structure where adults, as a superior force, exercise power over children as a subordinate minority group. Thus, we need to assert 'generation' as an important analytical concept that permits us to start thinking about generational power.

The works of Leena Alanen (2009) and Berry Mayall (2002) focus specifically on processes of 'generationing': children and adults are located within a generational structure that positions them, first of all, as categorical opposites in the same way that we can talk about class categories – 'middle class' and 'working class' – or gender categories such as 'male' and 'female'. Secondly, Alanen (2009) and Mayall (2002) also develop generational theory in terms of material, social and emotional processes through which children and adults take on and refine these positions. In other words, while a starting point for the analysis is to locate children and adults within these structural categories, the ways in which these positions are occupied within the social structure are also shaped by a range of material and emotional factors.

An explicit generational power approach is in danger of neglecting intergenerational power relations. As we will argue in Chapters 2–4, the conventional idea of kid power depicts it as reversed generational power in a zero-sum sense. That is, kid power is articulated as the balance of power shifting from adults to children and the rise of kid power is often viewed in terms of the loss of parent power. A zero-sum conception of generational power, however, is a limited and narrow means of conceptualising power, whether we are talking about the assertion of power by children or the reassertion of this power by adults. A discussion of generational power incorporates a conception of the family as a formative institution for the disciplining of children and an institution within which power is exchanged or distributed. It emerges from a binary framework for assessing generational relations and builds on a model of the nuclear family extolled by sociologists in the mid-twentieth century constructing sex/gender and generation as 'axes of power' (Parsons and Bales, 1956). Within this model, generation is conceived as a dominant, naturalised boundary between children and their parents, with the latter necessarily retaining power due to children's dependency and incompetence. We refer to this model as the bi-nuclear family and offer a critical examination of its main implications in Chapter 5. The focus on 'generation' may also lead to a neglect of intragenerational differences. However, an emphasis on more intersectional approaches is offered in the second section of the book, where we position generation alongside other differentiating approaches enriching the analysis of kid power (Crenshaw, 1991; Konstantoni and Emejulu, 2017).

## Agency and Empowerment

As the above has shown, feminist analyses of patriarchy tend to focus on the power of men over women and children (domination), and extending this to generation involves consideration of adults' power over children. As pointed out by Ansell (2014: 24), there has, however, also been an important shift, particularly among feminist geographers and within development studies, from 'power *over*' to 'power *within*' (self-respect, self-awareness, confidence and dignity), 'power *with*' (solidarity, alliances and coalitions) and 'power *to*' (capacity-building, decision-making and leadership). Consequently, power has increasingly come to be seen as a process of self-transformation. Within childhood studies, this focus is also prevalent and has formed the basis for extensive attention to agency and empowerment, sometimes conceptualised as almost synonymous with power.

There is a parallel between the way that power is theorised within broader social scientific theory and the assumptions often made about children's agency within childhood studies. In the former case, as we have noted, there has been a shift towards individual and independent exercises of power. Similarly, agency has predominantly been viewed as a property of individual children (White and Choudhury, 2007) but, more recently, also as a relational concept (Bjerke, 2011; Esser et al., 2016; Greene and Nixon, 2020). A number of 'sub-types' of agencies have furthermore been developed, to illustrate how agency can be deployed in and through relations with others in different ways. For example, Utas (2005) draws on Honwana (2000) to discuss 'tactic' and 'strategic' agency in the context of young women's coping mechanisms in war zones. Tactic agency is manifested in 'short-term responses' to a society's social structure and forms part of the 'trajectories travelled by the weak'. Strategic agency, on the other hand, is 'agency for those who can forecast future states of affairs and have the possibility to make use of other people's tactic agency' (Utas, 2005: 407). Strategic agency thus gives more space to develop longer-term strategies. In a critical volume specifically focusing on the agency of children, Esser et al. (2016) argue that agency can be usefully seen as a continuum. They draw on Klocker's (2007: 85) concepts of 'thin' and 'thick' agency, which bear some resemblance to Utas's notion of tactic and strategic agency. Thin agency describes 'decisions and actions carried out within highly restrictive contexts, characterised by few viable alternatives' and thick agency as having a broad range of options as the basis for one's actions.

The concept of agency is widely used in childhood studies, where children as previously mentioned are increasingly seen as active in the construction and determination of their own lives (Esser et al., 2016: 1–2). The similarity between agency and power goes some way to explaining why the former is a dominant reference point rather than the latter within childhood studies. However, the concept of agency is generally poorly defined with regard to children, and it is unclear how exactly it relates to other concepts such as participation and power (Esser et al., 2016; Punch, 2016a, 2016b). Valentine (2011) has argued that childhood studies tend to rely on 'liberal' models of agency, which see the moral and unconstrained agency of individuals as paramount and can be used to argue against autocratic and tyrannical subjects.

Theories of the social contract rest on a relationship between sovereign individuals, who are entitled by virtue of their agency to control how, and the degree to which, they are governed. Liberalism then appears to be to childhood studies 'that which cannot be done without'. (2011: 350)

However, contrary to this individual autonomous approach, Valentine (2011: 354) notes that agency may also be considered as 'inflected with power'. Whereas some forms of agency, such as 'thick' agency, may be seen as similar to having power, others, 'thin' agency, would be more questionable as a form of power. 'Tactic' agency furthermore seems to reflect one-dimensional power within particular spaces, whereas strategic agency may to a greater extent present as two- or perhaps three-dimensional power. Finally, there is the possibility that people with agency do not always act in their own best interest:

> Individual trauma and structural oppression may inflect agency in such a way that people act as their own 'worst enemy', or act to resist power, and of course resistance to power may be interpreted as self-defeating behaviour. These sometimes, uncomfortable dimensions of agency are rarely taken up in childhood studies, which has so far focused on examples of positive, competent, rational activity. (Valentine 2011: 354)

The same can be argued in relation to another power-related term, used extensively within childhood studies: empowerment. Empowerment is a term derived from community psychology, where it has been described as 'a process, a mechanism by which people, organizations, and communities gain mastery over their affairs' (Rappaport, 1981: 122). The individual level of empowerment is described by Lawson and Kearns (2016) as including individual capacity building, personal control and the ability to make informed decisions, and the collective level as involving families, communities and organisations in processes and structures which facilitate change. Specifically discussing the individual level, Zimmerman (1995: 583) has distinguished between processes and outcomes of empowerment, the former describing processes whereby 'people create or are given opportunities to control their own destiny and influence the decisions that affect their lives', and the latter, people's perceived degree of control, mastery and competence, their awareness and understanding of the context in which their options and choices are taking place and any particular actions taken.

The concept of empowerment has gained popularity across disciplines, including childhood studies, education and health, where its individual elements are often emphasised. As described by McLaughlin (2016), the way the concept of empowerment is commonly used stems from the social and political movements of the 1960s and 1970s where it was used to emancipate and improve the conditions of disadvantaged groups. By the mid-1990s it had, however, become a buzzword in both Western policy circles and international development work, and has also since been increasingly used to argue for a more individual and neoliberal notion of self-responsibility. He cautions against this development:

> There is a need to be aware of the ideological assumptions and practical consequences surrounding the discourse of empowerment, and to be alert to both the overt and covert workings of power. In other words, we need to view empowerment not as a fixed, a priori good, but as embedded within social and political relationships, and therefore as a concept that can be used for either progressive or regressive social policies and social work practices. (McLaughlin 2016: 6)

As we will discuss in Chapter 8, empowerment forms an important part of the rationale for children's participation in research, as well as more generally. It is usually described relatively uncritically as a positive concept, but as with McLaughlin (2016), we caution that its applications need to be seen in their social and political context. This involves acknowledging where structures and institutions may not only limit children's empowerment but also attribute them with power over situations that they cannot in fact control.

## Conclusion

In her chapter on gender and power, Davis (1991: 84) concludes by noting that 'considering the dazzling variety and complexity of social life, it seems highly improbable that any one theory – regardless of whether its starting point is gender or power – can ever hope to explain it all'. Rather than looking for the 'perfect theory', she recommends a grounded approach, which takes people's experiences as the starting point and uses theory as a way to come to terms with the relations between them in their specific contexts. Davis's (1991) analysis of gendered power relations has many similarities to our work on kid power, and like her point about the variety and complexity of gender relations, the chapters in this book all emphasise the diverse and highly contextual power relations between children and adults, as well as within groups of children. In the remainder of the book, we present our analysis of kid power, using a grounded approach based on empirical material on children's everyday lives. The following three chapters first critically analyse common conceptions of kid power in relation to children's rights, child-centredness and the thesis of the loss of adult power. In the second section of the book, we take children's experiences in their families and communities, on social media and in research as the starting point, and build up an alternative framework for kid power which uses the theory introduced in this chapter to understand its complex intergenerational, intragenerational and multidimensional character.

# Chapter 2

# GLOBAL RIGHTS AND KID POWER

Children's rights are a key reference point for common understandings of kid power. The history of children's rights goes back to the early twentieth century, with intermittent international commitment to supporting children's welfare (Wyness, 2019). There was a libertarian moment in the 1970s when a group of academics argued that children should be empowered to escape the 'shackles of childhood' by offering them a range of civil and political rights (Holt, 1975; Farson, 1978).[1] However, it is the relatively recent version of children's rights, the 1989 UN Convention on the Rights of the Child (CRC), which has had most impact, heightening – sometimes controversially – the position and condition of children globally. The CRC is a legal document obligating nation states to respect the integrity and status of children as human beings. It has been ratified by all UN member countries, except the United States, and adopted by a multitude of national and international agencies, resulting in children becoming an integrated part of the global discourse on childhood. The global focus has been on children's rights to provision, protection and participation (Franklin and Franklin, 1996), with the latter often singled out as a distinctive and controversial feature of the CRC. Participatory rights have sometimes been associated with an increase in child power and a shift in power relations between children and adults. This chapter explores the question of whether the greater global focus on children and their rights has led to an increase in kid power.

The chapter focuses on two related themes in teasing out the difficulty of equating rights with power. First, the CRC developed as a result of increasing realisation of the suffering of children in conflicts and in poor living conditions

---

[1] Historically the libertarian moment came at the end of the civil rights movement in the United States in the mid-1970s. A group of philosophers and educationalists argued that children should have the same minority status as women and be liberated from the arbitrary political and social constraints known as childhood. By arguing that children should have the same rights as adults, the work of Farsons (1978) and Holt (1975) attacked the notion that children should be excluded from these rights on the basis of any imputed social, moral and cognitive inferiority.

due to their age-related vulnerability. Consequently, it emphasises the role of adults, institutions and states providing for and protecting children:

> The main argument for a separate international human rights law for children was the reality of reports from all over the world indicating that children, indeed, needed special rights because of their vulnerability. Children suffered so badly that their protection required special attention. (Hammarberg, 1990: 99)

The Convention is important in asserting the status of children as holders of human rights entitled to be treated with respect and dignity in the same way as adults. However, given global concerns over the exploitation of children, the Convention also encourages adults to have greater control over children's lives. This may lead to tensions between 'participation' and potential power, on the one hand, and 'protection' and 'provision', on the other.

Second, one controversial area of the Convention is the idea that children should have a say and access to public spaces and knowledge, also known as their participation rights. While this might suggest potential conflict between adults and children, participation rights are also heavily regulated, as children have to prove to adults that they are capable of participating. Furthermore, children's participation in particular areas of their lives may be severely limited, in some cases due to national reservations, in others because their age renders them unable to have a say, for example, in the sphere of politics. Thus, while there are major changes to children's status globally as a result of the CRC, there is little sense that their participation rights in themselves lead to an increase in kid power. In addition, and as we will discuss in further detail in the second part of the book, participation may take various forms, which include not only having a voice but also material participation within families and communities. Kid power thus needs to be explored more broadly, acknowledging children's varying levels of power within different contexts.

## Children's Rights and Power

The articles in the CRC are commonly described as falling under three broad categories, first described by Hammarberg (1990: 100) as *provision* (the right to fulfilment of basic needs, such as food, healthcare and education), *protection* (the right to be shielded from harmful acts and practices, such as exploitation, abuse or warfare) and *participation* (the right to be heard in matters of importance to one's life). However, the way in which these three 'P's are understood and prioritised has been widely debated. By acknowledging children's devolving capabilities and the duty of adults to provide guidance and act in the child's best interest according to these, the CRC provides ample opportunity for conflicting views and practices (Lundy, 2007). Furthermore, as noted by Hammarberg (1990: 100), the Convention is 'stronger on the first two aspects – provision for basic needs and protection – than on rights relating to participation'.

Quennerstedt (2010) has traced the origin of the narrative around the three Ps. She shows that while these categories were initially developed as an analytical tool, they are increasingly perceived as a depiction of the rights themselves. She furthermore notes that while children's rights are often described as part of the universal human rights framework, the terminology used to describe children's rights is significantly different than that of adults, with a focus on 'protection' rather than 'social rights' and 'participation' rather than 'civil and political rights'. This, Quennerstedt argues, has resulted in a reproduction of the view of children as 'passive' and 'non-agentic' receivers of rights. A similar point is made by Sandberg (2015), who notes that the Committee on the Rights of the Child explicitly describes children as universally vulnerable until the age of 18, due to them not being fully developed physically, mentally, emotionally and spiritually. This is made explicit within the Convention, where children are defined as different from adults. For example, the preamble states that children should have 'special care and assistance' (UNICEF 1990: preamble).

Children's vulnerability can be defined in terms of their limited capacity to protect themselves from harm, but also as a result of their position within the social structure (Goldson, 2002). Children are seen as dependent on others for protection, provision and decision-making, with connotations of children being their parents' property and objects of charity, rather than subjects of rights (Goldson, 2002: 22). Pells (2012) describes well some of the contradictions between a rights-based approach to children's participation and the notion that particular children are vulnerable. Drawing on two case studies of rights-based interventions by NGOs in Rwanda, she illustrates that children's participation is often limited to the implementation stage of intervention and focuses more on the process of participation (e.g. skills development, with focus on the child) than outcomes (e.g. addressing structural inequalities). Many interventions tend to focus on orphans, as they are perceived to be more vulnerable, although vulnerability is not always related to orphanhood. She thus argues that 'Rwandan children's lives and subsequent interventions are constructed between the notion of vulnerability on the one hand and agency on the other' (Pells, 2012: 429).

John (2003) points out that the notion of childhood depicted in the CRC is a Northern conception of children as safely propelled along individualised trajectories by adults. The CRC forms part of a global discourse on childhood where schooling has become the dominant feature of childhood (Wyness,

2018) and children outside this model, for example, street children, are seen as marginal and deviant. By working for themselves, caring for and respecting each other and not asking society to rescue them, John (2003) argues that street children challenge the hegemony of Northern conceptions of the schooled child. In addition, she notes that adults tend to avoid talking about adult power in their relationships with children and instead use words such as 'care', 'authority' and 'firm control'. This illustrates the point we raised in Chapter 1 – that the concept of 'power' is only likely to be used where authority and control are viewed as excessive and where the generational relationship has broken down, for example, within contexts where adults exploit and abuse children. This reflects some of the previously mentioned links between vulnerability and generational power inherent in the CRC, the former implying that children are most at risk and the latter predominantly framed in terms of disproportionate and overt actions by adults on children. These notions tend to draw on a conflictual zero-sum notion of power, where one person's gain of power involves another person's loss of power, and describe children and adults as opposing dichotomous categories. As noted by Reynaert et al. (2009: 526), focusing on the idea of individual and autonomous rights of children 'increases the likelihood of social conflicts and inhibits a dialogue that could lead to consensus'.

## *Reservations*

The common conflation of rights with power is particularly evident where countries have made reservations to their ratification of the CRC. That is, countries that ratify the Convention can limit the extent to which they are bound by specific articles and thus retain the power of their own national legislation which diverges from the CRC without having to make adjustments. John (1995) argues that the UK government's support for the CRC was at best ambiguous. Despite ratifying the Convention, various exemptions were claimed in relation to the rights of migrant children and the imprisonment of children in adult prison. These exemptions are legally defined as reservations. All Islamic countries have ratified the CRC, but some have made reservations where the Convention is seen to compromise faith-based principles. For example, Iran has invoked a reservation that positions sharia law in conflict with the CRC and 'reserves the right not to apply any provisions or Articles of the Convention that are incompatible with Islamic laws and the internal legislation in effect' (cited in Schabas, 1996: 478). Schabas (1996) argues that the reservation is so general that it is tantamount to a rejection of the CRC.

While there have been significant shifts in Islamic law in recent years towards more child-specific policy, there is still a strong emphasis on children having obligations towards their elders and families rather than possessing rights (Rajabi-Ardeshiri, 2009). Children are not seen as individual rights holders but deferential subordinates within an explicit generational hierarchy. To give children any legal rights is viewed, in an Islamic sense, to position them on the same level as adults. In this important sense, the CRC is viewed as legitimating a shift in power from adult to child, and there is an apprehension that, at the very least, rights put children at the same level as adults in terms of power. Reservations, then, are invoked to protect the cultural and faith-based integrity of states, where children's rights are perceived to breach these values.

The position of the United States can be viewed in similar terms. As stated earlier, it has not ratified the Convention and thus has not had to add reservations. However, the United States, along with various other states, was involved in drafting several articles of the Convention throughout the 1980s (Gainsborough and Lean, 2008). While there was some support for the Convention in the 1990s among the political elite, including President Clinton, the Convention was never passed on to the US Senate for ratification, and so the United States never became a party to the Convention. Gainsborough and Lean (2008) refer to 'procedural and political barriers' to the US Senate ratifying the Convention. Powerful constituencies within the United States, including faith-based groups, and home schoolers viewed the Convention as giving the state a charter for empowering children and thus negating or at the very least challenging the proprietorial rights of parents. American politicians were fearful of losing political support among their constituents due to the idea that children ought to have participatory rights (Gainsborough and Lean, 2008). Moreover, Article 37 of the CRC abolished life sentences and capital punishment for all children. Until the mid-2000s there was some ambivalence over this issue, with six federal states retaining capital punishment for juveniles (Human Rights Watch, 2005). Thus, as with Iran and other Muslim states, the United States viewed the CRC with some suspicion, with children's rights being equated with disempowering adults and elevating children politically.

### Political rights

Various authors have referred to the way that the CRC constrains children's power by invoking provision and protection as features of children's 'welfare' rights (Wyness, 2019). Adult 'caretakers' regulate children's welfare as they develop towards maturity and adulthood (Archard, 2015). Murray (2010) refers to children's rights as hierarchical: provision and protection rights are basic welfare rights that need to be established before children can assume participation rights. One important requirement of these welfare rights and highly illustrative of the relationship between rights and power is that in all countries, children have no formal political rights – 'the very status of the child means in principle that the child has no political right' (John, 1995: 106). Children were not viewed as a constituency or acquired 'stakeholder' status throughout the 11 years of the CRC's drafting from 1978 until 1989. They were not consulted on their needs or their interests during this period. The UN belatedly organised 'special sessions' where children as delegates reported back on the progress of the CRC in 2002 (UN Special Session on Children, 2002, https://sites.unicef.org/specialsession/), but there was little sense that children played any consultative role in policies that directly affect them. This represents a paradox, as legislation that furthered the position of children was constructed, debated and implemented without any contributions from children themselves. As children have no right to vote, they were not in a position to directly influence any change in policy that might have strengthened their position. Children were not able to endorse the political parties that formed national governments, who in turn, with the exception of the United States, endorsed the CRC. There is little sense that children were able to exercise any political power with respect to the drafting of the Convention. Importantly, this has shaped the absence of ways in which children's rights can be deployed politically by children themselves. In political terms, 'children's rights are alien to children' (Liebel, 2018: 34).

## Children's Rights and Participation

The one area that has provoked most discussion over the CRC is the third 'P', the child's right to participate. While provision and protection arguably strengthen the power of adults over children, participation suggests a degree of autonomy and control for children. Thus, rather than provision and protection rights which need to be enacted by adults on behalf of children, children in some ways 'possess' participation rights, and provisional assessments of the Convention suggest that children are in a position to do things for themselves. Articles 12 to 15 focus on rights in terms of children taking ownership of decisions that affect them. Article 12 states that children, who are 'capable of forming their own views shall have the right to express those views freely', and Article 13 extends the idea that children have a right to knowledge, information and 'freedom of expression'. The latter includes children's access to knowledge in both physical and virtual forms. In some respects the advent of digital technology complicates the capacity of adults to regulate children's access to knowledge, and there is potential for children's digital capacities to be in conflict with adults' responsibilities to protect children from 'harmful' data

(Livingstone et al., 2018). Article 14 grants children the right to freedom of thought, conscience and religion, and Article 15 focuses on children's right to more collective forms of participation, for example, in associations or peaceful assemblies.

Article 12 has come in for particular attention[2] and is often seen as one of the most innovative parts of the Convention (Perry-Hazan, 2016). It focuses on children's access to lines of communication that allow them to articulate their interests; in other words, children now have a say. Article 12 has been associated and sometimes conflated with the concept 'voice'. Children have a right to participate largely because the CRC challenges children's hitherto 'muted' status, in giving them a say in affairs that affect them (Wyness, 2018). However, and importantly, there are conditions attached to this article, as the child's views are to be given 'due weight in accordance with the age and maturity of the child' (UNICEF, 1989: A.12).

Countries and institutions offer varying levels of opportunity for children to have a say: in schools (Wyness, 2013a), within the research process (Dunn, 2015; Leitch et al., 2007; O'Brien and Moules, 2007), in relation to family matters (Mayall, 2002) and in terms of policy developments (Tisdall and Bell, 2006). In the school context, Article 12 legitimates a dominant form of participation, predominantly found in schools in the Global North, which is based on consultation between pupils and school staff, including, for example, surveys, school councils and suggestion boxes (Yamashita and Davies, 2012). The agenda is primarily shaped by adults, however, with children in a position to comment on some of the decisions, actions and expectations of adults.

The emphasis on children's participation and voice is also reflected in other global legislation. Regionally, in Africa, the African Charter on the Rights and Welfare of the Child (African Union, 1990) includes various principles such as non-discrimination, the best interests of the child, and survival and development. The Charter also, importantly, includes respect for children's views (Viviers and Lombard, 2013: 10). The European Union makes a very brief reference to participation in the Charter of Fundamental Rights: children should be able to 'express their views freely. Such views shall be taken into consideration on matters which concern them in accordance with their age and maturity' (European Union, 2000: Article 24). Article 12 has also been integrated into national constitutions in Europe such as those of Austria, Lithuania, Belgium and Spain (European Commission, 2015: 13–14):

---

[2] Several campaigning organisations are named after the article, for example, Article 12 in Scotland, https://www.article12.org/; the Children's Rights Alliance for England was formerly known as Article 12.

'The public authorities shall promote the conditions for the free and effective participation by the young in political, social, economic and cultural development.' (Spain)

'Every child has the right to express herself/himself on all matters of interest to her/him; her or his opinion is taken into consideration depending on age and capacity of discernment.' (Belgium)

Other countries such as England, Scotland, Poland, Romania and Sweden have child-specific legislation where forms of participation are built into the legislation (European Commission, 2015). In England and Wales, the Children Act 1989 was passed as legislation in the same year as the CRC, and although the act had little to do with the CRC, it required professionals working with families to 'ascertain the wishes and feelings of children' before making decisions (Barker and Weller, 2003). The Children Act was updated in 2004, furthering the idea that children have a voice. Local authorities are to 'give due consideration (having regard to his age and understanding) to such wishes and feelings of the child as they have been able to ascertain' (DCSF, 2004: 2). In England, the idea of 'Gillick competence' developed from the notion that children could be judged competent by professionals such as doctors and social workers to make important decisions that affect their lives and futures. Thus despite children not having legal capacity, they may be judged mature enough to make these decisions, for example, around medical treatment (Cornock, 2007).

However, the notion of participation may be understood differently depending on local and contextual ideas about childhood. For example, Twum-Danso (2010) describes the Ghanaian context, where children who express their views or show signs of assertiveness are seen as social deviants, disrespectful and bringing shame on their parents. Consequently, she argues,

Despite the fact that almost all governments in the world have ratified the Convention, this particular article [Article 12] has faced seemingly insurmountable obstacles in societies around the world where children are seen as the property of their parents who must do as they are told and not question. Culture and its attendant values are central to the limited implementation of this article, due to the fact that they guide the way parents and other adults perceive and react to the principles on which Article 12 is based. (Twum-Danso, 2010: 133)

Burr (2002) describes similar tensions in her research on the implementation of the CRC in Vietnam. In the Vietnamese context, where child-care norms are based around children's deference and communal obligations, Vietnamese aid workers had some misgivings about granting children participation rights:

> I consider the UNCRC is 'good' if society is developed. But for us we have many customs which prevent us raising children to say what they think to their elders. They [the international aid workers] say children should not work … but for many this is an impossibility. Many of us aid workers know this and there is a difference between ours and the foreigner's approach, but we do not voice this. We know our country is not ready for the changes. (Aid worker interviewed in Burr, 2002: 149)

As this illustrates, communities may fear that advancing children's participation poses a threat to adult power. This is similar to countries and cultures which, as we have previously discussed, display ambiguity over a commitment to the CRC due to concerns that it challenges the integrity of adults' superiority.

## Participation and Regulation

While cultural factors may challenge the idea of empowering children, a cursory glance at Article 12 and related articles suggests that children's participation is also significantly conditional on judgements made by adults. There are two parts to Article 12: (1) it is formally recognised that children can now articulate their interests and (2) these interests may be taken seriously (given 'due weight') by adults and institutions. Both stages are regulated, with adults able to select who can act as a spokesperson (the 'capable' child) and decide whose views will be taken seriously. Similarly, Article 5 refers to the way that parents and family members provide for and protect children but take account of the 'evolving capacities of the child'. While Article 12 offers decision-making opportunities for children on the basis of assessments made by adults, Article 5 suggests that children are granted autonomy and space by parents based on a careful assessment of their capacities. This connects with the second part of Article 12, the idea of giving due weight to children's voices on the basis of their competence. Decisions around process and outcomes of participation are thus structured by adult political, institutional and social interests and practices. In this section, we discern different modes of adult regulation, by exploring the range of meanings and interpretations of the child's right to participate and their ability to express opinion and be taken seriously (Lansdown, 2010).

A number of typologies have been developed with regards to children's participation rights. Hart's (2002) widely cited 'ladder of participation' includes eight rungs with varying roles for children and adults. The bottom three rungs are defined as forms on non-participation, including (1) manipulation, (2) decoration and (3) tokenism. Rungs 4–8 are defined as legitimate forms: (4) assigned but informed, (5) consulted and informed, (6) adult-initiated but shared decision-making with children, (7) child-initiated and directed decision-making and, finally, (8) young people and adults share decision-making. Critics of Hart's model have argued that its hierarchical nature neglects the many ways, dimensions and contexts of children's participation (Smith and Haslett, 2017). However, Hart's (1992) typology continues to be hugely influential and used in child participation literature and reports globally. Drawing on Hart, but focusing only on activities that can be considered participation, Shier (2001: 110) has suggested the following levels of participation:

1.  children are listened to;
2.  children are supported in expressing their views;
3.  children's views are taken into account;
4.  children are involved in decision-making processes; and
5.  children share power and responsibility for decision-making.

A novel element of Shier's work is his distinction within each of these levels between three levels of commitment: *openings* (when an individual commits to the given level, although there may not be any opportunities within his or her organisation to carry it out), *opportunities* (when there are opportunities within an organisation to carry out at a given level) and *obligations* (when an organisation commits to a given level). This emphasises the importance of analysing participation over time and as a continuous process.

Other typologies have been developed to describe children's participation, including Lansdown's (2011: 147–50) distinction between consultative, collaborative and child-led forms of participation, which all three involve various levels of cooperation between children and adults.

*   *Consultative participation*, in which children's views are sought to understand their lived experiences, and where participation is initiated, led and managed by adults. Children do not have an impact on outcomes or share decision-making, but adult decision-making is informed by their expertise and perspectives.
*   *Collaborative participation*, which resembles more of a partnership between adults and children, and children have the opportunity to shape decisions and challenge both process and outcomes.
*   *Child-led participation*, which gives children space and opportunity to initiate activities and advocate for themselves, with adults taking their role as enablers.

Whereas these models focus specifically on participatory activities, Thomson and Holdsworth (2003: 373–74) define child participation, or more specifically student participation, in much broader terms. Their typology identifies five ways in which 'participation' has been used in Australian educational policy:

1. being physically present at school, measured through attendance and retention data;
2. being involved in school and taking part in school activities and in lessons;
3. involvement in formal school decision-making;
4. children initiating, deciding and acting in the school and beyond the school boundaries; and
5. community or social activism and 'organizing'.

Within childhood studies, only the last three would generally be considered participation as they go beyond the idea of mere presence and generalised engagement in school. Model 3 prescribes participation in more conventional terms where children are consulted in school but have little involvement in agenda-setting. Model 4 offers a more advanced level of involvement with children working alongside adults on a range of participatory initiatives. Model 5 views the school as a medium through which children participate on a range of community-based projects where they might be expected to have more agenda-setting powers.

These ladders, levels and types of participation provide a useful tool to consider the respective roles of children and adults in participatory activities and an important language for talking about the distinction between non-participation and participation. All of them incorporate a developmental logic with lesser forms of participation leading to more sophisticated and elaborate forms. Thomson and Holdsworth's (2003) typology furthermore suggests that school democracy, pupil engagement and consultation presuppose an earlier period, where children establish patterns for regularly attending schools. Children are able to participate in more democratic practices because they are physically present in schools and in a position to engage with the curriculum and the teacher. They are socialised into attending school regularly, which allows them to absorb the various rules and regulations of the school and classroom as well as acknowledge the significance of formal learning trajectories. Children are thus incorporated into participatory structures inside and outside school while agendas and practices are still set by teachers and other adults in authority. The remaining types of participation involve less adult input and control, but there is still little sense that any of these forms of participation, including child-initiated forms, have radically altered power differentials between children and adults.

Where the developmental logic might lead to a more radical change in power relations between children and adults is in Lansdown's (2011) typology. The model offers the potential to see child participants moving from 'consultation', to 'collaboration' to 'child-led' forms which suggest a move towards having more say over the conditions of participation as well as some agenda-setting powers. At the very least we can suggest here that although these powers may be structured by local community-based or institutional interests, there is possibility of adults and children sharing agenda-setting powers. Hart's typology also depicts participation as becoming progressively more child-centred, with adults having less involvement in developing the participatory initiatives. The highest rung of Hart's ladder of participation converges with the idea that the most advanced model of participation in terms of intergenerational relations is where adults are working alongside children in developing a stronger collective capacity for intergenerational communication (Wyness, 2013a).

## Participation and Change

Two further points are worth making in relation to models of participation and power. First of all, combining insights on participation with standard definitions of power necessitates a consideration of the potential of participation to facilitate or instigate changes (making other actors do something differently). However, models of participation often focus on the process rather than the outcomes of participation, making it difficult to make any firm conclusions about changes to practice, priorities and dominant regimes of knowledge. The importance of considering both processes and outcomes of participation is also emphasised in studies of young people's view of participatory activities. Stafford et al. (2003), for example, show that the young people in their Scottish study called for respectful and genuine consultation of children and young people, recognizing their status and contributions, but also had a clear sense that participation should be about achieving outcomes. Hill's (2006) research on children's involvement in consultations similarly showed that the children were committed to making a difference and that for them participation involved changes to practices that would benefit children as well as others. Acknowledging the importance of outcomes, Lundy's (2007: 933) conceptualisation of Article 12 includes four elements: that children need to be given the *space* and the *voice* to express their views, as well as an *audience* that listens to these voices and implements *changes* as appropriate.

This relates to the second point about children's participation in relation to power. As noted by several authors, discourses on participation are predominantly focused on decision-making. Percy-Smith (2010: 110) has critiqued the 'widespread preoccupation with involvement in decision making' in the United Kingdom, which tends to ignore other activities that young people engage in to realise their well-being, identity and citizenship. He furthermore argues that young people's participation has been weakened, as they are most often consulted or given a voice, but without granting them any 'real power'. Participation tends for the most part to be on adult/organisational terms and these tend to reinforce power inequalities between adults and children rather than challenge them. This limits the achievements of young people's participation and the extent to which outcomes can be achieved within the context of powerful adult-dominated forces, priorities and interests. Percy-Smith (2010: 109) thus calls for

> more attention to opportunities for children and young people to participate more fully in everyday community settings – home, school, neighbourhood – through the actions, choices, relationships and contributions they make, rather than being preoccupied with participation in political and public decision-making processes in organisations and systems which are removed from young people's everyday lives.

In almost all of its current legitimate forms, participation affords children little power in terms of agenda-setting and structuring change (two- and three-dimensional power). A shift away from the focus on institutional and discursive forms of participation would potentially allow for a more multi-dimensional understanding of children's power which goes beyond consultation and decision-making (one-dimensional power) and which, to a larger extent, includes the practical experiences of a diversity of children. In the second part of the book, we provide our interpretation of such a shift, by analysing children's participation in a diversity of contexts through the lens of power.

## Inequality and the Distribution of Participatory Rights

Percy-Smith (2010) has alluded to the narrowness of dominant formats within which children participate, and Pells (2012) has furthermore argued that children's inclusion in a programme does not always equate with participation. Hidden barriers within and outside the programme may prevent engagement and act as an obstacle to the participation of particular groups. Some children are in a better position to participate than others, and while this does not automatically lead to their empowerment, participatory initiatives, at least formal versions, are likely to reinforce the advantages that some groups of children have over others.

As illustrated by Thomson and Holdsworth's (2003) typology, children who may not attend school regularly due to work or caring commitments are less likely to be in a position to participate in various 'democratic' initiatives within schools. Pells (2012) questions whether school-based programmes are the best way to engage all children, as some will prefer to participate outside of the school context as they get on with their daily lives. Moreover, even where children from different cultural and socio-economic contexts regularly attend school and engage with the various school-related tasks, some groups of children are less likely to take part in consultation exercises or take on the role of representing their peers through councils or forums. As we will discuss in Chapter 7, formal participatory structures in school are less likely to connect with children from more challenging backgrounds. Power resides at the managerial centre where agendas, surveys and projects reflect the demands of the school for more educationally centred children. The 'usual schooled child', the confident child with sufficient social and cultural capital, is likely to represent the interests of children from similar backgrounds rather than all children within their classroom or year group (Wyness, 2009). Children who connect with the managerial centre will be in a position to take advantage of any participatory initiatives, which reinforces the education and social advantages they have over other groups of children.

### The distribution of children's rights

At the more global level, the conventional conception of kid power implies that children are empowered and that this leaves adults in a much weaker position. The CRC is a global and universal mechanism for ensuring that all children are recognised as rights holders, but exemptions or 'reservations' represent cultural and political obstacles to their realisation. As we discussed earlier in the chapter, formal claims made by individual states can exempt them from implementing specific articles, and this can have major implications for any material and symbolic differences that the CRC makes for child populations. More informally, the CRC may also have a more limited connection to the lives of particular groups of children, for example, those living in extreme poverty or in situations of conflict. Consequently, rather than talking about the global *universal spread* of rights, it is useful to focus on the global *distribution* of children's rights, with some groups of children in a significantly stronger position than others to take advantage of their rights. A focus on the distribution of rights involves two issues: first, material advantages of particular groups of children exacerbate levels of inequality between groups of children in relation to rights, and there are significant global, national and local differences between groups of children in terms of access to resources and protective structures (Bourdillon and Boyden, 2014). For example, in the case of young girls in sub-Saharan Africa with significant caring responsibilities, rights to provision, including education, and protection from sexual predators and bodily mutilation are severely routinely compromised (Andersson et al., 2008; Bourdillon and Boyden, 2014; Reig Alcaraz et al., 2014). More generally, evidence from the Millennium Development Goals and the Education for All initiative suggests that although there is global progress in reducing extreme poverty and improving the registration and completion rates of schooling at primary level, in certain global regions such as sub-Saharan Africa and Southern Asia key targets have not been met (UNESCO, 2015; UN, 2015). The life worlds of many children in these regions thus do not connect with children's rights in terms of provision.

Secondly, the uneven distribution of rights globally can also be understood in terms of the recognition of children's rights among different populations and societies. Children may have agency and make major contributions to the material and social well-being of their families and communities, but many of these activities are not acknowledged in the CRC as part of their rights to participate. In part, this is due to the way that children's participatory rights are defined as *discursive* forms of participation. Throughout this chapter, we have emphasised the importance given to the concept of 'voice' through forms of consultation and processes of decision-making. While there is a material and physical dimension to all forms of children's participation, there is a predominant global recognition of the discursive voice-based dimensions of participation (Wyness, 2013b).

There has been considerable critical examination of any universalised notion of children's rights (Bessell, 2009; Boyden, 1997; Twum-Danso, 2010). Despite almost universal legal commitment to the CRC, children's rights connect with particular cultures, societies and states, and this is of particular relevance to participation rights. Culture can be defined in terms of global differences that affect the routines, representations and expectations of populations generating differences in the way that participation is understood. While in some societies there may be an expectation that children participate in economic and domestic work, this is seldom articulated in terms of rights which grant children a voice in affairs that directly affect them. The CRC rejects particular *material* forms of participation such as labour: Article 32 goes along with a broader discourse on ending child labour, with an emphasis on

> protect(ing children) from economic exploitation and from performing any work that is likely to be hazardous or to interfere with the child's education, or to be harmful to the child's health or physical, mental, spiritual, moral or social development. (UNICEF, 1989: Article 32)

This includes all forms of 'labour', including caring and armed combat (ILO, 2017). The International Labour Organization (ILO) makes it clear in their strategy for ending child labour that a major concern is to tackle the worst forms of labour, 'work which, by its nature or the circumstances in which it is carried out, is likely to harm the health, safety or morals of children' (ILO, 1999). The global discourse on participation offers limited political recognition of material forms of participation (Wyness, 2013b), and a network of global organisations are committed to the ending of child labour and the heightening of children's formal schooling (Wyness, 2019). Through education systems, agencies and organisations are promoting more discursive 'educational' forms of participation. Thus, the rights agenda prioritises discursive educational forms, in the process consigning those groups of children involved in more material forms to the status of social deviants. Moreover, the distinction between discursive and material forms of participation is strengthened by the assumption that the former takes place in safe and heavily protected contexts such as the school, whereas the latter implies lack of adult regulation with children exposed to the dangers and hazards of the street, the factory and the farmyard.

At the same time, it is not simply that we have 'legitimate' and 'deviant' forms of participation, or that we may be able to define them as culturally and socially different forms of participation. These forms are often in conflict. Banks's (2007) analysis of the 2003 report to the Committee on the Rights of the Child for Bangladesh nicely brings out the contrast between routine 'participation' and greater involvement in decision-making processes:

> As children get older, increasing account is taken of their views, although adults display striking inconsistencies in their attitudes to the participation of adolescents in different aspects of life. On the one hand, the family and community expect them to act like adults – arguably overestimating their capacity – on matters such as work and responsibilities towards parents and other family members. On the other, their potential is underestimated and they are insufficiently consulted on issues on which they have a right to express an opinion, such as the course of their future studies or career, decisions regarding their marriage and other future plans. (Banks, 2007: 410)

Material forms of participation thus clash with discursive forms, with the former in some cultural contexts seen as a routine part of growing up, and the latter a breach of generational rules. As we will discuss in Chapter 7, collective forms of voice among groups of child workers, such as the International Movement of

Working Children, challenge the conflict between material and discursive forms of participation (Liebel, 2012a). However, in some contexts, norms of deference and obedience appear to be out of step with the idea that children have a say about the level and forms of participation within their families and communities. In sum: the distribution of rights can be seen to exacerbate inequalities between children in two ways. First, unequal access to provision and protection, what we might term welfare rights, reinforces material support structures where Northern and affluent groups of children are located. Second, a global discourse on participation rights prioritises discursive and voice-based activities over more material forms of participation, and these are more likely to connect with the life worlds of children from more affluent individualistic regions of the world.

The school is a central regulatory context for children's participation. The curriculum within different school sectors in most countries is structured along age-related developmental lines. Teachers follow these pathways and incorporate process- and curriculum-based modes of participation in these terms with older children having more access to voice than younger children (Wyness, 2009). Children are incrementally introduced to more sophisticated forms of participation, and as they move up the age-related hierarchy, we would also expect to find them participating at the upper rungs and levels of participatory typologies. Moreover, much of these discursive forms of participation are located within educational contexts where adults are moulding children into future citizens, workers and voters (Tisdall, 2010). UNICEF advocates child participation both as a means of giving children a say as children and as an educational initiative that gives them the necessary skills and knowledge for living in liberal democratic societies as adults (Skelton, 2007). Thus, dominant forms of participation are future oriented, having important educational and developmental functions.

In effect, this is a normative model of participation that emerges from a dominant Northern conception of childhood, emphasising welfare support and formal education (Hendrick, 2015). Welfare systems were initiated in many states in the Global North during the first half of the twentieth century. This created legal and social frameworks for children and their families, generating individual entitlements to material support. Mass compulsory schooling developed earlier in the nineteenth century across Europe, slightly later in England and Wales, offering forms of educational, social and moral regulation for children. The emphasis is on the development of the individual child who is incrementally introduced to the outside world through forms of participation. As children gradually engage with the world, they are carefully incorporated into decision-making processes.

## Conclusion

In her critical examination of the language used in the children's rights framework, Quennerstedt (2010: 620) argues that

> with the basic assumption that the meaning and understanding of societal phenomena, such as children's rights, are formed in and by language use, it is necessary critically to analyse the language that children's rights is couched in. Accordingly, we need to examine what is indicated in children's rights thinking as 'normal', 'acceptable', 'right', 'real' and 'the way things are'.

In returning to our discussion of power in the previous chapter, we might argue that children's rights are related to Lukes's third dimension of power, in terms of taken-for-granted levels and forms of adult regulation. We have referred to two dominant forms of rights, a child's right to *welfare*, putting adults, institutions and states under pressure to take more responsibility for children's physical, moral and social welfare, and a child's rights to *participation*, which are often considered as an indication that children are becoming more powerful. Participation, as well as children's welfare rights, is incorporated within a framework of basic assumptions about the nature of childhood, appropriate forms of work, and engagement with and treatment of children by adults, institutions and states. Adult power is instantiated within this framework: children's rights to provision, protection and participation are normalised through the CRC, helping adults and institutions to improve the welfare and well-being of children globally. The language used to establish children's rights emphasises normal and acceptable forms of intergenerational relations, which obscure underlying social and political structures of power. This may thus be seen as an expression of Lukes's third version of power (Lukes, 2005) and converges with Foucault's (1977) ideas about 'regimes' of truth and knowledge.

In relation to the first dominant form of rights, providing for and protecting children may be felt and viewed as an imperative or, on occasion, a threat, particularly from a higher political body. As we will see in Chapter 4, the concept of 'responsibility' is a double-edged sword which empowers adults to structure children's growing up but also puts adults on the defensive in terms of discharging their obligations. Nevertheless, welfare rights reinforce underlying positions of adults in structuring children's development and future. In an important sense, 'acceptable' and 'normal' forms of adult–child relations implicit in Quennerstedt's quotation above are more directly found in the expectations that adults provide for and protect children. Moreover, the simple fact that we still talk about concepts like 'child development' suggests that adults retain power with respect to children.

In relation to the second form, children's rights to participation, there would appear to be more potential for children to refine if not challenge the assumption that children's lives are best directed and structured by adults. We discussed several forms of participation which focus on the child's capacity to engage with adults in terms of their own development as well as make contributions to institutional and community practices and contexts within which they inhabit. Much of the work on children's right to participate extends the meaning and practice of children's engagement from consultation through to child-focused initiatives. The dominant model of participation lies closest to the former, with adults structuring children's participation across Lukes's three dimensions of power (Lukes, 2005). Institutional forums encourage children to engage with their peers, but this is often carefully choreographed by adults, who also have the final say, giving 'due weight' to the voices of particular groups of children on particular areas. Adults are also often expected to retain participation within narrowly defined institutional, and often educational, boundaries. While children may have particular grievances and ideas that they wish to promote, the means through which they can be readily articulated and legitimated are seldom available to them within such institutional contexts.

Based on the discussion in this chapter, we question whether the global child rights movement, in spite of having led to major changes to children's status globally, has also led to children becoming more powerful. We have argued that, contrary to the idea that participation usurps the position of parents and teachers, the global rights agenda offers a narrowly constructed idea of participation, which is more likely to connect with the life worlds of affluent world children living in more liberal democratic societies. Fundamentally, children's rights is an adult concept – a way for institutions, parents and professionals working with children to take more responsibility for children's welfare and offer them heavily regulated forms of participation.

# Chapter 3

# CHILD-CENTREDNESS, SCHOOLING AND KID POWER

In this chapter, we analyse 'child-centredness' as a concept and address the question: does child-centredness equate with more power for children? We offer an analysis of this question by focusing on social and professional trends, variously referred to as child-focused, child-friendly and child intensive. These are all part of the trend we identify as 'child-centredness' – reflecting the emphasis on late twentieth-century ideas around repositioning children more centrally within relations, networks, media, policy and practice. One area where the idea of child-centredness is apparent is within school settings, where it is understood as an ideology, a pedagogy and a powerful form of professional practice (Langford, 2010). Using case studies from primary school contexts in different countries, we analyse some of the different ways in which child-centredness is applied and practised and the implications this has for power and power relations within schools and in the home. In the previous chapter, we argued that the children's rights agenda has led to a trend towards strengthening children's voices. While schools increasingly include children's voice in their daily work, the way this is sought and executed is often based on adult modes of communication and thus works to reinforce existing power relations. Child-centredness generates new ways of regulating children at a distance and as such has little to do with children having more power. As with children's rights in the previous chapter, child-centredness furthermore favours particular groups of children, making child-centredness unequal in its process and potentially also in its outcomes.

## Child-Centred Pedagogy

The theoretical and philosophical basis of child-centredness draws on the work of developmental psychologists such as Jean Piaget and the early twentieth-century educational philosopher John Dewey. Piaget emphasised the need to nurture and shape children's capacities as they learn to develop (Piaget, 1932; Burman, 2007). He furthermore focused on play as a way in which teachers are able to apply elaborately constructed measures of a child's development in the classroom (Walkerdine, 1984). In line with this, nursery and early-years teachers in the Global North often focus on children's developmental capacities, by setting them play-based activities. For the youngest children, sensory motor and cognitive skills are developed through these activities. As they grow up, children gradually move through various stages of development, away from physical skills towards more abstract and three-dimensional cognitive capacities that allow them to see their world and the worlds of others in progressively more sophisticated ways. Teachers adjust learning tasks accordingly, focusing on how the individual child responds to these tasks, how they manipulate objects and start to think through the relationship between these objects. Child-centred pedagogy thus becomes a form of applied developmental psychology, what some have referred to as 'developmentally appropriate practices' (Fowler, 2017; Woodhead, 2009).

Piaget's ideas on the child's invariant upwards movement towards full cognitive and emotional competence can be visualised through the checklists of capacities that children develop as they get older. The development of skills is observed, monitored and assessed by teachers as they move between different groups of children in class. Walkerdine (1984) refers to the nursery record cards used in the 1980s in the United Kingdom as an instrument for monitoring children's development. One of the criteria on a nursery card is 'Perception – Motor' followed by a number of questions including, 'Is he reasonably coordinated? Can he understand and use simple tools and construction toys?' (p. 158). Similar 'learning records' are used in British nurseries today, as part of the Early Years Learning framework. These leave little need for didactic teaching as nursery teachers are able to tick off a checklist of activities and skills while children perform and demonstrate them through play. This implies more horizontal relations between the teacher and children interacting in groups as the children master the various play activities.

Dewey's conception of education was based on principles that challenged more conventional didactic approaches to children and teaching. He rejected the top-down controlling capacities of teachers and conceptualised education in terms of 'assisting through cooperation the natural capacities of the individuals guided' (Dewey, 2014: 17). First, children were viewed as active learners and learning as a quintessentially social activity where children were expected to continuously engage with others. Education was thus a means rather than an end. Second, knowledge was seen as relative and grounded in reality. Children were to respond to their social environments, and through their engagement with others they developed their linguistic and cognitive capacities. Drawing on the work of G. H. Mead (1934), Dewey described how children come to learn about the world in and through the way that others respond to them in a range of diverse settings. Third, and following this, he viewed the school as a workshop or laboratory, where children learn through various forms of experimentation. Importantly, Dewey rejected the dualism between the school as the sole arbiter of knowledge and the commonsensical and partial learning that children experience within the home and the community. Schools were seen as more organically located within the community, with teachers helping to bridge the gap between formal and informal knowledge. Just as schools were displaced as the repository of legitimate knowledge, Dewey also clearly argued that the teacher was displaced from a sovereign authority role within the classroom:

> The teacher is not in the school to impose certain ideas or to form certain habits in the child, but is there as a member of the community to select influences which shall affect the child and to assist him in properly responding to these influences. (Dewey and Archambault, 1964: 432)

Moreover, the disciplinarian role of the teacher, a crucial feature of more traditional conceptions of teachers, was displaced with 'the discipline of the school [proceeding] directly from the life of the school as a whole and not directly from the teacher' (ibid.). Fishman and McCarthy (1998: 20) refer to this as a form of 'indirect' teaching where the classroom is a highly interactive space within which teaching and learning activities take place between student and teacher and between student and student.

Myagmar (2010) discusses the features that differentiate teacher-centred from child-centred approaches. She argues that while the former emphasises whole class teaching, the latter focuses on the individual child and the unique capacities of each child to learn. This has led to a concomitant interest in the diversity of children as pupils within the classroom. Furthermore, children are assumed to have 'an instinct to play' and this has become a frame through which children's learning is constructed (Myagmar, 2010: 65). Finally, rather than an emphasis on discrete subjects transmitted by the teacher to the whole class, child-centred approaches emphasise more integrated topic-related work which connects with the lifeworlds of the children.

One example of the way that the teacher can focus on the grounded social interests of children is in the kinds of contributions that children themselves can make towards the curriculum. Let us take a fictional example of this: April was a 9-year-old girl living in London who went back to her parents' home country in Barbados for three weeks during the summer holidays. On returning to her primary school at the beginning of September, the teacher spent the first day back asking the children to talk about what they did over the summer holidays. April talked about her trip in front of the class and the teacher decided to use her holiday in Barbados to teach a range of subjects including geography, science, English and social relationships. The holiday formed the basis of a topic through which parts of the curriculum were being taught. The teacher drew on an activity or event that was personal to the child and built some of her lessons around it.

Capturing children's interests is one important feature of a child-centred pedagogy, and in some cases children are able to take the initiative (Sugrue, 1997) and introduce a topic which is then transformed into an educational theme by the teacher. However, teachers will translate their interests in developmental terms and mould their learning through these 'interests'. Another important feature of child-centred pedagogy is that children tend to work in groups with their peers rather than have a linear relationship on an individual basis with the teacher. Group work is unpredictable in terms of the dynamic of the classroom and may generate complex relations among the various classroom participants. Moreover, a child-centred approach generates movement and noise among pupils within the classroom. In teacher-centred terms, the noise and physical movement of children in class is associated with disruptive behaviour. However, within group-oriented work, children are expected to engage with their peers and noise and physical movement is thus viewed differently. Teachers surveil their activities drawing on their experience and knowledge of managing young children in regulating classroom activities. Thus, while child-centredness encourages activity and movement among children, it cannot be equated with taking control of the curriculum, the teaching or the spaces within which both take place.

For example, in returning to the case of April, she was unlikely to be informed or consulted about the curriculum. Neither was she in a position to suggest or dictate the content of her lessons. The teacher was able to 'scaffold' her teaching around the child's experiences, which had the effect of engaging with children in terms of how their own experiences help to shape their learning and at the same time allow the teacher to justify the lessons in terms of recognisable subject areas. However, there is little sense that she, even within such child-centred practices, exercised power over her teachers or that the teachers redistributed their power. Alexander (2001: 555) gives short shrift to the idea that primary teaching in England has mitigated the power of teachers in favour of pupils: there is 'no obvious democratic commitment within the classroom, but rather a strong allegiance to a developmental view of the individual within a framework of unambiguous teacher authority'. Teacher control is a generic term for a range of quite diverse strategies adopted by teachers in exercising power over children. Child-centredness constitutes one popular means of keeping control in class, although by some it has been interpreted as giving too much power to children.

## Child-Centred Practices

In England and Wales, the move towards a national curriculum in the 1980s was partly a response to an alleged rise in child-centred practices in English and Welsh primary schools. Various policy documents during the Thatcher era referred to what was seen as a liberal, if not left-wing, tendency within the teaching profession towards loosening classroom structures, generating more space for children to inform the curriculum (Alexander et al., 1992). Particular concerns were articulated over a perceived decline in subject work leading to lower levels of literacy and numeracy. An emphasis on topics rather than subjects was argued to lead to 'fragmentary and superficial teaching and learning'. Teachers were not deploying their authority and control over children in providing a standardised curriculum (ibid.: 2). In Bernstein's (1971) terms, classroom interactions were weakly 'framed', with teachers having limited levels of control over the curriculum.

In some ways this focus on child-centred teaching was simply a shift from more teacher-centred rote learning approaches, typical of the first half of the twentieth century, towards more topic-based discursive approaches which encouraged children to engage with the curriculum through forms of interaction with peers. Sugrue (1997: 1) refers to this in terms of the 'two grand narratives of teaching': 'traditional' and 'progressive' forms. The former emphasises content-driven teaching where teachers instructed children across a range of curricular subjects. Children here were 'actively passive and industriously receptive' as they internalised the knowledge directly from the teacher for most of the school day (Sugrue, 1997: 6). Ryan offers a definition of the latter:

> In a child-centered education, the curriculum begins with the needs and interests of the child and responds to the unique characteristics of childhood. Teachers use their knowledge of how children develop to structure learning experiences that facilitate children's learning through play and discovery. Children, therefore, are viewed as active learners who require freedom from adult authority to explore ideas independently and make sense of their world. (Ryan, 2005: 99)

The references to 'freedom' and 'independence' are anathema to conservative critics of child-centredness. These are also concepts that characterise adulthood, a state that children aspire to as they grow up. However, although child-centredness places emphasis on the child rather than the teacher, there is little sense that the practice as advocated in early years and primary schools globally offers us an absence of teacher power and authority. There is no one-to-one transmission of knowledge from a powerful source to a powerless child;

however, there is a more refined hierarchical relationship as teachers seek to encourage children to learn in and through active play with their peers. We define this more refined generational relationship in the following sections.

## Pedagogical Approaches and Global Variation

There has been a trend towards child-centred teaching and learning globally, particularly where countries have expanded their provision of institutional early years' education. The international commitment to preschool education through the Education for All (EFA) initiative has underpinned this trend with a commitment to 'expanding and improving comprehensive early childhood care and education, especially for the most vulnerable and disadvantaged children' (UNESCO 2015: Goal 1). The UNESCO report notes that by 2012, 184 million children were in pre-primary education worldwide, representing a 60 per cent increase since the inception of EFA in 1999 (UNESCO, 2015). Much of the global investment in early childhood education has been accompanied by a move towards more Northern child-centred approaches with an emphasis on play and development (Education International ECE Task Force 2010; Wyness, 2019).

However, the professed claim to child-centredness has been viewed as tokenistic in some countries. In Mongolia, for example, a stated shift to a child-centred pedagogy has been challenged by researchers arguing that there is little or no space created for children in class to engage with children's interests (Myagmar, 2010). While some teachers might profess to adopting a more child-centred approach, the pedagogy and curriculum are driven by the interests of the teacher and the school. Furthermore, other countries show little commitment to child-centredness, and there is considerable pedagogical variation between countries. In some instances, adult-centred approaches prevail particularly in early years and elementary schools. Traditional forms of teaching are still apparent within many education systems where teachers perform a more sovereign didactic role within the learning process. For example, Partovi and Wyness (2020) examine the contemporary pedagogic situation in Iranian primary schools where teachers play a more overtly powerful role over their pupils. Iranian teachers refer to a 'monologue pedagogy', a top-down unidirectional form of communication between children and teachers in the classroom.

Iranian classrooms, similar to many classrooms across the world, are likely to be square-shaped with few possibilities for children to display their work publicly. Primary school children sit as pairs in a regimented fashion on individual chairs in linear rows facing the black or white boards. The teacher's desk is usually raised above pupils, which affords a degree of surveillance within the class, and the relationship between teacher and pupil is much more formal with children facing the front rather than peers, expected to sit and listen to the directives of the teacher. The teacher remains at the front of the class in her 'sovereign' position surveilling all forms of pupil activity. The architectural space within the classroom renders it difficult for the teacher and the children to move around the class; the children are rooted to their own individual spaces, which makes it difficult for them to engage with interactive forms of participation. This emphasises the link between spatial layout and teaching practices (Allan and Jørgensen, 2020). Furthermore, topic-based group work does not feature in routine classroom activities in classrooms, such as these, and the emphasis is predominantly on teacher 'instruction' rather than 'active learning' (Partovi and Wyness 2020). As we discussed in the previous chapter, the Iranian state has reservations over the child-focused nature of the 1989 UN Convention on the Rights of the Child (CRC), and this top-down focus is also reflected in the teacher-centred pedagogic approach in schools.

It is also worth referring to cultural contexts where play, a vehicle for the expression of child-centredness in nurseries and primary schools, is still viewed in pejorative terms. For example, Sarangapani (2003) found that in rural Indian schools, play was perceived as antithetical to discipline in both behavioural and pedagogical terms. Teachers had 'absolute' authority and parents exercised a 'parallel' authority, from which children's dominant predisposition towards adults was 'obedience'. Overt discipline was a key feature of teaching approaches, with teacher authority and power 'naturalised', through common community-based ideas and practices that highlight generational hierarchies. Also in a more recent study of a rural Indian school, Sriprakash (2010: 304) observed that while educational reforms emphasised more democratic and holistic learning, the way the teacher implemented child-centred pedagogy tended to reinforce 'social messages of control and hierarchy'.

In China, play is often not seen as having educational value but viewed as an additional activity for children after the work of teaching and learning has finished. There have been attempts in recent years by early-years practitioners to introduce more child-centred approaches to teaching in early years' and elementary schools. Nevertheless, the influence of Confucian principles, particularly in Chinese nursery schools, still powerfully counters any Northern-influenced pedagogies of play (Lau and Cheng, 2010; Yang, 2013). Confucianism highlights a clear deferential and hierarchical relationship between child and teacher. From an early age, children develop the capacity of 'self-cultivation', through a highly formal relationship with their teachers. As with rural Indian and Iranian teachers, Chinese practitioners are expected to have a formal and highly structured role within the classroom. Children learn through the top-down transmission of knowledge and rules, and power is overtly exercised by teachers as sovereign figures within the classroom.

### Early years' education in Reggio Emilia

Progressive and radical versions of child-centredness have developed in Europe, for example, in schools inspired by Maria Montessori, Rudolf Steiner and the Reggio Emilia approach (Edwards, 2002). Particularly, the Reggio Emilia approach has been highly influential in some circles. This approach, developed after the Second World War in Reggio Emilia, a city in Northern Italy, celebrates the capacities of young children to engage with processes of teaching and learning. Reggio Emilia preschools were funded and organised by the Catholic church until the 1960s, when they were taken over by the local authorities. With an immediate historic and political context of fascism, the founders set out to create a generation of creative and independent young people, a generation who would challenge the rise of powerful political forces (Thornton and Brunton, 2015). Reggio Emilia currently functions as an intricate web of educational and social support for preschoolers involving formal and informal agencies and groups. Professionals, local authority personnel and parents are involved in running the various activities that young children dip in and out of within the city. Networks of learning are developed through the set-up of 'learning groups' where children work with teachers, artists and sometimes parents in developing the children's social cognitive and emotional capacities (Thornton and Brunton, 2015). Reggio Emilia thus follows Dewey's idea that schooling and learning should be located more organically within the local community.

In many respects, the Reggio Emilia approach has been advocated and, in some instances, adopted globally because it offers a model of a community-based and non-bureaucratic version of teaching and learning. As with the shift towards child-centredness in English primary schools in the 1970s, it is a child-centred approach to teaching and learning (Giardiello and McNulty, 2009; Thornton and Brunton, 2015). As we argued earlier, child-centredness as a pedagogy in England was based around child development principles, with teachers playing a prominent role as monitors and facilitators. Reggio Emilia, on the other hand, is based more on the principles of children having the capacity and freedom to develop and engage with the various learning activities on offer. Whereas English children's curriculum initiatives are ad hoc and dependent on the time and capacity of the teacher, in Reggio Emilia children's initiatives are an integral feature of classroom agendas. The focus is very much on what children bring into school rather than how adults can shape and mould children. Reggio Emilia has no formal curriculum and nothing written down which teachers can consult. There are thus limited structures and guidelines; Reggio Emilia classes have very little adult intervention in the content of what children are taught. Much of the documentation is produced by the children themselves: working with local artists and teachers, the children generate more personalised portfolios of work, quite often in the form of drawings, paintings and photographs.

Moreover, the conception of childhood implicit in Reggio Emilia is more focused on the contributions that children can make within their communities. Moss and Petrie (2002) refer to the 'rich child', and Dahlberg et al. (2013: 122) define this model of childhood as the 'child of infinite capabilities, a child born with a hundred languages [...] foregrounding relationships and encounter[ing] dialogue and negotiation, reflection and critical thinking'. The child is competent and enabling as well as being enabled. The standard global model of the (schooled) child is a product of neoliberal conceptions of competitive individual achievement, carefully regulated until developmentally ready and socially peripheral with limited expectations of any social contributions. The Reggio Emilia child, on the other hand, is a more social being, fully immersed within the social and political world from an early age, and working alongside parents, professionals and city officials. Children learn and are creative in and through ongoing relations they have with the different kinds of adults around them.

Following a similar intergenerational approach, some European countries employ pedagogues as professional child workers in early childhood settings to engage with children, working alongside them and encouraging dialogue between themselves and children. The pedagogue has a strong intergenerational focus, and Moss and Petrie (2002: 143) argue that employing pedagogues encourages a more relational approach: 'The child is not regarded as an autonomous and detached subject, but as living in networks of relationships, involving both children and adults.' Adults, such as pedagogues, teachers, parents, professionals and members of the community, are central, along with the children, in developing relations that further children's learning (Dahlberg et al., 2013). Yet the agentic possibilities and capabilities of the 'rich child' emphasised in the Reggio Emilia approach and the work of pedagogues do not automatically equate with the altering of adult–child power relations in a zero-sum sense. Adults have not capitulated to children, and there is also little sense that adults have receded into the background (Wyness, 2013a).

Dahlberg et al. (2013) refer to all forms of pedagogy as 'technologies of power' where children are subjected to different forms of disciplinary power which act on children, both regulating and normalising them. Through a range of techniques which have little to do with the unilateral impositions of teachers, children are both learning forms of self-discipline and incorporating the common practices and the expectations of the school in positioning themselves within the classroom. The significant difference between the child-centred and the teacher-focused classroom is that power in the latter is exercised in a unilateral and unambiguous sense. However, in child-centred classrooms, power in the Foucauldian sense has a normalising capacity which is both restrictive and productive. Children are unlikely to be constantly aware that power is being exercised over them, particularly where the activities may be more child-focused and generated. Furthermore, where adults are perceived as being powerful participants, they are in a position to use this power positively. Ghirotto and Mazzoni (2013) argue, in their analysis of children in Reggio Emilia, that the adults working with the young children were in a position to encourage greater participation and creativity. Nevertheless, the genuine attempts to create more democratic relations between children and adults provide little basis for viewing Reggio Emilia as an expression of lost adult power. Dahlberg et al. (2013: 123) as proponents of Reggio Emilia have asserted that 'the child and pedagogue' are viewed 'as co-constructors of knowledge and identity', thus emphasising the potential for a more consensual and positive-sum notion of intergenerational power.

## Child-Centredness as a Form of Control

Various theorists and researchers have argued that child-centredness offers a genuine pedagogical alternative to more traditional teacher-centred approaches. We have argued that, although this may be the case, in its conventional sense, it does not lead to a major shift in the balance of power towards children, despite a common perception that bottom-up child-focused approaches disempower adults. In their classic ethnography and Marxist analysis of a London primary school in the 1970s, Sharp and Green (1975) provide an example of how child-centredness may in fact work as a form of social control. They highlight the difficulties that working-class children had with the curriculum and illustrate how teachers drew on child-centred pedagogy as a means of keeping order in class. Teachers articulated a particular version of child-centredness as a progressive approach to working with the children in their classrooms. There was the eschewal of a formal curriculum and the top-down whole-class approach in favour of more group-oriented activities in the classroom. The children were, furthermore, given a degree of autonomy in how they engaged with the materials and resources, and the focus was on the individual child and his or her interactions through play. There was a rhetoric of freedom and engagement among the teachers as children interacted with their peers in groups through forms of discovery with minimal teacher intervention. However, in effect, group play was a strategy for keeping children occupied while teachers attended to the educational needs of a minority of more able children within the classroom. Teachers permitted children to choose an activity with which they could engage with their peers with minimal supervision – they were, in effect, kept busy. This 'busyness' could be mistaken for child-centredness as children worked on various 'self-directed' activities in groups with their peers. However, in Sharp and Green's analysis, the strategies of the teachers for keeping order in class resembled a form of social control. If children could be engaged in activities within their groups, it made it less likely that these same children would get bored and become disruptive. This interpretation provides little sense that the children were being empowered. Despite the perception that groups of children were being left to their own devices, child-centredness had limited purchase in terms of power and individual freedom.

Another, post-structuralist, analysis of child-centredness as a form of control was offered by Walkerdine (1984), who argued that the elementary school classroom is a site for the production of knowledge and identities for both children and teachers. Under the banner of child-centredness, children interact more regularly with their peers and teachers as they engage with educational material. This, however, also involves a translation of developmental concepts into educational practices and children being grouped according to teacher-determined criteria and given tasks to complete with their peers. The 'instruction' takes the form of teachers surveilling children by moving around the classroom and monitoring the progress of children within their groups. Whereas assessment in more traditional pedagogical approaches is outcome-based with children being ranked according to how well they have performed in tests, child-centredness involves continuous assessment (Walkerdine, 1984). Teachers observe, monitor and assess children's progress against a normative model of the developing child and make judgements on how well children are learning by referring to this model through charts and lists – what Walkerdine, as we discussed earlier, refers to as 'developmental records' (1984: 450). The latter are used to tick off the various developmental milestones that children achieve as they engage with their peers through play, giving central importance to emotional and cognitive development. While there is little overt top-down attempt to prescribe a curriculum that all children should assiduously follow in relative silence, teachers through this surveillance are able to strategically intervene and shift the focus of the activities. There is thus little sense in which children are free from teacher intervention or direction. Walkerdine (1993: 454–55) in a later article similarly argues,

This freed child has every action calibrated so as to assure that development will be normal and natural, go according to plan because abnormal and pathological development has to be noted, classified and corrected.

The notion of a 'universal' development, however, is strongly based on European and male-centred 'norms' and, as argued by Walkerdine (1993), constructs 'otherness' around gender, class and cultural variation. Drawing on Foucault, she shows how universal development is produced as a 'truth' which works as a form of social control to define 'what is understood and why' (Walkerdine, 1993: 454), for example, in the school context. In a more recent study, Langford (2010) has also offered a critique of child-centredness in terms of processes of normalisation. She argues that children are closely monitored in developmental terms, with teachers working from a 'normal' model of the child as a rational, autonomous, developing proto adult. Children are 'shaped benevolently into rational beings' (Langford, 2010: 24), and those children who do not conform to this model are liable to further and more intensive surveillance to bring them in line with this construct of 'normality'. Power et al. (2019: 573) have similarly pointed out that developmental stage theories 'provide idealised models of how children learn, they do not encompass either the diverse social circumstances in which children are socialised or the characteristics of the institutions in which they are educated'. Consequently, they argue, child-centredness works better for some children than others.

## Child-Centredness and Inequality

Both Marxist and post-structuralist interpretations of child-centredness in English primary schools in the 1970s and 1980s showed how child-centred teaching involved the teacher nurturing, regulating and, in some instances, controlling children from a distance. Issues of power surfaced in the role that teachers played as 'facilitators' rather than instructors with sovereign authority within the classroom. However, and crucial to our discussion of kid power, while the shift towards the former from the latter might have provided more opportunities for children to innovate and take initiative, it did not lead to more power to children. Furthermore, as Walkerdine (1993), Langford (2010) and others (Power et al., 2019) have critically discussed, child-centred learning is based on assumptions about universal development, play and learning, which tend to neglect sociocultural and gendered contexts of development and learning.

The child at the centre of this pedagogy can thus be seen as overly individualized, as 'the pilgrim, the cowboy, and the detective on television – invariably seen as a free-standing isolable being who moves through development as a self-contained and complete individual' (Kessen, in Morss, 1996: 43–44). Public commentary also generally takes for granted that the benefits and limitations of child-centredness have a universal effect on the child population, irrespective of background. This section explores diversity within the child population and how it plays out in relation to child-centredness. In challenging the conflation of child-centredness with kid power, we focus on how school-based practices may not only appear to favour and free up particular groups of children but also further rigidify the hierarchical relationship with other groups of children by assuming a universal model of the individual developing child.

As demonstrated by Sharp and Green (1975), keeping order in a child-centred classroom may feed into broader social processes of inequality. In their study, a minority of high attaining children in the class took up disproportionate amounts of the teachers' time, and other groups of children, often children from lower-income or disadvantaged backgrounds, were left to get on playing with their peers. Teachers loosely applied child-centred teaching practices among the better-off children, those who they believed were developmentally ready, but the bulk of children in the classrooms were regulated at a distance by the teacher. In this analysis, it thus seemed that it was predominantly middle-class children who benefited from the shift in focus from the teacher to the pupil. In effect, child-centredness in school became about control and differentiation along social class lines, rather than a blanket empowerment of children.

A more recent study of the Welsh Foundation Phase curriculum (Power et al., 2019) further supports the argument that child-centred learning strategies tend to favour particular students. Power et al. (2019) argue that such strategies are based on 'invisible pedagogies' which assume that learning in school is supplemented at home. Child-centred pedagogies furthermore require greater investment of time and space than traditional teacher-centred pedagogies. This, they argue, leaves working-class children doubly disadvantaged as they not only 'lack the requisite resources and educationally oriented activities in the home, but they will also experience a relatively impoverished and less supportive pedagogy in the classroom' (ibid.: 586). The authors also found that girls fared much better than boys in child-centred classrooms, highlighting the importance of gender alongside class in the analysis of child-centredness and power.

Exploring generational relations in the home in relation to child-centred practices at school further allows us to identify 'empowering processes within middle class families that permit teachers to develop their child-centred strategies' (Sharp et al., 1975: 79). Drawing on the work of Bourdieu, Lareau (2011) has focused on the origins of child-centredness within middle-class families in the United States. For Lareau, differences in life chances between working-class and middle-class children are located within the home, where children's capacities to engage in school are shaped in meaningful ways. Child-rearing practices underlie socio-economic differences and shape the nature of relations that children have within the school. Middle-class parents view their children as individualised projects to be shaped and prepared for school and life beyond the family as they grow up. Lareau refers to this child-rearing strategy as *concerted cultivation*. Children develop a sense of entitlement, a self-confidence in terms of their relations with others through the way that parents communicate with them within the home. Children are encouraged to have a voice, to articulate in a rational manner and to engage with others in a more confident and assertive way. In Bourdieu's terms, children develop the cultural capital enabling them to thrive within a predominantly middle-class context, the school (Bourdieu and Passeron, 1977). In Lareau's analysis, working-class parents, on the other hand, provide a culturally and socially more constraining context through which their children grow up. Their strategy is based on *accomplishment of natural growth* and emphasises children's emotional well-being rather than their cognitive capacities. Communication here is limited and constrained by social conventions. Parents are more likely to leave their children's educational development in the hands of teachers and tend to view their children's capacity to learn as a product of nature or genetics. Children thus learn about constraints rather than developing an 'entitlement' mindset generated within middle-class families.

In one sense, concerted cultivation may be seen as approximating to the idea of child-centredness. Issues of entitlement converge with the idea of centring on the child and children developing communicative strategies for asserting their interests and needs. They generate a sense of who they are, a more individualised and autonomous self from which they are able to make claims on society. This also links in important ways with children's status as rights holders, which we discussed in the previous chapter. For example, children's right to a voice advances the idea of the assertive, self-confident middle-class child. However, an alternative interpretation could be that concerted cultivation strategies may be more about gaining advantage in a competitive education and labour market (Vincent and Maxwell, 2016) than about the individual child's interests and abilities. Just as child-centredness in school is arguably a way for educationalists to prepare middle-class children for more powerful positions within the broader society, so middle-class parents provide the space, resources and mindsets within which children are able to both connect and compete within a more individualistic school system and society. Vincent and Maxwell (2016) have furthermore critiqued Lareau's binary analysis of working-class versus middle-class parents and emphasised the importance of considering a range of intersecting motivations and strategies. For example, they discuss findings from a study of middle-class Black parents in the United Kingdom (Vincent et al., 2013), which showed that the parents pursued enrichment activities for their children for a number of reasons, including to gain advantage and obtain credentials in the context of racism, as well as asserting their middle-classness in a society that often portrays Black families uniformly as having working-class backgrounds (Vincent et al., 2013; Vincent and Maxwell, 2016). Studies of parenting strategies and priorities among minority ethnic and migrant families further complicate class-based analysis as they show how class may intersect with other more cultural perceptions and be influenced by the specific context of race and/or migration (Bodovski, 2010; Dumais et al., 2012; Fischer et al., 2009).

Another concept which further links children's diverse homes with child-centred pedagogies is the concept of 'readiness'. The idea of readiness assumes that the teacher in many respects will be working with the labours of others: parents. Children starting school between the ages of 4 and 7 are already socialised into (ready for) particular ways of thinking and behaving. As the early years are now taken up with children spending progressively more time in preschool contexts, the concept of readiness is also likely to apply to children at a much earlier age moving into the nursery or the preschool (e.g. Houri and Miller, 2020). Readiness is a frequently used term in the child development and educational psychology literature (Hojnoski and Missall, 2006; Slicker and Hustedt, 2019), where the strategies and behaviours of different groups of parents have been associated with more or less likelihood of their children being ready for school or preschool settings (e.g. Bono et al., 2016; Xia et al., 2020; Xie and Li, 2018). The idea of readiness thus directs us towards understanding the moral, social as well as educational investments that parents make in their children from birth. Parents are supposed to provide children with a home-learning environment (Goodman et al., 2010), and judgements are made by various professionals about the extent to which children are developmentally, emotionally and socially ready to move into different social settings such as the nursery or the school and, if not, what interventions can be suggested for parents to aid their children's school readiness.

## Conclusion

Whereas traditional pedagogies are based on unambiguous downward lines of power and authority between teacher and pupil, child-centredness is more regulatory with teachers surveilling children at a distance and always in a position to change the task or alter the combination of children in the group. Teaching arrangements are much less vertical, and the primary school becomes a learning nexus within which children are engaging actively with their peers as well as the teacher. Children are the focal points within this nexus both individually and collectively, and this has led to a common assumption that child-centredness also involves them having more power.

Conservative commentators from affluent countries have also in the past associated child-centredness with a decline in education and behavioural standards (Alexander et al., 1992). There is a barely concealed attempt to return to deferential and hierarchical relations within the classroom. These views converge with top-down pedagogical practices found in many non-Northern countries. Despite the global influence of child-centred approaches, countries such as Iran, India and China retain more traditional teacher-centred approaches. In the context of China, Confucianist influence in teaching emphasises knowledge being formally handed down from teacher to child. Teaching is suffused by children's deference and their adherence to the overtly powerful position of the adult educator. Child-centredness clearly contradicts this conception of teacher–child relations. However, also within countries that have embraced child-centredness as an educational approach, international and national agendas increasingly focusing on standards, accountability and individual performance have resulted in more rigid curricular practices and testing, both of which necessarily limit the creative inputs of children. Furthermore, it has been suggested that a combination of approaches might benefit those children who find themselves disadvantaged by the invisible pedagogies inherent in the child-centred approach (Power et al., 2019).

In this chapter, we have critically explored the idea that a shift towards child-centredness, particularly in school, reflects an underlying shift in the balance of power between children and adults. We have focused on child-centredness in its various manifestations, as a pedagogy centring on the interests and the development of the child and as a process of democratising relations between pupils and teachers. In thinking about teaching and learning and the curriculum in terms of the interests of the child, the impression is given that educationalists in some way shift power towards children, at least for some groups of children and adults. However, while there has been a shift towards centring teaching around the interests of children, there is little sense that children shape, let alone dominate, the agenda within schools. Teachers in the early years draw heavily on developmental psychology as a supposedly universal framework within which they can shape children's formal education, but this may connect more closely to some children than others. Teachers also occupy a different position both spatially and pedagogically within child-centred learning, eschewing a single dominant line of communication and static and highly visible hierarchical relations. Teachers favour more movement within and between individual pupils and groups, surveilling children's development and refining children's classroom-based activities.

It thus seems that child-centredness can be seen as a process whereby adults shift from a more overt 'power over' position to shaping and constructing children from a distance. In this chapter, we have argued that in the context of child-centredness, power can consequently be understood in a more Foucauldian sense, with developmental psychology seen both as a regime of truth in terms of its perceived universality and a series of techniques for the surveillance of children as they develop and grow up. There is a shift to more subtle, sometimes concealed, horizontal forms of control as teachers provide the resources and spaces within which younger children's development can be shaped. There is almost a panoptical effect with teachers at a distance monitoring, assessing and classifying the movements of children. In Lukes's (2005) terms, power inheres in the capacity of teachers to regulate the activities and education of younger children through encouraging more child-directed activities. However, teachers and educationalists retain agenda-setting powers and offer children highly regulated spaces within which their interests are accommodated. Furthermore, as children are being surveilled by teachers, so teachers themselves are under pressure to perform as measured by inspectors and pupils' academic output (Ball, 2003).

A class analysis reveals child-centredness as an ideology or a regime of truth, which gives the impression that teachers focus on the children's development and educational well-being irrespective of their family and class backgrounds. Child-centredness focuses on the individual child claiming to provide an educational space through which children develop and thrive. However, child-centredness in the form of group work and play may also constitute a strategy for controlling groups of 'difficult', less engaged children, in effect keeping them busy. Furthermore, child-centredness is an individualising strategy which tends to connect better with the lifeworlds of middle-class rather than working-class children. Some have also suggested that the opportunities and capacities of children to engage individually with learning is shaped by gender and ethnicity and have critically commented that child-centred pedagogy is decontextualised and denies social differences between children (Langford, 2010). The emphasis on the freeing up of children from more traditional didactic practices where power is explicitly and overtly exercised by teachers and parents has thus neglected other less overt expressions of power and overly focused on the free and decontextualised individual child (ibid.). In the following chapter, we continue to critically examine the assumed shift of power towards children by focusing on the position and status of adults.

# Chapter 4

# THE LOSS OF ADULT POWER?

In this chapter, we address the question of whether a move towards more power and influence for children inevitably leads to the loss of adult power. As we have previously noted, conventional conceptions of kid power have predominantly viewed the relationship between children and adults in zero-sum terms. In this view, kid power involves either a shift in the balance of power from adults to children, or quite simply the loss of adult power and authority and a concomitant increase in the capacity of children to wield forms of power over adults. This chapter examines the alleged rise of kid power from the vantage point of adulthood – the position, roles and responsibilities that different kinds of adults occupy within generational structures. We argue that adult power is to some extent compromised by the way that various external forces converge on the capacity of adults to shape children's welfare and, in effect, their ability to mediate between children and the wider world. We explore several related themes. In the first part, we discuss the loss of adulthood in terms of the rise of technology and the expansion of the global marketplace that incorporates children as economic actors. We draw on Postman's (1982) classic thesis on the disappearance of adulthood, to analyse the rise of digital technology and its implications for generational relations. We critically examine the thesis that the advent of technology has led to the blurring of boundaries between child and adult spheres, and the concomitant disempowering of adults.

In the second part of the chapter, we focus on the political context for adults' loss of power. We examine the role that global discourses and national policies play in replacing the mediating role of parents with a political framework that centres on the welfare and needs of children. A number of related themes are discussed here, including state intervention and the rise of the 'responsible parent' as a discursive mechanism for disciplining parents, the role of the state and the move from bipartite to tripartite relations, and the decline of corporal power. In the final section, we explore children's narratives on adult power and discuss whether children themselves support the idea that adults are losing power.

## Adulthood, Technology and the Global Market

To some extent, arguments around the loss or disappearance of childhood make it difficult to provide equivalent analyses of adulthood. The dominant ontological assumptions of childhood as a transitional period locate children along educational, social and developmental trajectories en route to completion as adults. Adulthood is the implicit benchmark with social scientists, developmental psychologists, educationalists and marketers preoccupied with getting children up to an 'adult' standard (Wyness, 2019). In an ontological and social sense, children are lesser than adults.

Historically, evolutionary arguments have focused on recapitulation theory,[1] where childhood recapitulates human development. A parallel is drawn between the evolution of humankind and the development of children towards adulthood, both equated with civilisation (Burman, 2008). Childhood equates a natural state to be tamed and adulthood the end and high point of civilisation. However, rather than theorise the nature of adulthood, this implies a model of the fully constituted social being. Children's movement towards this end state – what is referred to as childhood – is measured against the end point of adulthood. At the same time, traditional sociological theory views adult power as a necessary and temporary state. In order for children to grow up, they take on a powerless dependent role and, gradually over time, assume powerful positions as they move towards adulthood. The power relationship, as it were, withers away (Parsons,1951). However, just as children grow up towards adulthood, so they are replaced by other children who, like them, start off in positions of powerlessness. In structural terms, adulthood is a permanent position which adults occupy as a position of power vis-à-vis children (Qvortrup, 1994). Children, like adults, are part of a generational structure, which is arguably under threat from the rise of kid power.

One way of exploring imputed challenges to adulthood is to analyse technological trends which have been argued to disempower adults. The specific role of contemporary digital technology in shaping intergenerational relations will be discussed in more detail in Chapter 6. Here we focus on the early work of Postman (1982) on the disappearance of childhood, and the distinction that Prensky (2001) has made between digital 'natives' and 'migrants' which emphasises the challenges that technology poses to contemporary notions of adulthood. Postman explicitly argues that just as childhood disappeared due to the rise of television in the mid twentieth century, so did the concept

---

[1] Recapitulation theory was put forward by Ernest Haeckel in 1866. In essence, the development of the human organism (ontogeny) reflects the development of the human species (phylogeny). This development of an individual follows the same developmental stages as the history of societies and civilisations.

of adulthood. There is a clear assumption that generational power prior to the advent of analogue technology located children and adults within an unambiguously hierarchical conception of generation.

According to Postman (1982), the invention of the printing press in the middle of the fifteenth century in Germany both shaped and symbolised structured hierarchical differences between children and adults. It set in motion a series of political and institutional changes leading to the monopolisation of knowledge by adults. Localised knowledge was superseded by educational processes that were carefully and incrementally distributed to children by adults in a hierarchical sense: as children got older, so their knowledge and intellectual capacities grew. The institutionalisation of this process was the expansion of mass compulsory schooling. Adults were professionalised as teachers and in a much stronger position than previously to distribute this knowledge. Hendrick (2015) argues from a British perspective that the restructuring of children's time and space, an increasing need to protect children and the importance of knowledge in economic terms necessitated educators rejecting experiential and localised knowledge. '(Teachers) threw aside the child's knowledge derived from parents, community, peer group and personal experience. Instead [they] demanded a state of ignorance' (Hendrick 1997: 46).

Contrary to the printing technology, which generated a structured and socially sanctioned difference between children and adults in terms of power, the rise of analogue technology, in particular television in the post-war period in the United States, challenged the hierarchical distance between generations. The 1950s were suffused with advertising images of the nuclear family watching television together, but for Postman this symbolised the breakdown of the generational hierarchy. Television opened up a realm of knowledge for children, ideas which were hitherto monopolised by adults and gradually distributed to children as they grew up. For Postman, the classic image of the nuclear family happily watching television together was thus highly disjunctive. It romanticised the way that all members of the family shared television, while at the same time it broke down the generational boundaries, fundamental to children growing up.

The analogue television has in some sense been superseded by the digital framework that currently dominates education and leisure for many children and adults. The Internet and social media provide a broader virtual landscape within which children have instantaneous access to the same material as adults. Moreover, the shift towards viewing children as economic actors has, for some, presaged more aggressive forms of advertising directed at children. In updating Postman's (1982: 77) thesis, digital technology can thus be seen to destroy or compromise the generational 'information hierarchy' in two ways. First, the process of learning to read, which previously marked off children from adults, allowed the latter to structure the process of growing up in developmental terms. However, digital technology is a visual medium and, paraphrasing Postman from an earlier era, emphasises 'perception' rather than 'conception' (Postman 1982: 78). It thus limits the capacities of adults to structure the process of growing up. Secondly, the messages that are sent via this medium are often 'adult' in nature. Various attempts have been made to regulate children's access to the Internet globally with some success (*The Economist*, 2013). Nevertheless, the various digital platforms open up the worlds of sex, crime and economics to children, arguably before they are developmentally ready.

Kitzinger's (2015) conception of the 'knowing child' is useful here as it connotes ideas of precocity and danger. The knowing child is both cynical and streetwise, challenging dominant constructions of childhood innocence. Technology loads up children with knowledge that they are not always able, in Piagetian terms, to assimilate (Piaget, 1932). Children are unable to make sense of the unlimited and often chaotic representations and text generated by various social media and Internet sources. In more social terms, children may have difficulties engaging with peers and forming friendships. It may be argued that children become more cynical and streetwise and more likely to become risk-takers (Selwyn, 2001), at the same time developing increasing resilience (Smahel et al., 2020).

Postman (1982: 98–119) refers to both the 'adultifying' of children and the 'infantilising' of adults. He views television as the crucible of these trends, as it offers instant answers and knowledge. Whereas literary sources involve having to work at discerning meaning, television watching is a form of immediate gratification. Broadcasters and entertainers furthermore appeal to our childish instincts, by emphasising visual images rather than intellectual ideas. Postman's thesis on the disappearance of childhood has been superseded by a global protectionist discourse in the twentieth century, which places concerns around safeguarding as a central feature of the relationship between childhood and technology. In addition, the rise of digital technology has generated concerns over children's status as dependent innocents. Nevertheless, Postman still offers us a zero-sum conception of power, where analogue or digital technology is seen as radically shifting the balance of power in favour of children, and consequently depriving them of their childhood.

Prensky's (2005) work is not explicit in its insistence on the rise of kid power, but it still sets up a binary distinction between child 'natives' and adult 'migrants', and places the latter in a less advantageous position in relation to the distribution of power. Prensky's focus is on the imputed difficulties that teachers have engaging with their students within a fully digitalised teaching environment.

We [adults] have adopted many aspects of the technology, but just like those who learn another language later in life, we retain an 'accent' because we still have one foot in the past. We will read a manual, for example, to understand a program before we think to let the program teach itself. (Prensky 2005: 9)

Children or students are viewed as 'digital natives', fully immersed within the digital world. Adults, on the other hand, are defined as 'digital migrants', who have to adapt and adjust to a context where they have less monopoly over the access to knowledge. However, it would be a mistake to conflate the 'digital migrant' status of adults with a parallel loss of adult power. Just as television helped to flatten the hierarchical distinctions between adults and children, there is no obvious sense in which children have superseded or replaced adults with the digital world as a dominant frame of reference. Various authors have been highly critical of the way that the binary native/migrant distinction overstates the power of children and the extent to which the distinction accurately depicts the influence of digital technology on generational relations (e.g. boyd, 2014). Selwyn spells out the implications of this binary opposition:

The apparent lack of leeway has prompted growing numbers of commentators to argue that the digital excesses of young people should be tempered and checked, with adults and formal institutions working towards a depowering of the digital native where-ever possible, through the increased regulation and control, blocking and filtering of young people's technology use. (Selwyn, 2009: 370)

Selwyn (2009: 372) argues that children tend to use technology as the 'passive consumption of knowledge' rather than to challenge the way that knowledge is monopolised by adults. There is little empirical support for any loss of adult power here, with adults still setting the agenda within which digital technology is deployed within school, and also often within the home, at least for younger children. As we will discuss in more detail in Chapter 6, children often require guidance, support and regulation in ensuring that they are in the best position to utilise digital technology, supporting a more positive-sum and intergenerational notion of power.

Moreover, issues of capacity and competence cannot be reduced to a generational binary. Various researchers have focused on intragenerational differences, where the status of a generation of children as digital natives is compromised by significant levels of *intragenerational* inequality (Holmes, 2011; Howse, 2014; UNICEF, 2017). The digital divide between children manifests itself not only in terms of access and ownership but also in varying levels of digital skills and competence and autonomy of use. More affluent children are in a stronger position to have regular access to a computer than less affluent children (Livingstone and Helsper, 2007) and are also more likely to use the Internet for educational reasons (Courtois and Verdegem, 2016). While various initiatives have been set up globally and nationally to reduce digital inequalities within the child population, different forms of inequality in relation to digital technology affect adults as well as children in socio-economic terms. The global market in media and technology, like all other markets for consumption, favours middle-class educated families and thus implies a complex web of inter- and intragenerational power relations.

### The global market and the mediating roles of parents

In further exploring the loss-of-adulthood thesis, it is instrumental to focus on the relative position of parents and children within the global market. Until the 1960s, marketers tended to address children's consumer preferences indirectly through mothers, considering the nuclear family as the dominant economic reference point (Seiter, 1993). The idea of the nuclear family provided a relatively unambiguous model of a generational hierarchy. Arguably, global capitalism disrupted this relationship and, in their search for new markets, multinational corporations have since the late twentieth century targeted children more directly. Marketers draw on a range of research approaches to generate refined age-related data in trying to second-guess the way that children interpret prospective merchandise, toys and media (Buckingham, 2007). According to Seabrook (1998: 41), children are viewed as 'another continent ripe for opening up and exploiting, the colonies of the future, the expanding markets of tomorrow'. The dominant ontological assumption of childhood as a temporary stage en route to adulthood prevails. Nevertheless, it is depicted alongside a rapacious global market, which bypasses the mediating role of parents in exploiting children as an extant and future market. Similarly, Giroux focuses on the way that children have been successfully exploited by multinational corporations (MNCs) and marketers:

> Childhood at the end of the twentieth century is not ending as a historical and social category; it has simply been transformed into a market strategy and a fashion aesthetic used to expand the consumer-based needs of privileged adults who live within a market culture that has little concern for ethical considerations, non-commercial spaces or public responsibility. (Giroux 2001: 18–19)

Marketers have for some time cultivated the capacity of children to choose and addressed them in their relatively new 'adult' roles as economic actors. Considerable pressure has been placed on governments, public bodies and MNCs to regulate the form and level of advertising that directly addresses children (*The Economist*, 2013). Nevertheless, children represent a dominant group of consumers with approximately 4 billion dollars spent worldwide on advertising to children in 2018 (Guttmann, 2020). This includes a marked rise in digital advertising to children from 0.3 billion dollars in 2012 to a forecast of 1.7 billion dollars in 2021. Moreover, a panoply of researchers and marketers use age segmentation, gender and ethnicity as critical variables in shaping and refining the forms that advertising takes (Seiter, 1993). As Dan Cook states,

> Observe a child and parent in a store. That high pitched whining you'll hear coming from the cereal aisle is more than just the pleadings of a single kid bent on getting a box of Fruit Loops into the shopping cart. It is the sound of thousands of hours of market research, of an immense coordination of people, ideas and resources, of decades of social and economic change all rolled into a single, 'Mommy pleeease!' (cited in Shah, 2010: 2)

In effect, what is being argued here is that parents have been supplanted as mediators of children's consumption by a global media market that directly speaks to children. Parents are no longer the central arbiters of children's preferences and tastes, and global capitalism has furthermore had major implications for parents' capacities to retain some authority over their children. MNCs and advertisers are complicit in targeting children as extant and future economic actors, sidestepping the powerful mediating role of parents. Marketers insinuate the importance of various fashion items and Internet games, implying that these are necessary acquisitions, in some instances almost viewed as a precondition of peer group membership. At the very least, children are incorporated within the global marketplace reinforcing a culture of individual consumerism and making it more difficult for parents to guide their children morally and socially.

Critics have viewed both consumerism and the rise of digital technology as dangerous and destabilising influences on children's lives, in the process marginalising parents as dominant reference points and role models (Palmer, 2016). Where there has been a particular focus on the loss of influence and power among adults is arguably within the home where parents are allegedly in a weaker position to assert control over the Internet as a dominant source of knowledge and marketing, distributed directly to children. If adopting a loss-of-adulthood perspective, the digital world may be considered an unwelcome third party within generational relations, but as we will discuss in Chapter 6, other interpretations are possible. In the following section, we analyse the rise of another third party, the state, and discuss the way in which the power and authority of parents is sometimes viewed as being usurped by external institutional and legal forces.

## State Intervention and the Decline of Parenthood

Throughout much of the twentieth century, most Northern liberal democracies defined children legally and politically as dependents, absorbed within the family where parents represented their 'best interests' to the outside world (Lewis, 2006). Family was viewed as a private realm, at a distance from the state, with parents as the powerful arbiters of children's welfare. Political theorists and commentators from disparate ideological perspectives viewed the family as a haven or sanctuary from the rigours and interventionist propensities of the state and what are often referred to as forms of 'welfarism' (du Bois-Reymond et al., 1993; Lasch, 1995; Mount, 1992). US culture, in particular, conflates family with the 'rugged' individual warding off incursions from the bureaucratic state (Whitman, 2003).

Where state agents came into contact with families a 'rule of optimism' pervaded. That is, there was a presumption among social workers or 'agents of the state' that parents were always acting in their children's best interest (Dingwall et al., 1995). Family was viewed as the natural and necessary site for child development and social workers' and teachers' intervention seen as a last resort. Implicit within these claims was the natural power and authority of parents as arbiters of children's 'best interests'. A laissez faire approach to families was typical of late nineteenth-century thinking in English-speaking countries, and there was a sense that the state had to have pretty strong reasons to intervene. However, during the latter part of the twentieth century a number of high-profile cases came to light through the mass media in the United States and the United Kingdom over allegations of physical and sexual abuse of children (Parton, 2011). This brought the uneasy relationship between family and state to a head, highlighting a tension between the general interests of the state in the protection of all children and the proprietorial and particular interests of parents.

Consequently, from late twentieth century onwards there was greater political focus on the welfare and needs of children. This opened up the possibility of a move from a bipartite relationship between family and state to a more tripartite configuration, with children, parents and the state as related but legally separated parties. For example, the 1992 Child Protection Act in Norway and the Care of the Child Act (2004) in New Zealand centre specifically on children's needs and welfare (Goldson 2002; Vis et al., 2011). Similarly, the 1989 Children Act in England and Wales focuses on the welfare of children being paramount. Whereas the unit of analysis had hitherto been the family, it shifted to the child. Much of the recent politicising of child protection in the second half of the twentieth century has focused on the tension between the integrity of the nuclear family and the protection of children. As Dingwall et al. argue,

> They (the social services) cannot be given the legal power to underwrite an investigative form of surveillance without destroying the liberal family. At the same time, the state cannot opt out. There is a collective interest in the moral and physical well being of future citizens, in the quality of social reproduction. (Dingwall et al., 1995: 220)

As child protection became a policy priority (Parton, 2011), political and professional expectations shifted. The natural authority of parents was increasingly seen as the romanticising of the private nuclear family, and it was acknowledged that the family home to some was a place from which children needed to escape rather than a retreat from the pressures of the outside world (Hancock and Gillen, 2007). These ideas were reinforced by the rise of feminism within public discourse. Increasing attention to domestic violence focused on the abuse of women within the home, but it also overlapped with public concerns around the physical and emotional integrity of children. The prominence of child abuse became a public concern, generating less trust in families' ability to protect children, with more questioning of parent–child relations (Parton, 2011).

A perceived lack of trust in parents in European and English-speaking countries was reinforced by a policy framework that emphasised the obligations or responsibilities of parents towards their children (Gilbert et al., 2011). Parental responsibility as a concept, on the one hand, contradicts the dominant policy focus on the child, as various issues and problems relating to children become centred on the actions of parents. However, while there is an emphasis on the capacity of parents to protect, nurture and guide their children, the responsibilities delegated to parents are also in some respects a means of disciplining 'errant' groups of parents (Walters and Woodward, 2007). The emphasis on the parent as the responsible agent ensures that children develop appropriately, following moral and social trajectories. In policy terms there is an emphasis on parents as blameworthy. Parents with economic and social challenges, those parents most likely to come into contact with agencies, are more likely to view 'parental responsibilities' as a threat from the state. The links between parents and children are articulated in terms of the imputed inadequacies of the former. Family–state relations are hierarchical, with various agencies having legal and social powers over families.

Donzelot's (1979) notion of 'the social' invokes the idea that low-income working-class families' responsibilities are heavily circumscribed by welfare professionals. Power takes on a Foucauldian meaning, as the state regulates the population judged to be more prone to crime and ill health at the macro level. At the micro level, regulations work their way through individual families and normalising processes, with mothers targeted as responsible agents in the socialising of their children (Donzelot, 1979). As an illustrative example of this, Widding (2018: 487) discusses parental responsibility in the context of children's health in Sweden, drawing on the concept of parent determinism. She argues that 'in order to be regarded as proper parents […] today's parents are expected to keep themselves "up-to-date" with respect to the latest developments regarding good parenting'. This narrative governs parents 'according to current family ideals about the responsible and "good parent"'.

Within various policy realms, normalising thus takes place by invoking the notion of the responsible parent. For example, in various affluent countries parents have responsibility to ensure that children regularly attend school. In the early 2000s parenting orders were introduced in the United Kingdom rendering parents responsible for their children's actions. Educational forms of these orders were administered to parents whose children persistently truanted (Walters and Woodward, 2007). Truancy is occasionally discussed in the media in the United Kingdom and the United States, where parents are pursued by the authorities in situations where they are unable or unwilling to send their children to school:

- 'Parents serve jail time with children for truancy', *News Channel 25*, 27 May 2010.
- 'Parents fined £24m for children's truancy and term time holidays', *BBC News*, 15 March 2018.

Parents are seen to be abdicating their responsibilities as they fail to ensure their children regularly attend school. The notion that parents are responsible for children's actions, and consequently should be sanctioned for non-compliance, is also evident in recent Danish policy, where measures were introduced in 2019 to allow withdrawal of child benefits for a term if a child's school absence was more than 15 per cent (Regeringen, 2018). The fact that these measures were first introduced as part of the former Danish government's 'ghetto-plan', and thus mainly directed at families in socially disadvantaged areas, illustrates a significant deficit approach and has received criticism from social workers, who fear that they will damage their work with vulnerable families (Fransson, 2020; Lessel, 2020).

Finally, as evident in the criminal justice system in England, there is often a marked discrepancy between the age of criminal responsibility and the expectation that parents are responsible for their children's criminal acts (Hollingsworth, 2007). In the 1990s there was a public discourse on the idea of 'responsibilising' children, particularly after high-profile cases of young children committing serious criminal acts. Children are legally liable for crime at age 10, but judicial practice eschewed the criminalising of those under the age of 14 through the legal device *doli incapax*. The Labour government in the United Kingdom abolished the latter in a 1999 legislation, paving the way for younger children to be held legally accountable. However, legislation throughout the 1980s and 1990s focused more on ensuring that parents became more responsible for their children's welfare. In England and Scotland parents are subject to a range of orders: for example, they are 'bound over to take proper care and exercise proper control over the child' (Hollingsworth, 2007: 193; Cleland and Tisdall, 2005). Anti-social behaviour orders (ASBOs) were introduced ostensibly to deal with localised misdemeanours but quickly became associated with controlling the public behaviour of children and young people. Curfews were introduced in towns and cities where children under a certain age were picked up by police if they had broken the curfew and were returned home to parents. Again, these tended to affect families living in poorer housing estates, putting more pressure on parents to conform to normalised conceptions of 'good parenting'. As Cleland and Tisdall (2005: 414) argue, 'parents become part of a moralising strategy of responsibilisation'. While the intention may have been to make parents more vigilant, the unintended effect was to put more pressure on parents struggling to control and discipline their children. Family may still be viewed as a private sanctuary within which parents have special powers over their children. Giesinger (2019) argues that parents have 'proxy powers' over children in that within a framework of duties towards their children they are in a position to shape children's lives. Arguably, what is at stake now is the breadth of this 'obligations' framework, the extent to which these obligations are under public scrutiny and the implications this has for parents' power within the home.

### Tripartite relations and children's participation

As we argued earlier in the chapter, a bipartite relationship between state and family throughout most of the twentieth century meant that parents spoke on behalf of their children when professionals and agencies became interested in children's welfare. The move towards a tripartite relationship puts parents in a position where their obligations towards their children are more explicitly articulated legally and politically. Up until now we have focused on tripartite relations in more legal and political terms: that is, the 'child', and in particular the 'child's welfare', has become an important discursive reference point, constituting a third space between parents and child professionals. This suggests a degree of ambiguity with parent power both redefined and challenged by the state. We can, however, also explore this tripartite relationship in terms of children *physically* occupying the third space between parents and the state with the potential for children to speak for themselves. In Chapter 2, we discussed this in terms of the invocation of children's global human rights to participate. Another possibility in exploring the alleged weakening of parental' power is to focus on how children are incorporated within decision-making processes involving parents and the state.

Work on family group conferences within the child protection context has highlighted the potential for conflict between parents and social workers, with the former feeling disempowered by the latter (Appleton et al., 2015; Barn and Das, 2016; Burford et al., 2011). While the inclusion of parents is a well-established professional practice within social services, Holland et al. (2005) explores the more radical practice of including children within family group conferences in the Welsh context. Group conferences, which involves a type of child welfare intervention, were set up by social workers involved with safeguarding the children. Cases involved the social workers, parents, the children involved and other professionals engaging in group work in an attempt to improve relations within families between parents and children. The very presence of children within these forums is significant in indicating a shift from bilateral meetings between professional and parent, with the child absent, to more trilateral arrangements where children are expected to be present.

Holland et al.'s research (2005) illustrates the centrality of a tripartite or triangular relationship and the implications this has for parental power. Children were in a position to exercise some agency in the way that they talked about their feelings and requested more input into domestic decision-making processes between them and their parents. However, the issue was less about the role that children played within these forums and more about the agenda-setting powers of the state and the social workers as 'experts' who, among other things, were promoting children's participation within these forums. The authors argue that this has resonance with the 'client parents' who generated some resistance towards being advised to incorporate their children's voices in their normal family routines at home.

One interpretation of this new dynamic is the pressure placed on parents as a consequence of the state's insistence that children ought to have a say. In the case of Holland et al.'s (2005) sample of families involved with the social services, parents were expected to go home with their children after the group sessions and practice often scripted narratives, where children would be given space to articulate their interests. Families were then expected to return to further group sessions and report back on progress. In most instances, parents reported in positive terms about the effects of the conferences on family relations during periods in between the sessions. The researchers referred to this as democratising processes, where children were central and accorded more space to have a say. At the same time there was a very thin line between encouraging greater intergenerational dialogue in families which hitherto had been limited, and state facilitation and direction designed to alter family dynamics. In the latter case we can refer back to the work of Lareau (2011) discussed in Chapter 3, with social workers 'engineering' a shift from the 'accomplishment of natural growth' towards more 'concerted cultivation', incorporating a 'sense of entitlement' in the child. With respect to Holland et al.'s (2005) research, this was, on occasion, perceived by working-class parents as the unjustifiable rise of children's power within the home.

We might draw on Donzelot's (1979) key concepts 'protected liberation' and 'supervised freedom' in comparing the different relationships that parents have with the state. Middle-class parents have more autonomy from the state and are more likely to work alongside state professionals through forms of 'protected liberation' (Donzelot 1979). Structural forces highlight the involved 'responsible parent' as a standard set of expectations, a construct generated through policy and professional practice in schools. This discourse of the 'responsible parent', however, is experienced very differently by different groups of parents, and state power takes very different forms. Middle-class parents use the state in supporting their children by drawing on the expertise and resources of various agencies when necessary in augmenting and endorsing their responsibilities. For example, affluent parents are more likely to be engaged with schools through parent–teacher associations and school governing bodies. Parents here draw on the state as a resource in the pursuit of academic excellence for their children. Moreover, this emphasis on schools heightens expectations that parents can make a difference to education outcomes. Doherty and Dooley (2018), for example, argue that middle-class families are under pressure to enter the education economic marketplace and shop around for additional private tuition for children. Middle-class parents compete for additional education resources so that their children have an edge in competing for the highest levels of attainment.

Working-class parents, on the other hand, are more likely to experience forms of 'supervised freedom'. Parents are closely surveilled in ensuring that children, who hitherto had limited constraints on their movement, were shepherded 'back to spaces where he could be more closely watched: the school or the family dwelling' (Donzelot 1979: 47). Schools offer a mixture of incentives and penalties in structuring parents' expectations; teachers here are disciplining parents in terms of their obligations towards their children's well-being and education (Wyness, 2020). Some critics examine the fateful consequences of this supervised freedom for working-class parents or other groups of parents from minority backgrounds. Luet's (2017) ethnographic work with a small urban population of African American families, for example, refers to forms of mutual misrecognition. Schools and teachers viewed parental practices as abnormal and deviant and minority parents misrecognised the institutional power of schools as normative taken-for-granted values and practices. What was viewed as normal by schools and teachers had little resonance within local communities, yet minority families were under pressure to normalise their practices. Miscommunication between schools and families and deficit views of families were similarly identified in Jørgensen et al's (2020) review of European school approaches to migrant children with special educational needs. Some of the papers reviewed reported that school  professionals sometimes blamed migrant parents for lack of their involvement in school, although the parents were constrained by employment and caring responsibilities and experienced language difficulties which meant that they did not always understand the teachers or the activities they were asked to participate in.

### *Power, punishment and parenting*

In more global terms, the rise of a discourse on the ending of adults' corporal power over children provides a potent example of intervention that challenges the mediating roles of parents. While some states have acted to end, or at least to limit, the power that adults have to physically chastise children, the rise of an International Aid network made up of non-governmental organisations and intergovernmental organisations such as UNICEF has also acted as an important political interloper (GIEACPC, 2018). However, most parents globally still have the power to physically chastise their children. There has been a shift away from assuming these powers across the different contexts where children come into contact with adults, including home, school and juvenile justice settings. By 2018, 53 states (27 per cent) had abolished corporal punishment across all sites including the home; 131 states (66 per cent) had abolished corporal punishment in schools; and 165 (83 per cent) of all countries had banned corporal punishment as a form of judicial punishment (GIEACPC, 2018).[2]

---

[2]  The most recent country to ban corporal punishment within the home is Scotland (BBC News, 2020).

The home context has been the most debated and most controversial, with the great majority of states (73 per cent) still allowing parents the legal capacity to impose some form of physical punishment on their children (Rowland et al., 2017; Saunders, 2013). However, the moral and utilitarian arguments for retaining parental power now have much less potency Saunders's (2013) review of the effects of corporal punishment suggests a general scientific consensus that physical chastisement has little positive impact on modifying children's behaviour in both the short term and the long term. Nevertheless, the retention of corporal power has important symbolic and cultural value. Imoh (2014), for example, refers to physical punishment as a common practice in many African states where smacking and using a leather strap are often viewed as 'domesticated' and 'dignified' forms of punishment. In Malaysia, where corporal punishment is practised across all sites including home, school and juvenile justice contexts, smacking children is associated with keeping children in line, reinforcing the deference and respect that children ought to have towards adults (Pak, 2014). Moreover, in the Global North, the recent ban in Scotland on parents smacking their children generated several media headlines that appear to suggest that there is still a powerful constituency of support for smacking within the United Kingdom.

> Mum says 'every loving parent' should slap their child to properly discipline them. (*The Sun*, 10 October 2019)

> New smacking law 'will turn loving parents into criminals'. (*The Times*, 7 June 2019)

> Smacking ban will see hundreds of parents sent to jail after it becomes law, police say. (*The Sun*, 5 May 2019)

In England, while parents are still able to exercise corporal power, the agendas around safeguarding and children's rights have severely curtailed this form of punishment for parents. The most recent relevant legislation, the 2004 Children Act, narrows the forms of corporal power that can still be practised within the home. While there is still the invocation of 'reasonable harm' as a rationale for parents physically chastising their children, there are now limits on the forms that this punishment takes. Thus, parents are no longer able to leave a mark on children's bodies when smacking and all implements that were hitherto used by parents are now prohibited.

## Loss of Adult Power – Children's Narratives

One of the ironies of the debate about adults' presumed loss of power is that the concerns over the resulting gain of power by children are usually expressed by adult commentators. Despite the perception that children have now assumed power, there is very little evidence from research on children's perspectives to support the view that children have been empowered. From the adult perspective, there has been some commentary on the loss of adulthood as a consequence of the politicisation of children. In Chapter 2, we argued that the children's rights agenda fails to incorporate a political role for children in any formal sense. However, we can find instances where children are exposed to the same political pressures as their parents. For example, children and young people in South Africa were thoroughly politicised during the anti-apartheid period in the 1970s and 1980s (Bundy, 1987). Children were immersed in the political struggle experiencing the racist nature of the education system, and at times they took on the mantle of leading the fight against the apartheid system. Despite a Northern narrative that saw Black South African children as victims, interviews from South Africans who were involved as children in the anti-apartheid movement in the 1970s and 1980s argued that they were politically informed and committed to challenging the structures of apartheid (Bridger, 2016). The trigger for the Soweto demonstrations in 1976 was the introduction of Afrikaans, the language of the White minority, in school as a compulsory part of the curriculum. Children went to the street to protest only to be met by force from the Afrikaner state, resulting in the deaths of around two hundred school children.

Ndebele (1995) analyses the aftermath of Soweto, in terms of South African youth rejecting what was seen as the inadequate attempt by Black South African adults to challenge apartheid. Children rejected the idea that they should be insulated from the political struggle and continue to attend school. They coined the phrase 'Liberation now, education later' to emphasise the idea that children were immersed within the apartheid system just as much as their parents. Thus, education would materialise only once the apartheid system had been overturned, and children were an integral part of this struggle. Ndebele interpreted 'Liberation now, education later' as a loss of adulthood, viewing 'pupil power' in terms of the loss of adult authority, with a breakdown in adult–child relations, due to the incapacity or unwillingness of adults to offer children guidance and support:

> Adulthood has itself been threatened with destruction. The progressive loss of parental authority in the wake of the 1976 student uprisings was a significant sociological phenomenon. Hemmed in between children on

the one hand, and a hostile state on the other, black parents suffered an ontological crisis. Dismissed by children for having failed to protect them as well as having failed to bring about liberation, relentlessly bludgeoned into submission through the state repressive laws and other forms of state terrorism, the confidence of the black adult was seriously shaken. (Ndebele, 1995: 331–32)

Ndbele's thesis is provocative: while we may question the extent to which parenthood was ontologically challenged, children here are questioning an imputed abdication of parental responsibilities. We might speculate that the children have reluctantly filled the void left by Black adult political leaders. Ndbele hints at this in the way he describes how Black South African children and young people had to quickly fill a political void left by adults, who had either been imprisoned, exiled, killed or were simply unwilling to maintain the fight against a White minority political elite. Thus, far from any commitment to usurping the role of adults, politically charged children and young people were arguably calling for the reassertion of parent power and authority.

Within more recent global concerns over environmental issues and climate change, children have, as we will discuss in more detail in Chapter 7, also been quite vocal in driving the debate. As with the calls for 'liberation now education later' and the reinstallation of adult power in Ndbele's (1995) analysis of South Africa post-Soweto, much of the focus of the young people's environmental movement is to make various adults and organisations more responsible for protecting the environment. Greta Thunberg has become the public face of a global campaign, where school children in some instances have challenged the power of adults through walkouts from schools. While much of the controversy over Thunberg surrounds her age and her capacity to confront world leaders, she herself has explicitly called for adults to take the lead in tackling climate change, as, for example, in a written statement to the US Congress:

I am submitting this report as my testimony because I don't want you to listen to me … I want you to listen to the scientists. And I want you to unite behind the science. And then I want you to take action. (BBC News, 18 September 2019)

More generally children also seem to display both caution and pragmatism before getting too involved in initiating activities such as research and consultation (Hill, 2006; Maes et al., 2012). The role that children play in divorce proceedings and research will be discussed in further detail in Chapters 5 and 8. However, it is worth briefly mentioning Maes et al.'s (2012) example of Belgian children of divorced parents who were found to prefer that adults took the key decisions over their custody. While it was important to the children that they were informed about where they would live and with which parent, they had little desire to have an integral role within decision-making processes and were happy for adults to have the final say on custodial arrangements. Hill (2006) also shows how a group of Scottish children were willing to be occasionally consulted on research but wary about taking the initiative when setting up and running research projects. While there is a paucity of research on children's conceptions of adult power, these examples illustrate some resistance among children to the idea of challenging the powerful roles of parents and teachers.

## Conclusion

In line with the argument we proposed in Chapters 2 and 3, this chapter has challenged the idea that kid power involves a simple transfer of power from adults to children. While previous chapters have focused on the position of children within the generational hierarchy, this chapter has focused more explicitly on the position of adults. Postman's thesis on the disappearance of childhood implies the disappearance of adulthood: the flattening of generational boundaries and differences, which consequently disempowers adults. However, we have argued that there is little evidence to support the contention that the rise of analogue and digital technology has disempowered adults. There is also little sense in which we can conceptualise generational relations in binary terms, such as digital 'natives' and 'immigrants'. Undoubtedly, children have embraced the full range of digital innovations in recent years. Nevertheless, the distinction between natives and migrants is difficult to sustain, as economic and educational barriers compromise the idea of the child as a universal digital 'native'.

If we focus on the economic and political context of childhood since the late twentieth century, there is again little evidence that children are able to wield power over adults. At a global level, a discourse on banning physical punishment provides a powerful moral and social counterweight to teachers and adults with corporal punishment incorporated within their punishment regimes. Nevertheless, the majority of parents globally retain the capacity to smack their children. This contradicts the UN Convention on the Rights of the Child and the broader idea that children have human rights to physical integrity (Alderson, 1994). The retention of corporal punishment is part of a broader discourse that extols the virtues of the private family. Parents view children as their own property with a carte blanche in terms of methods of discipline and punishment. One of the last bastions of traditional power that adults have over children, a right to physically chastise their children, remains.

Furthermore, social class persists as a significant marker of difference in terms of how parents negotiate a political and legal discourse on safeguarding. Critics view this as a direct infringement on the powers of parents within the home, particularly where parents come into regular contact with state professionals. As with the argument on the role the global economy plays in debilitating poorer parents, there may be some traction in the loss-of-adult-power thesis in the way that political forces target less affluent parents. Here, intragenerational rather than intergenerational forces seem to come to the fore. While the postmodern state delegates responsibilities to parents at a distance, middle-class parents may be more able to take advantage of the resources available and be in a stronger position to interpret the discourse around the 'responsible parent' in more positive terms. The responsible parent here is the listening parent, able to draw on the repertoire of consultative and dialogical skills needed to engage with their children. Working-class parents and other parents from disadvantaged backgrounds may, on the other hand, feel disempowered by state officials and unable to act on an agenda that supports their own conception of their responsibilities.

In the final part of this chapter we have focused on the loss-of-adulthood thesis with reference to children's own narratives on their imputed empowerment. For both proponents and critics of this argument this may seem a surprising line of argument to take. Within the debate over children's empowerment, children's own voices are still barely audible. Nevertheless, we have been able to provide a few examples of children being more assertive and engaging. As we discussed in Chapter 2, children are in a stronger position to articulate their interests as a result of global political developments asserting their rights. However, there is a major distinction to be made between being able to effectively articulate concerns that are already within the public domain and having agenda-setting capacities that impinge on the responsibilities of adults. Where children have been most publicly assertive in recent years is in their chastisement of adults for failing to take on their responsibilities, for example, for climate action. Economic and political factors have refined generational relations, and adults are now instantiated within powerful global discourses which centre on the child's welfare. However, there is no simple transfer of power from adults to children, and the thesis that adults have lost power to children is difficult to sustain.

# Section 2

# RECONSTRUCTING KID POWER

# Chapter 5

# FAMILY, GENERATION AND MEDIATION

One of the key themes to emerge from our previous analysis of kid and adult power was the rise of third parties that provide an economic, legal and political framework for challenging and refining traditional forms of adult power. Children are central within this framework, but beyond providing them with highly regulated channels for communication, there is little sense that they have gained more power. In Chapter 4, we discussed the way that economic and political trends that intercede in generational terms compromised the capacity of some parents to mediate between their children and the outside world. In this chapter, we argue for the importance of *mediation* as an important conceptual device for refining generational relations and generating interstitial spaces within which adults and children are able to work together. The chapter focuses on family as a social and political context within which children play a mediating role and may exercise kid power, in the positive-sum and intergenerational sense.

Mediation often refers to the capacity of a mediator to intercede in disputes, offering parties a channel of communication through which some form of resolution can be reached. Mediators are drawn on to work through conflicts at a number of levels, including political global resolution, between countries or military forces, and economic disputes between trade unions and employers (Jolobe, 2019). At a more localised level, there have been examples of young children in various countries being trained to mediate in low-level disputes between peers as peer mediators or buddies, for example, by ensuring that there are positive social relations within the playground (Ay Çeviker et al., 2019; Salmivalli et al., 2011). More broadly, mediation refers to an interstitial position between two social institutions or groups of people. A mediator brings these disparate, sometimes warring groups of people together for a particular purpose. As we have argued previously, adults provide an important link between children and the outside world. Parents, in particular, are charged with responsibility for the welfare and well-being of children, which includes both introducing children to and shielding them from various external forces (Lightburn, 1992). In a recent paper on parental responses to the Israeli-Palestinian conflict, Golden and Erdreich (2020) discuss how middle-class Palestinian and Israeli mothers regulate talk about the conflict between themselves and their children. In this way, the mothers argue that they are able to mediate between their children and the conflict, insulating them from the public discourse on violence and war and constructing and maintaining boundaries between the family as a discrete private realm and the outside world.

The idea of mediation focuses on the dominant role of parents exercising their power in regulating children's physical and intellectual access to the outside world. The nuclear family suggests a clear generational divide: parents mediate children's lives as they grow up in the way that they exercise power over their children. The conventional model of the nuclear family thus presents a binary intergenerational relationship and a clear generational divide, with children as vulnerable dependants and parents as caretakers and responsible agents. The concept of the binary nuclear conception of family is borrowed from Moxnes's (2003) analysis of post-divorce bi-nuclear families. While we apply the concept to post-divorce contexts for children in the first part of the chapter, we also argue more broadly that the 'bi-nuclear' model of family flows from the zero-sum conception of power discussed in Section 1 of the book.

While parents are still expected to take on the primary role of mediation, in recent years more awareness has been growing of how children support their parents and other adults by taking on a mediating position. In this chapter we explore the different ways that children occupy the interstitial space between the family and the outside world, by playing a mediating role within their families and between their family, the community and the external world. We argue that this space challenges the bi-nuclear conception of family and offers a more nuanced framework within which we can assess the level and forms of power in intergenerational terms. In some ways we are borrowing Bhabha's (2004) conception of 'third space' here. Where this idea is commonly associated with the hybridising or mixing of different and dominant cultures, we use mediation as a form of third space. Children's mediation creates a hybridisation of two dominant generational references that typify the bi-nuclear family and the zero-sum conception of power: the dominant adult and the subordinate child.

In the first part of the chapter we discuss the contemporary restructuring of Northern families, and how this potentially creates new generational relations and responsibilities, presenting challenges and opportunities for children. We focus on the way that the restructuring of families has resulted in children negotiating multiple transitions as parents separate and divorce. Through this, we demonstrate the mediating roles that children play in helping to sustain a network of links between parents in different households. We furthermore discuss children who mediate for social and economic reasons. We are aware that divorce affects families across the socio-economic spectrum and that children from all backgrounds may play a mediating role in post-divorce households (Raley and Sweeney, 2020). However, our focus in this chapter is the role that children play in mediating poverty, which is often an outcome of family breakdown.

In a second illustration of children's mediation, we consider the role of migrant children in helping their families, often acting as mediators between their families and the host country. Migrant families may lack economic and cultural capital in relation to external agencies and larger institutional structures, and this may complicate their process of settling in host countries (Sleijpen et al., 2017). Migrant children are an effective means of social integration, as they and their families negotiate an unfamiliar language and culture (Bauer, 2016; Orellana, 2009). We explore the practical roles children take on in helping their families to settle and consider the impact of these roles on children's power.

Finally, we attend to the myth of the 'absent' parent, by critically examining political and professional conceptions of deficit childhoods in the developing world where adverse circumstances often leave children with less conventional adult contact (Wyness, 2013b). We construct a case study of child-headed households and examine the social and economic networks often initiated by children in search of provision and protection. The focus here is on the ways in which children connect with external adults as forms of proxy parental support, due to economic and social necessity. In the absence of biological parents, children mediate between their households, often containing younger family members and schools and various aid organisations.

## Family Restructuring and Post-divorce Families

The changing nature of family is complicated by economic, social and demographic factors, and while there is no linear global trend, since the mid-1970s families have generally become smaller (Prout, 2005). This is particularly marked in many countries in the Global North where, since the 1970s, more children have been experiencing parental separation and divorce. Currently, around a quarter of all children under the age of 16 in the United Kingdom have experienced parental separation and divorce and are living in a lone-parent household (Office for National Statistics, 2015). In the United States, the proportion of children living in lone-parent households has similarly increased from 9 per cent in the early 1960s to 28 per cent by 2014 (Child Trends, 2015), and in Europe, almost a third of all households (32.5 per cent) contain a single parent and children (Eurostat, 2020). While more recent research is cautious on the effects that divorce can have on children, there is still a dominant discourse that views divorce as damaging for children in terms of their schooling and emotional development (Kelly, 2003; Wallerstein et al., 2014). The evidence is strongest for the short-term effects, particularly among pre-adolescents and their social and emotional development, but there is less support for the contention that long-term effects are damaging (Hetherington, 2003). Focusing on the ways in which children adjust to the changes brought on by divorce, the evidence suggests that children demonstrate high levels of social and emotional competence and are quite capable of adjusting to the transitions that they experience within the post-divorce period. Recent research on children and divorce thus centres less on the idea that children are victims of parental separation and more on the agentic role that children play in post-divorce settings within more complex networks of households, including the homes of separated parents, containing biological, step- and half-siblings as well as step-parents and their extended kin (Haugen, 2010; Neale and Flowerdew, 2007; Sadowski and McIntosh, 2016). While there is considerable work involved in children negotiating these new family members, in the following section we focus mainly on the ways in which children challenge the bi-nuclear family through mediating the different parental households.

### *Children mediating separated parents*

As has been argued in Chapter 2, global and national policies increasingly focus on the role of children as active participants. Children's inclusion within decision-making processes relating to custodial issues was also particularly discussed in Chapter 4. The emphasis on inclusion and consultation highlights the relational nature of children's ability to deal with and negotiate the break-up of their biological families. As an example, the 1989 Children Act in England brings public and private law together by focusing on the children's welfare. Adults involved in decisions on the children's future relations with their separated parents and siblings are supposed to 'ascertain the wishes and feelings of children' (section 8), and children are to be consulted. However, it is not always clear that children want to play a prominent part in decisions relating to custody after parental separation. Hogan et al.'s (2003) sample of young Irish children emphasised the importance of maintaining contact with both parents but had no interest in being involved in decision-making processes relating to custody. Maes et al. (2012), in their analysis of Flemish children's conceptions of divorce, similarly argue that the most important feature of generational relations during the process of divorce is 'the feeling of mattering', that children are taken into account and have a good understanding of the reasons why their parents are divorcing. Children were clear that having a say or at least being informed about possible custody arrangements was important. However, some of the children stopped short of wanting to have any input into decision-making processes and were happy to let parents make arrangements as long they were informed. In some respects, power can thus be understood in this context as the possibility of playing a subordinate role and not being overburdened with responsibilities. An alternative interpretation is that children want to have some control over the conditions of having a voice. Some professionals and parents may interpret children having a say more vigorously in terms of articulating a position or a preference. However, children staying silent without this being interpreted as disinterest or suspicion is equally important. As Oswell (2013: 106) argues, children need to be able to find a role within decision-making processes that 'allows (them) not only to speak but also to stay silent, to have some control (whether actively or passively) over the conditions of communication'.

Recent research has also identified the voices and participation of children in post-divorce periods through the various strategies and contributions that children make in keeping the lines of communication open between separated parents. Marschall (2014: 523) refers to this as children 'hooking up' the different households in order to maintain a 'coherent flow of everyday life'. Children mediate between the different post-divorce households, for example, by communicating with one parent via phone or text while staying with the other. They may cycle to the other parent's house to take the dog out for a walk or check on the other parent. Much of these activities are routine and mundane, integrated into the new post-divorce situation and over time becoming second nature. Routines and practices are created by children as a way of keeping channels open, mediating between different households and ensuring that separated parents are an integral part of their lives.

In this lens, children can thus be viewed as agents rather than victims of change. Moxnes (2003: 142) refers to the role that children play in shifting from a 'pre-divorce nuclear family to a post-divorce bi-nuclear family', which helps children in some respects to 'keep their families'. Moving between households is one way to maintain a network of open communication between different households, and custodial arrangements that highlight 'shared time' are prominent. Between 17 per cent and 35 per cent of children of divorced parents in different countries divide their time up between their separated parents' households (Haugen, 2010; Sadowski and McIntosh, 2016). Children are committed to dividing their time with their parents in the different households as equitably as possible (Haugen, 2010).

Movement between different households also allows children to mediate in situations where parents are in conflict over custody and other issues. For some children it can be emotionally painful and draining to try to maintain a positive line of communication where there is considerable conflict and bad feeling between their parents (Neale and Flowerdew, 2007). Shared time also allows the children to capture brief moments when both biological parents are together, often where one child is being 'handed over' to the other parent. Sadowski and McIntosh's analysis, for example, captures the joy expressed by an 11-year-old Australian boy, Shane, as he is able to draw and photograph his parents physically together, albeit fleetingly:

> For Shane, security and contentment in shared care is evoked by this reminder of the foundation of his family of origin and his parents' continued ability to share friendship and delight, and be in the 'same frame'. (Sadowski and McIntosh, 2016: 74–75)

Older children from an earlier study based in the north of England reflected on the difficulties of shared time and the adjustments they had to make. For instance, 17-year-old Rachel had been living in different households since she was 8 years old. She discusses the impact this has had on her and her sister:

> They both arranged their lives around us [...] They both sued for custody, cos both my parents wanted to have an equal part in my growing up [...] I was going back and forth between them [...] I was with my Dad on Mondays and Tuesdays, my Mum on Wednesdays and Thursdays and then we would alternate weekends. And then it was mad on Sundays. [...] So, they sorted this very complicated system. [...] It was confusing at first, but like second nature now [...] I've got this huge bag that I carry back and forth between my houses. [...] You've got to settle in, because you sort of change, depending what house you're at. [...] I find I'm a different person at each house [...] they're both your homes it seems more [weird]. [...] It takes a while to settle in, to being the other person. (Neale and Flowerdew, 2007: 33)

Much of the research on children's perspectives focuses on the way that children mediate different households, maintaining fluid and hospitable relations between their parents (Davies, 2015). Children negotiate complicated family dynamics, particularly where at least one of the households has become a step-family. With 10 per cent of all children in the United States living in step-families, and an average of around 8 per cent of all European households being step-households, shared time also comes to be about shared attention and attempts to create an equitable weighting of love and care within households where new step-relations have to be negotiated (Steinbach, Kuhnt and Knüll, 2016).

> In cases of divorce, different caring practices must be reinvented and rearranged when the family members attempt to re-establish the *family-we* with only one parent at a time, but the contents from nuclear family life is often reproduced. (Marschall, 2014: 521, emphasis in original)

Marschall's (2014) work resonates with other research emphasising the critical concern of children's mediation as a way of keeping their original biological family together, albeit in the form of a phantasy. Thus, psychologically, mediation of their parents' households allows children a sense of ownership of their original nuclear family (Moxnes, 2003).

### *Mediating family poverty*

A recent global review of research on family structures argues that 'divorce is a stratified and stratifying life event' (Raley and Sweeney, 2020: 81). Although there has been an increase in the educational attainment and earning power of women, fathers still earn more than mothers. This contributes to the 'feminization of poverty',[1] with disproportionately high levels of women from poorer backgrounds moving into poverty after divorce (Chant, 2006). Women hitherto reliant on their partners' income have to make ends meet on their own, often through the benefits system, where one is available. As they are likely to be the custodial parent, women are also often dependent on their former partners to support them financially in providing for their children (Raley and Sweeney, 2020). Since the early 1990s, there has been a particular focus from the UK state on 'absent' fathers – those biological fathers who do not pay maintenance to their former partners who have custody for their children. Children within these families have less resources, and are less likely to be given pocket money and maintain a presence within an increasingly dominant peer consumer culture. Ridge (2017) argues that children are often drawn into the complex financial relations between their separated parents. While there is a tendency to think that children play each parent off in asking for money, in some instances, children maintain contact with their fathers as

---

[1] The 'feminization of poverty' is a term which reflects the fact that the majority of the world's people living in poverty are women due to a combination of factors, including lower salaries, denied access to resources and property, and gender-disproportionate negative impacts of globalisation (McLanahan and Carlson, 2001; UN Women, 2000).

long as they are able to mitigate poverty within the maternal household. Ridge shows that there were also occasions where children deployed moral agency in asking for money from their fathers. They were well aware of the lack of finance within their maternal households and the problems their mothers were having because of this. On occasion, children used money from one parent to help the other parent out. As one 11-year-old boy in Ridge's study stated when talking about how he spent the money given to him by his separated father, 'all the pocket money and allowance I got from my Dad, yeah, tried to use it to help my Mum as much as I could with it' (Ridge, 2017: 91). Importantly, the children were also mediating between their mums and dads, acting as go-betweens and trying to maintain an equilibrium between parents who were intermittently in conflict. As one 13-year-old girl commented,

> I try to please my mum and my dad at the same time and that, and like if I phone my dad too often my mum's like 'ah you're dad's best person in the world here', I'm like 'he's not' and if I don't phone him he's like 'why aren't you phoning me' and stuff, I'm like 'I can't win'! (Ridge, 2017: 94)

Where children are living mainly within one parental household, there are more possibilities for them to take on domestic and caring responsibilities. As Marschall (2014: 521) argues, 'in cases of divorce, different caring practices must be reinvented and rearranged'. While the bi-nuclear family focuses exclusively on the physical, emotional and psychological responsibilities of mothers and wives, more recent versions of family have provided different models of care and domesticity. Mayall's (2002) analysis of working-class family life in London highlights the domestic work that children routinely carry out within multifamily settings. Her focus was on the agency of young girls aged 9–14 who often had to mediate ill health and poverty within their families, where mothers were the only parents around. As with the research on divorce and separation, children were often working to maintain links across various family and household settings.

Karen and Sandra were two 12-year-old girls interviewed by Mayall (2002: 90–96). Both lived with their siblings and their mothers and had little contact with their fathers. Despite their economic circumstances and their mothers' ongoing mental health problems, they emphasised the responsibilities that their mothers had for their welfare. Sandra's mother, for example, immediately after giving birth at midnight, had to phone for a taxi to ensure that Sandra and her siblings, who had been at the hospital, were safely taken home. However, Sandra had a range of domestic roles to play within the home, including running errands for her mother and looking after her younger siblings. These were compounded after the birth by her mothers' post-natal depression.

> We help out, like if the baby's crying, instead of saying, mum, the baby's crying, just go and pick her up. Or if there's loads of dishes in the sink, don't say Mum shall I wash the dishes, just go and wash a few dishes. Just to help her, cos there's lots of things get my Mum down, get on top of her ... Sometimes I moan about it. (Sandra, quoted in Mayall, 2002: 93)

Children are also involved in helping out their mothers by trying to restrict levels of food insecurity. Cairns's (2018) sample of Afro-American and Hispanic teenagers in Camden, New Jersey, talked about the 'relational work' carried out with their mothers and referred to the various ways in which they helped out. First, they were more actively involved in taking responsibilities for the preparation of meals, which gave them an insight into the difficulties of providing regular food for the family. Secondly, they were sometimes able to gain access to free food as food markets were closing within the local community. Thirdly, most of the children attended high school and also held down two part-time jobs in order to augment the family income. Finally, the children helped out emotionally through reaching out to their mothers when they were struggling to put food on the table. Cairns refers to Sheylinn, a 17-year-old girl:

> It is noteworthy that when describing food as a stress in her life, Sheylinn speaks not about her own hunger, but about the emotional experience of her mother's strained foodwork. In this narrative, Sheylinn and her mother are tightly bound in foodwork relations. (Cairns, 2018: 181)

## Child Migrants and Mediation

Migrant families are another example of families who may be faced with a range of adverse economic circumstances. In addition to poverty, they may also have to deal with separation, isolation, discrimination/racism and cultural dissonance once they reach and try to settle in a host country. There are parallels with divorced children in the way that children support their parents in the process of resettlement and mitigate some of these challenges (Bauer, 2016; Orellana, 2009; Estrada, 2013) through various forms of mediation. One area where children are adept at supporting their parents is through 'language brokering'. Mediation here refers to the mundane and routine ways that children are able to act as translators in social settings and translate documents for their parents. First- and second-generation migrant children are often in a stronger language position than their parents because of their exposure to schooling, social media and peers and may act as interpreters. This is, for example, described by Sime and Fox (2015) in their study of Eastern European migrant families in Scotland, where the mother of Daniel, a 10-year-old Polish boy, reported,

> My husband sometimes starts talking in English and Daniel finishes his sentences. Daniel translates for my husband, finds things on the Internet, as he doesn't always understand and Daniel even found out if we could register with the dentist. (Sime and Fox, 2015: 531)

Orellana's (2009, 2001) work among migrant families in California similarly documents the way that migrant children help out their parents with their English. One girl of Mexican origin acted as a translator for a range of tasks and activities:

> If we are watching TV, and it's English, my mom asks us what they are saying so we have to tell her. Sometimes I also translate letters and bills. When I go to the pharmacy at Walgreen's, I have to translate for my mom. Usually the person that works there talks English, so my mom doesn't understand. (Orellana, 2009: 1)

Children also sometimes have to mediate between their families and the varying levels of racism and discrimination they meet within their new communities, illustrating the overlaps between language and culture brokering. In Bauer's (2016) study, children would often protect their parents from localised racism and discrimination. This involved censoring information and utterances from others; children would deliberately mistranslate racist name-calling. There was a strong protective and caring element in the way that some of these children mediated the discrimination directed at their parents. One boy aged 13 tried to protect his Italian mother from the humiliation of not being understood in a shop:

> She'd gone in to repair a watch, and she was certainly the first person there [...] The woman behind the counter ignored her for ... quite a long time, serving other people. My mother was holding my hand [...] She was squeezing it very hard and I could see that she was just building up the courage or the strength to push herself to be served. So, she demanded attention in the kind of English that would make us wince. I remember sending her a message when I realised what was going on. A kind of message through my hand because I knew she was doing

something very hard. And she did [calm down] and she did get served. (Bauer 2016: 31)

Rather than try and translate over his mother as she tried to make her request in broken English, this boy thus used physical signals to support her in making her request in the shop.

The migrant families in Orellana's study also often had to struggle to make a living and maintain a distance from the authorities, particularly where they had no papers and were trading illegally. In these contexts, children sometimes played a more cultural/political role in working between their families and the wider society. In Estrada's (2013) research, children also mediated between their families and the police, as the children were often second-generation migrants and thus in a politically stronger position to represent their families. The children were born in the United States and had automatic citizenship, which gave them some leeway when their undocumented parents came into contact with the authorities for illegally trading on the Californian streets.

Although the children acted as mediators between their families and the wider society and had some language and legal advantages in relation to their parents, these examples provide little evidence of a generational inversion of power. In some instances, the children complicated the generational lines set out in Postman's (1982) thesis of the disappearing childhood. In Postman's thesis, power was related to the ability of adults to distribute knowledge or 'secrets' downwards to children in an appropriate developmental manner. The power of adults is seen as challenged by children's access to technology, but child protection is also an issue here: children are to be shielded from inappropriate knowledge about the outside world, including sex, money and death. As we have described, migrant children intermittently cross these lines, particularly when they are working on their parents' behalf, as brokers of language, culture or politics. For example, in Orellana's study, Cindy, a 14-year-old girl of Chinese origin, often had to deal with bureaucracies when helping her parents to pay bills and taxes, and this made her feel different from other children:

> Sometimes I think I am invading people's privacy, like, they have to tell me over the phone, like deposit statements and stuff like that. I know exactly the house's wages ... and I tell my parents, and they don't really care. I just know and I translate it. While like other kids, they ask for things. I'm not trodding down people of my own age, but some people they just ask for things like 'Can I have a bike, can I go swimming, can I go to summer camp, can I have a new pair of Nikes?' ... Their parents keep saying 'Do you know how hard I work for the money to pay the

bills?' They don't know exactly how much is in their bank deposits, the bills and stuff. But I know personally because I write the bills. I write the cheques. (Orellana, 2009: 9)

However, for many migrant children, mediating on their families' behalf is a routine and unexceptional feature of family life. Estrada (2013) argues, with respect to his sample of young street vendors in Los Angeles, that the majority of children from the families that he studied were not involved in the family businesses. The ones that were involved were not compelled to work with their parents. Most were expected to attend school and help out parents when they had time – they thus helped out and worked alongside parents, rather than replacing them, and the more family members involved, the more money their family could earn. Children were an integral part of family decision-making processes, and older children had the skills, the street knowledge and in some cases the status to make a difference to family economic ventures. As Estrada concludes in his paper,

> the adolescents in this study are not marginalized, exploited family members, but rather co-economic providers with parents. This type of family–work relation allows us to see that parent–child relations do not always fall into a top-down hierarchical model. Here we are able to see that parents also learn and benefit from their children's skills and knowledge. (Estrada, 2013: 63)

While the children in Orellana's (2001) sample were very positive about the difference they made to their families' welfare and happy for others outside of the family to know about their mediation, other children may feel that they have to conceal their mediating responsibilities from school. For example, Crafter et al.'s (2017) sample of language brokers and young carers based in the south coast of England were generally ambivalent about disclosing to teachers their mediating roles. In the case of the children who had caring responsibilities, some were fearful of the perception that teachers would have of the parent that was being cared for, and some were worried that any disclosure to the authorities would result in punitive action being taken against them and their families. Where children had struck up a relationship with a sympathetic teacher, they appeared to be less concerned, illustrating the importance of considering children's relations with different types of adults. Their fear of teacher perceptions and authorities furthermore emphasises the complex dynamics of power between different adults in their lives and their consequent attempts to mediate them.

## Mediation and Child-Headed Households

In the final illustration of the mediating roles of children, we focus on contexts where children have to mediate outside the protective structures of the parent-dominated families. In Southern Africa, concerns have been expressed for some time over the implications of the HIV/AIDS pandemic for children, both as children and as a future generation of adults. By 2013, 15.2 million children in sub-Saharan Africa had lost at least one parent to the pandemic (Avert, n.d.). As the numbers of AIDS orphans[2] rose in the 1990s and early 2000s, the capacity of the extended family network to take in these children was exhausted (Germann, 2006; Haley and Bradbury, 2015). A key concern here was the alleged lack of social structure, as spelled out by two contributors to an edition of the *British Medical Journal* devoted to the AIDS pandemic:

> The potential for these children to form a large group of dysfunctional adults which could further destabilise societies already weakened by AIDS, has increased the urgency of finding an effective solution to the orphan crisis. (Matshalaga and Powell, 2002: 184)

The problem of order is clearly set out here: without the guidance, tutelage and regulation of adults, children are likely to grow into chaotic rootless adults with little or no sense of purpose, and a weak moral compass.

Many sub-Saharan countries have a strong cultural commitment to take in children from extended kin, when there are problems with them staying in their biological family. The extended family traditionally absorbed orphaned children with cultural norms concentrating on orphans being cared for from the father's bloodline. As a consequence of the AIDS pandemic, this was expanded to allow children from either parent's bloodline to be taken in by the extended family (Germann, 2006). However, even this more inclusive support structure struggled to cope with the numbers of orphaned children. One result was the creation of child-headed households (CHHs) or, as some have coined this phenomenon, the child-headed family[3] (Underhill, 2015). The numbers of CHHs tend to be under-reported, but there is estimated to

---

[2] Although we use the concept of AIDS orphan in this section, we acknowledge that this term needs to be approached with caution, as it may carry derogatory connotations and cultural stigma in local contexts (Harms et al., 2010). Community definitions of orphanhood may, furthermore, differ significantly from definitions used by governments and external agencies (Skinner et al., 2006).

[3] The language is significant here with 'household' viewed as a neutral statistical category, and 'family', a term invested with social and moral value. Child-headed households in these terms are viewed as tenuously and temporarily related to the social order, and

be around 90,000 children living in 50,000 CHHs in South Africa (Stats SA, 2018) and 77,000 children living in CHHs in Ethiopia. In the immediate post-genocide period in Rwanda, around 90,000 children lived in 45,000 CHHs (Pells, 2012), illustrating that not only AIDS but also military conflict may result in a rise of this type of household.

In theory, children in CHHs create their own order in the sense that they take care of themselves, with older siblings and peers providing for and protecting younger members of the households. However, this in itself is viewed as a social problem. Children who head households are neither dependents nor responsible agents. As Haley and Bradbury (2015: 396) contend, the CHH 'places young adolescents in ambivalent social positions of differential power – still positioned as children even if they are performing adult roles. They assume responsibility without authority in an adult dominated culture.' Childhood is constituted in and through generational relations with adults, where children play a subordinate role as the younger generation. The family structure is defined by generational differences, and this is the case regardless of whether we are referring to the Northern nuclear family, the bi-nuclear family or the extended multigenerational form. There thus seems to be a general universal principle that, irrespective of cultural and social contexts, all families are organised according to a generational hierarchy with adults as heads of household.

The problem of 'order' is a perennial one within sociology. Since post-war developments within sociology, the bi-nuclear family has been viewed as a lynchpin of the social and moral order. Structural functionalists focused on the nuclear family form constructed along two axes of power: generation and sex/gender (Parsons and Bales, 1956). In the former case, an unambiguous hierarchical relationship between parents and children was seen to ensure that the latter have the appropriate characters and personalities. Clear generational boundaries with parents as protectors and providers at an emotional and psychological level produced children with a degree of 'inner directedness', a developing independent moral focus (Riesman, 1950). Social order is conflated with adult power, as parents provide an unambiguous moral framework within

---

child-headed families, on the other hand, as a core feature of the social structure (Tsegaye, 2009). Local understandings of CHHs may furthermore differ from policy definitions, as illustrated by Payne's (2012: 294) Zambian study, where CHHs were seen to include also 'children and young people living with alcoholic, sick or disabled parents and grandparents, and young couples who were co-habiting and had their own children but were considered children themselves because they had not completed recognised initiation practices'. CHHs exist also outside Africa, although information about the extent of these types of households in Latin America and Asia are 'practically non-existent' (Phillips, 2011).

which children are able to develop their emotional and moral capacities. The generational hierarchy creates a necessarily temporary period of dependence through which children develop the moral and social capacities as independent entities. Within this structure, parents have unambiguous authority over children and power is viewed as natural, emerging out of biological relations. As we have discussed in Chapter 1, there is also a general expectation that parents exercise this power in a beneficent manner – that parents are always acting in their children's best interests.

Research on the perceptions of AIDS orphans living in CHHs highlights complex and often contradictory conceptions of childhood and adolescence. Despite the devastation wrought by the AIDS pandemic, civil war, extreme poverty and the difficulties the extended family had in coping, CHHs are still viewed with some suspicion. Haley and Bradbury's (2015) analysis of CHHs in KwaZulu-Natal, South Africa, even refers to some hostility towards children living in CHHs, and the children themselves reported a heightened level of surveillance from their surroundings. On the one hand, this was positively framed as looking out for the children where no parents were around. Yet, the emphasis on protection also sometimes turned to distrust and animosity. Adolescent boys in particular were likely to be viewed as 'thugs' potentially out of control and at risk of committing crime within the neighbourhood. Adolescent girls, on the other hand, were sometimes viewed as both at risk from sexual abuse and behaving in an unacceptably sexual manner. As described by one 16-year-old girl, 'Oh they talk and say these kids stay alone they do whatever they want, they are whores, they say whatever they like because they know that there is no adult' (Haley and Bradbury, 2015: 402). The absence of an adult within the household is viewed as a license for children to behave promiscuously, and there is a slippage from protagonist to victim. Teenagers also felt less protected because of the absence of a parental figure at home. One 16-year-old girl vividly illustrates this point:

> The problems in my life is the fact that here in Etete even if a person is abusing you there is no one you can talk to [...] the other day I was walking here by the road near the stop street and these two guys took me to the field ground and raped me [...] I think sometimes if there was an older person at home this wouldn't have happened to me cause people do such things knowing that 'well they stay alone' [...] even if I can go home anyone can just come in because they know that we stay alone [...] I think sometimes even if there is a problem and I run home to hide it's useless cause anyone can just come in so... (Haley and Bradbury, 2015: 401)

These gender and generational structures illustrate the idea that children living in CHHs are out of position, 'unchild'-like in the absence of conventional social and moral structures that shape and mould them. Nevertheless, a closer analysis of the way the CHH functions and the position of these households within their communities suggests that they only really function if they are closely linked with agencies and other families within their communities. CHHs are unlikely to be socially and economically self-sufficient, and adult support from outside of the CHH is thus crucial. Older children will take responsibility for the well-being of younger children and help structure activities within the household. Nevertheless, there is little attempt to try and mimic the individualistic and proprietorial notion of the liberal family household, and consequently the CHH has to be viewed in more relational terms.

Kendrick and Kakuru's (2012) analysis of CHHs among Ugandan AIDS orphans highlights the different ways that orphans reach out to various adults and local organisations in trying to maintain these households. The children attended the local schools in order to improve their life chances, and schools functioned in the conventional education sense of providing the children with the possibility of achievement and future investment. One girl, Winnie, was doing well at school. She also took on many of her late mother's former responsibilities for the remaining members of her family. This included ensuring that her younger siblings continued to attend school by providing them with books and pens that they could take to school and by helping them with their homework (Kendrick and Kakuru, 2012). For some of these children, staying on at school after their parents had died was an important way of accessing adult support from the teaching staff, and in some instances, teachers were the only consistent source of adult support for their families.

The school became a central node in an expanding network of material and social support, with peers and teachers working with them in their search for material resources and food supplies. Other children passed on information about non-governmental organisations moving into the area; former friends of their parents and neighbours helped out with maintaining their properties. Through this network of ongoing support, children developed a capacity to take care of themselves. In Haley and Bradbury's (2015) research with children living together in KwaZulu-Natal, South Africa, neighbours were also an important source of support. For example, children had regular access to their neighbours when there was illness, and children also referred to the moral guidance they offered:

Maybe I am going with people who drink and come back home at night. They [the neighbours] tell me as a child sometimes that, like their children, I mustn't come back at night. I must come back in time just like other kids. (Mandla Ndebele, male, 17 years, quoted in Haley and Bradbury, 2015: 398)

Kendrick and Kakuru's (2012) research connects with Luet's (2017) work in deprived areas of the United States. Luet (2017: 679) combines 'funds of knowledge' with 'community cultural wealth', defining the latter as 'culturally developed bodies of knowledge and skills essential for household functioning and well-being' among poorer and migrant families. Luet's analysis concentrates on forms of knowledge found within working-class communities often marginalised through the education system. However, it might also be adapted to the analysis of the relationships between children from CHHs and their local communities. Thus, rather than being viewed primarily as dependants with little recognition of their cultural capacities, children living in CHHs are likely to be deploying as well as developing their funds of knowledge in meeting the challenges of poverty, food insecurity and discrimination. Children actively draw on this knowledge in advocating for their families; there is a constant need to seek out resources and connections in trying to maintain existing family relations in the absence of their parents. With the help of others within their communities, they are in a much stronger position to sustain levels of economic and social stability. The important point here is that the absence of parents does not need to be conflated with the absence of order. Children are quite capable of seeking out adult support and guidance, just as adults within communities ravaged by the AIDS pandemic are committed to protecting and providing for orphaned children living on their own as best as they can. These funds of knowledge provide a reservoir of information, local knowledge and judgements on the various sources of local support and the trustworthiness of those around in a position to support them. Within a context where conventional parental relations are likely to be absent, children draw on this knowledge and develop their mediating skills and capacity to work with those around them in maintaining the CHH. Older children mediate between younger members of the CHH and the community. While there is no clear generational line of power and authority for these orphans, members of CHHs are able to maintain the integrity of the household by reaching out to adults and organisations around them.

## Discussion and Conclusion

In constructing our theory of kid power, one of the key features is the role of children as mediators, which connects children with various groups of adults with varying degrees of authority. In this chapter we have focused on themes that relate to the broader issue of children's interstitial position as mediators within and between households and the linking up of families that are perhaps culturally alienated from broader and newer external contexts. While occupying this position might challenge a particular conception of generational power, the idea that children can mediate in different ways with respect to family, at the very least, complicates the common notion of a binary structural and generational position of children as subordinates and dependants (Prout and James, 1997). In effect, the idea of the child as mediator challenges the bi-nuclear family and by implication binary zero-sum notions of power.

There are three common threads that run through the discussions on children and divorce, children and migration, and CHHs. First, these are contexts of childhood and familial adversity underpinned by ongoing material poverty, problems of chronic illness and levels of cultural discrimination. These structural factors are overlain by new sets of familial circumstances to which families have had to adjust. If children do assume powerful positions, they are shaped by adverse sets of circumstances. More mundanely, children are adjusting to changing economic and social circumstances largely outside their control.

Second, all three examples involve issues of separation and dislocation of children from their families. For divorcing parents there are varying levels of distance between children and their biological parents. The separation is social, emotional and, in some instances, economic. Children's mediation here is about managing lines of communication and physical contact between parents in separate households. For migrant children and their families, there is a separation from their homelands and a cultural and linguistic dislocation which children sometimes manage more effectively than their parents. Children position themselves between home and host country, offering practical support in helping their families to settle. In the case of CHHs, children's separation from biological parents is permanent, robbing them of an economic, emotional and support network that many children take for granted. Agendas for living and for growing up are normally established within families for children by parents. Where parents are missing or where the parental dynamic radically changes within the home, mediation here often means children reaching out to other adults, households and organisations; taking on extra responsibilities; negotiating tasks; and generally having greater involvement with a wider range of other adults.

A third common factor is the way that these families challenge a dominant bi-nuclear family driven by structural factors, including poverty, inequality and discrimination. The families that we have discussed in this chapter have difficulties thriving within a context of global capitalism, inequality, discrimination and, in the case of CHHs, pandemics. In adapting to these forces, families and children are having to challenge cultural and social norms about family. We have provided illustrations of the way that generational relations are refined to take account of the mediating roles of children and the opportunities they have now in decision-making processes relating to custody. While the chapter has located generational relations, primarily within a context of poverty and cultural and social dislocation, it is important to note that middle-class families are not immune from separation and divorce. However, the implications of family break-up for poorer families are more far-reaching, potentially more damaging where parental separation leads to forms of economic deprivation. In mediating family break-ups, children are also helping to mediate poverty. Families migrate in search of economic and political stability, and as with children living in poorer post-divorce households, children occupy an interstitial space in providing practical and linguistic support for their parents. Again, children are often mitigating and mediating poverty.

Nevertheless, there is little sense that child mediators assert themselves as powerful agents. In most cases children are responding to economic and political exigencies; within their families they are adjusting to structural forms of inequality and discrimination. In the final example of mediation, children with primary caring responsibilities living in CHHs have to deal with poverty and discrimination outside the protective structures of parental support. They are doubly disadvantaged: having to find ways of tackling chronic food insecurity and finding support from within their communities, which intermittently censures them for living in a 'deviant' family form.

All three cases challenge the conventional binary relationship children have with powerful parents in nuclear forms. We might be talking about children connecting with post-divorce families for emotional, social and economic reasons; we might be focusing on the role that migrant children play in supporting their parents within their communities; we might be following the various links that children from CHHs make in providing for and protecting their siblings. Nevertheless, there is little attempt by child mediators to challenge adult agendas. Instead, there is a more horizontal focus on the contributions of children working alongside adults in securing the emotional and material integrity of their families.

# Chapter 6

# THE INTERNET, SOCIAL MEDIA AND KID POWER

Our previous chapter discussed the mediating role of children within families and households. In this chapter we go on to explore another area of children's lives which is increasingly becoming a key part of contemporary family relations but also requires specific attention on its own: the Internet and social media. Children and young people's lives have been transformed in the last decades due to the emergence of the Internet. One in three users of the Internet worldwide are children and adolescents under 18 years of age, and children are accessing the Internet at increasingly younger ages (UNICEF, 2017). Children and young people's use of social media sites has increased exponentially in recent years (O'Keeffe et al., 2011), and smartphones in particular have allowed for a more individual, personal and unmonitored access to online material. This has resulted in a variety of adult responses, on the one hand embracing the Internet as a source of educational and social opportunities and benefits, and on the other focusing on the risks involved and the need for better safeguarding against issues such as cyberbullying, online harassment, exposure to inappropriate content and targeted marketing. However, the access of children to the Internet and online devices is also highly unequal, and so is the digital literacy skills of both them and the adults around them. The balance between risk and opportunity is thus highly complex and the responses of adults significantly diverse, leading to many possible scenarios in relation to kid power in the context of the Internet and social media.

The image of 'digital natives', which we introduced in Chapter 4, has been used to describe children as having a better and more intuitive understanding of the Internet, a different language and a different skill set than their 'digital immigrant' parents (Prensky, 2001). This description often portrays 'young people as powerful social actors positioned to challenge the status quo' (boyd, 2014: 178) and, as also discussed in Chapter 4, could suggest that the Internet and social media might result in a reversal of the traditional power relationship between children and adults (Livingstone, 2013). However, the dichotomous and rather simplistic digital native/immigrant discourse is increasingly contested and replaced with a more complex understanding of the relationship of both children and adults to the Internet and social media (Livingstone et al., 2018). Not all children have the experience, resources and digital literacy skills to safely and competently navigate the Internet and the world of social media (Ní Bhroin and Rehder, 2018), and much depends on their access to technology and the support they get from the adults around them (Livingstone et al., 2012). Adults themselves may need education on how to understand both risks and opportunities posed by the Internet (Nawaila et al., 2018). Furthermore, studies have shown that the socio-economic and educational background of both children and parents will significantly shape not only their access to the Internet but also their experiences of using it (Mascheroni and Ólafsson, 2014). In addition, parents may practice different strategies to mediate their children's Internet and social media use, ranging from enabling to more restrictive approaches (Dias and Brito, 2020) and reflecting their general attitudes to the Internet (Nikken and Schols, 2015).

This chapter discusses some of the complexities and dilemmas posed by children's Internet and social media use through the lens of power. Drawing on our framework of power, we consider 'digital kid power' as *the ability of children to produce or share content which influences or has the potential to influence the actions of others*. By analysing some of the many different ways that children use the Internet, we examine the potential of the Internet and social media to connect children to diverse social and political realms and expand their economic capacities as consumers. We provide some examples of where this might be argued to increase kid power. However, we also consider the impact of the 'digital divide' which leaves some children more likely to experience benefits from the Internet and social media participation, and reinforces existing power differences between children, as some will have much better conditions for influencing the actions of others online. In addition, we discuss some of the intergenerational power paradoxes posed by the Internet and social media, where, on the one hand, safeguarding and adult protection dominate the agenda (Third et al., 2014) and, on the other, children are presented as having more intuitive and extensive knowledge and skills of the Internet and social media than the adults around them.

## Children, the Internet and Social Media Use

Across the world, children's access to the Internet is rapidly increasing. Smartphone ownership by children is becoming more common, and the average time they spend online is growing. However, within these general trends, large international and within-country differences prevail. A set of surveys carried out in Europe (EU Kids Online) and beyond (Global Kids

Online) presents important data on the international diversity of children's Internet and social media use over time and between countries. In the 2010 EU Kids Online II study, Livingstone et al. (2011) found that the average age when children first went online was 9 years of age across 25 European countries. However, the survey also found significant variation between countries with some, like Denmark and Sweden, having an earlier average age of first accessing the Internet (7 years) and others, like Italy and Germany, a much later average (10 years). The average time spent by the children online was 88 minutes a day, but with large differences according to age.

In a later survey of seven European countries, Mascheroni and Ólafsson (2014) found that the average age of first using the Internet had fallen to 8.5 years. This supports findings from UNICEF (2017: 1) that in 'high-connectivity countries, children are going on-line at an increasingly younger age'. The latest EU Kids Online survey (Smahel et al., 2020) furthermore shows that not only has there been a significant increase in the proportion of children using smartphones since the 2010 EU Kids survey, the amount of time that children spend online has also almost doubled in many countries. As examples, the report mentions that in Spain it had gone up from about 1 to 3 hours per day, and in Norway from about 2 to 3.5 hours. In 11 of the surveyed countries (Croatia, Czech Republic, Germany, Estonia, Italy, Lithuania, Norway, Poland, Portugal, Romania and Serbia), over 80 per cent of children aged 9–16 used a smartphone to access the Internet at least once a day, but within this group, children aged 15–16 were much more likely to use smartphones daily than younger children, and spent about twice as much time online than 9- to 11-year-olds (Smahel et al., 2020: 6).

These trends in use of the Internet, smartphone ownership and age differences are mirrored in the Global South, where the Global Kids Online surveys have found that children use the Internet at increasingly younger ages and that Internet use rises with age. UNICEF (2017) furthermore shows that children, also in countries not characterised as 'high-connectivity', commonly own their own phone before they become teenagers. For example, the report mentions that in 2013, children in Algeria, Egypt, Iraq and Saudi Arabia commonly owned a mobile phone by the age of 10–12, and in 2015, the average age for owning a mobile phone was 10 in the Philippines and 12 in Honduras. However, the Global Kids Online surveys have also identified significant inequalities of access. For example, the Brazilian Kids Online survey found that while about 80 per cent of Brazilian children aged 9–17 were Internet users, 6.3 million children were still not connected, and of these 3.6 million had never used the Internet. In addition, the study found that many children, particularly from low-income families, relied exclusively on mobile phones to go online, affecting their experiences and opportunities (http://globalkidsonline.net/brazil/).

This was similarly mentioned in the reports from the South African and Ghanaian Kids Online surveys, which found that children most often accessed the Internet via smartphones (Burton et al., 2016; Ministry of Communications et al., 2017). In both countries, identified barriers to accessing the Internet were cost of devices, cost of data and parental restrictions, and in Ghana, also the rural/urban divide in Internet coverage.

The increasing focus on the devices used for accessing the Internet, in combination with the question of access itself, illustrates what Mascheroni and Ólafsson (2016: 1658) have described as a move 'past an initial understanding of the digital divide as a binary opposition between those who have access to online technologies and those who do not, towards a focus on inequalities that lie in differential online experiences'. As Nawaila et al. (2018) have noted, differences between the Global North and South derive not only from the easier and earlier access to devices and technology in the Global North but also because children in the Global South are more likely to access the Internet in unsupervised cybercafes, making them more vulnerable.

The digital divide, however, manifests itself not only in differences between the Global North and South. This has become evident in the current Covid-19 pandemic, which has made it necessary for children and young people under lockdown to access education and communicate with their friends online. As commentators have noted, the crisis has highlighted the stark inequalities experienced by children and young people in relation to Internet use and devices also in the Global North. In the United States, for example, 4 million American households with school-aged children have been reported to not have access to the Internet (Floberg, 2020), and in the United Kingdom, some schools have reported that a very large proportion of their children may be unable to afford Internet access or may have to share one mobile device with their whole family, leaving a significant social gap in access to technology (Coughlan, 2020).

For others, the Covid-19 pandemic and ensuing lockdowns have resulted in children using social media earlier, differently and to a larger extent than what would otherwise have been the case, as for many children it has been the only way of communicating and accessing education. This has led to concerns being raised about some of the potential increased risks of online harm to children during lockdowns with ensuing recommendations and guidelines being produced on how to keep children safe in the current extraordinary circumstances (e.g. UNICEF, 2020; NSPCC, 2021). Evidently, not much is known yet about how children experience their increasing online lives, what the impact of digital divides are on social welfare and educational equality, and whether earlier and expanded access to the Internet experienced by some may in the long run have an impact on power structures between children and adults and/or between children themselves. In the following, we consider three broad themes of relevance to our discussion of digital kid power: social connectivity, political networks and consumption patterns.

## Social Connectivity

Children and young people's increasing access to social media sites via the Internet and individual smartphones has had clear implications for the ways in which they connect with their peers. In a clinical report for the American Academy of Pediatrics, O'Keeffe et al. (2011: 801) outline a range of social benefits from being on social media sites experienced by children and young people, including 'staying connected with friends and family, making new friends, sharing pictures, and exchanging ideas'. This is supported by international studies, showing that for children and young people, one of the key uses (if not the key use) of the Internet is to facilitate social relations and connect with friends (Ravalli and Paoloni, 2016; Smahel et al., 2020; Third et al., 2014). Findings from a UK qualitative study of 8–12-year-olds found that the children saw the Internet as a way to connect with their friends and find fun things to do and tended to associate social media with positive moods and happy emotions (Children's Commisioner, 2018). Similarly, the latest report from the UK communications regulator Ofcom (2020: 21) states that 'overall, children are more likely to feel positive, than negative, about social media [...] the majority of 8–15s who use social media say that it makes them feel happy or closer to their friends'.

Further confirming these benefits for children of being connected via social media, a literature review conducted by Richards et al. (2015) found that social media sites, such as Facebook, allowed young people to stay in touch with their peers, could help introverted young people learn social skills and had positive impact on well-being and self-esteem. Similarly, a study of 743 teens (13–17 years old) in the United States found that 81 per cent of the young people felt that social media made them feel 'more connected to what's going on in their friends' lives', and around two-thirds said that social media platforms make them feel 'as if they have people who will support them through tough times' (Anderson and Jingjing Jiang, 2018: 17). Those of the young people who were part of online groups generally had positive attitudes about these groups, which they felt helped them connect with new types of people, made them feel more accepted and helped them approach important issues and difficult times in their lives. However, some of them also expressed pressure to present themselves in certain ways online and reported feeling overwhelmed by 'social drama', and 26 per cent of the teens said that these sites made them feel worse about their own life.

This duality of experience is supported internationally, with more than 90 per cent of children in countries such as Egypt, India, Indonesia, Iraq and Saudi Arabia reporting that social media networking strengthened relationships with close friends, and many also finding that it helped them build relationships with more peripheral relations. However, at the same time, social media platforms were also experienced as an arena for conflict, drama among friends and a source of pressure to present themselves in a certain way (UNICEF, 2017). Other potentially negative consequences of children and young people's online social participation include cyberbullying (Alim, 2016; Canty et al., 2016), harassment, Facebook addiction (Ephraim, 2013), sexting with associated negative consequences (Jørgensen et al., 2019), exposure to inappropriate content (O'Keeffe et al., 2011), misuse of personal data (Livingstone et al., 2012) and negative impact on mental health (Richards et al., 2015).

As illustrated by the Global Kids Online surveys, many children are exposed to risks from their Internet and social media participation, including meeting strangers online, mistreatment and exposure to content which upsets them (Dodel et al., 2018; Ravalli and Paolini, 2016). In the European context, Smahel et al. (2020) found a large variation between countries in relation to the amount of children reporting having been bothered or upset by something online (from 7 per cent in Slovakia to 45 per cent in Malta), and a US study found that 59 per cent of American teens had experienced cyberbullying or online harassment (Anderson, 2018). A review by Sohn et al. (2019) found that one in four children and young people engaged in what they call problematic smartphone use (addiction) and that this raised their odds of poor mental health. The specific impact of social media on young people's mental health is addressed in Richards et al.'s (2015) review, where they identify some correlation between high use of social media sites such as Facebook with negative self-esteem and well-being. However, they also illustrate significant diversity in children and young people's social online experiences and argue that one of the key determinants of how young people are impacted by social media is the young person's circumstances or psychology, thus firmly locating causation within the child and the family.

As this shows, children's use of the Internet for socialising is not always unproblematic, and risks prevail both in the form of individual consequences of 'overuse' and in relation to the online interaction with others. The latter is of particular relevance to our discussion of power, as it shows that children may have significant potential power to influence the actions of one another through online interactions, for example, in relation to purchases (Thaichon, 2017), or lifestyle choices (Bevelander et al., 2013). Social media has also been described as a way for children and young people to reclaim agency, resembling some degree of social power in relation to their increasingly risk-averse and protectionist parents (boyd, 2014: 98). In this analysis, socialising via the Internet provides children and young people with a space free from parental power. In both cases, digital kid power predominantly comes in the form of one-dimensional power – potential ability to influence the decisions of other children or to be exempt from the decisions of parents, rather than two- or three-dimensional power, involving children in the social media agenda-setting and challenging dominant perceptions about children's online socialising. The power dynamics between children and adults and among children themselves are furthermore mostly framed in relation to them as individuals, who may experience an increase in their relative power (e.g. in relation to their parents) or be particularly vulnerable and disempowered. In contrast, our next theme focuses more specifically on the potential collective power generated by children and young people through their Internet and social media participation.

## Political and Community Networks

The Internet provides children and young people with a range of platforms to connect over political and community interests. This may enable them to 'amplify their voices and seek solutions to problems affecting their communities' (UNICEF, 2017: 22). Several examples of how young people use digital technology to connect, identify issues of interest and try to influence decision-making are presented in UNICEF's *State of the World's Children* report (UNICEF, 2017: 22–23). These include, for example, a climate change digital mapping tool, which makes it possible for young people across countries to map changes to their communities and use the results for advocacy, and a digital reporting platform (the 'U-Report') where 10 million youth reporters (of whom 19 per cent are between 15 and 19 years of age) in 68 countries share community issues and communicate with policy makers (https://ureport.in/). In Third et al.'s (2014) study of children's rights in the digital age, children from 16 countries reported that digital media helped them seek out information and enabled them 'to be informed citizens who can participate meaningfully in their communities [...] in friendship and broader community networks' (37). Nevertheless, only a minority of participants indicated that this enabled them to actually help drive social and cultural change. This shows that although the Internet and social media have provided new spaces through which children and young people can engage with one another, as we have discussed previously, having information and a voice does not necessarily translate into kid power.

The spaces generated as part of digital technology are described by boyd (2014: 9) as 'networked publics'. She draws on a broad understanding of 'publics' as spaces and communities where people 'gather, connect and help construct society as we understand it' and explains as follows:

Networked publics are publics that are restructured by networked technologies. As such, they are simultaneously (1) the space constructed through networked technologies and (2) the imagined community that emerges as a result of the intersection of people, technology and practice. (boyd, 2014: 8)

Similar to traditional physical publics, networked publics can be political or constructed around shared identities and social practices. However, four key affordances make them significantly different from offline spaces: (1) the persistence of the content shared, (2) their visibility (size of potential audience), (3) the spreadability and ease with which content can be shared and (4) searchability (the ability to find content) (boyd, 2014: 11). All of these create opportunities as well as challenges for those who engage within the networked publics. For example, spreadability can involve the rapid spread of rumours or 'fake news', but it also has high potential for mobilising people around a common cause.

The latter has been clearly illustrated by two recent youth-initiated campaigns:– the US Never Again/March for Our Lives Movement (https://marchforourlives.com/) and the global climate strikes (Fridays for the Future: https://fridaysforfuture.org/), which we will discuss in more detail in the next chapter. The Never Again/March for Our Lives Movement was initiated by the survivors of the Parkland Shootings in Florida in February 2018 and led to a series of mass demonstrations demanding stricter gun legislation. Analysts have been quick to point to the importance of social media for the speed with which the movement was able to mobilise, spread the message and organise activities across the United States (Klusener, 2019; Rahman-Jones, 2018; Salamon, 2018). The Parkland survivors have been described as 'social media savvy teens' who use social media to 'debunk conspiracy theories and amplify their voices in a way the world hasn't seen before' and through this have shaped the debate in ways that adults have struggled to do (Newcomb, 2018). The young people themselves have also recognised the importance of digital technology for the success of their movement: 'People always say, "Get off your phones," but social media is our weapon […] Without it, the movement wouldn't have spread this fast' (Jaclyn Corin, cited in Alter, 2018: n.p.).

Illustrating not only how messages spread via social media can mobilise young people but also the methods of doing so, Greta Thunberg has described how she drew inspiration from the Never Again/March for Our Lives Movement to begin her striking for the climate in 2019 (Rodrick, 2020). Similar to the Never Again/March for Our Lives Movement, the climate strikes were able to spread very quickly and mobilise huge numbers of young people due to the Internet and social media. As noted by one commentator,

> At a time of fraying trust in authority figures, children – who by definition have no authority over anything – are increasingly driving the debate. Using the Internet, young people are organizing across continents like no generation before them. And though their outsize demands for an end to fossil fuels mirror those of older environmentalists, their movement has captured the public imagination far more effectively. (Sengupta, 2019)

As this shows, networked publics, such as those generated around the Never Again/March for Our Lives and Fridays for the Future movements, are a powerful tool for young people who can utilise their persistence, visibility, spreadability and searchability to set the agenda, influence decisions and challenge the view of children and young people as apolitical.

That being said, it is important to note that political activism and civic participation still play a relatively small part of children's total use of the Internet compared to social and educational purposes. National and international studies have shown that only a minority of children use the Internet to discuss political and social problems with others or engage with community activities, and that this minority is almost exclusively composed of older children (Burton et al., 2016; Logar et al., 2016; Popadić et al., 2016; Third et al., 2014). Most online platforms and activities directed at community or policy engagement are also aimed at older children or young people, as are most studies of the effect of digital media on participation and citizenship. In addition, it is important to acknowledge some of the many challenges of children's digital activism and the different conditions under which children are able to express their opinions and take action. As noted by UNICEF (2017: 25), one major challenge is the fact that 'two thirds of all internet users – adults and children – live in countries where criticism of the government, military or ruling family is censored'. The Internet may furthermore present children and young people with many contradicting messages and causes which they, like adults, need critical digital literacy skills to filter out. As acknowledged by Third et al. (2014), digital literacy is a combination of technical, media and social skills, and some children's lack of these limits the extent to which they can make use of the Internet for political and community involvement and 'move up the ladder towards civic participation' (UNICEF, 2017: 28). While there are numerous examples of how the Internet and social media have provided children and young people with the means to exercise their collective power, it is thus important to acknowledge the wide disparities between children in terms of age, digital literacy and social settings. Our final theme further illustrates these disparities in the context of consumption.

## Children's Consumption in the Context of the Internet and Social Media

Children's direct access to the Internet and social media sites has opened up new patterns of consumption. It allows children not only to directly engage with the global economic marketplace but also to address others and be addressed within it. Particularly the latter is a focus of much concern, as it has been found that children are not always aware of if or when they are being targeted by advertisers. We discussed the potential for the Internet to act as an intrusive third party in intergenerational relations in Chapter 4. Specific concerns have also been raised about the impact of online advertising through social media sites, influencers and advergames, and the impact this has on children, for example, in relation to lifestyle or food patterns (An and Kang, 2014; Baldwin et al., 2018; Boerman and van Reijmersdal, 2020; Harris et al., 2012). In addition, Kim and Yi (2010) have discussed the extent of personal information collected through commercial websites targeting children and the subsequent implications for privacy. In the United Kingdom, Ofcom (2020) has shown that a majority of children are unable to recognise advertising and distinguish between commercial and editorial messages online. Marketing to children is thus predominantly conceived as a risk (O'Keeffe et al., 2011; Livingstone et al., 2011), resulting in calls for greater regulations, similar to those introduced in various countries with regard to television advertising (Wyness, 2018).

Emphasising the inherently social aspect of children's Internet use, children and young people may also themselves exercise significant influence over one another online (Thaichon, 2017). The children's commissioner for England found that some children may feel obliged to buy things in the games they play in order to keep up with their friends (Children's Commissioner, 2018), and others have commented that social media may increase children and young people's sense of having to keep up in the environment of 'constant comparison' facilitated by social media (Morlock, 2018). A growing number of 'influencers', both children and adults, shape children's views of lifestyle and consumption, for example, in relation to toys, eating habits or clothing

(Boerman and van Reijmersdal, 2020; Coates et al., 2019). Correspondingly, a growing proportion of marketing takes place via peers and influencers, illustrating several layers of potential power relationships. However, the extent to which peers and influencers may be considered as having power over those who follow them depends on a number of factors, not least that different children process and are influenced by what they see online in different ways (Richards et al., 2015). For example, in a Dutch study of 118 children from the 5th and 6th grades, Bevelander et al. (2013) found that similar to 'real-life eating situations', online peers model one another in relation to food intake, but also that some (those with low body or explicit self-esteem) may be more at risk to peer influences. This shows the importance of considering power, not only of adult producers over children, but also among children themselves and the way they are unequally positioned in relation to one another.

Most of the attention on children as online consumers has focused on the associated risks (e.g. unrecognised marketing and impact on lifestyle), and little is known about how or if children may use the Internet positively to expand their power as consumers. This may be because the idea of the 'consuming, desiring child' does not sit well with dominant understandings of childhood (Cook, 2013), or because children's use of the Internet to purchase things is still relatively limited internationally (Logar et al., 2016; Popadić et al., 2016; Ravalli and Paoloni, 2016; Smahel et al., 2020), especially in the case of young children. However, insights from the literature on adult consumers suggests that the Internet might offer significant opportunities for children to increase their power as consumers, and the link between children's consumption and the Internet thus seems in need of more analysis.

Labrecque et al.'s (2013) model of consumer power in the digital age provides an instructive analysis of the effect of the Internet and social media on the relative power of consumers and marketers/producers. Although the model does not explicitly consider different consumers' characteristics (e.g. age), it offers a useful framework to explore children's power as online consumers, as it considers both risks and opportunities and, furthermore, distinguishes individual from network-based power. This is important for our analysis of children as online consumers, as it allows us to explore the dilemmas posed by their online activities, both as individuals in relation to marketers and their parents, and in relation to one another.

Labrecque et al.'s (2013) model delineates four types of consumer power, the first of which they call *demand-based power*. This type of power describes the ability of individuals to purchase goods through an increasingly large and global pool of products, resulting in growing market variety and a lowering of prices. The second type of consumer power described in the model is *information-based power*, and this includes both consumption and production of information content.

The increased amount of information available to consumers online about products leads to 'better educated and more sophisticated consumers' (p. 261) and increases the relative power of consumers over producers as consumer awareness and attention are dispersed. Furthermore, some consumers not only access but also produce information and vocalise praise or complaints through 'electronic Word of Mouth' (p. 261). This constitutes an expression of a shift in power from the marketer to the consumer. However, the growing amount of information available about consumers due to their content production also enables the opposite effect, as firms are able to access data about search patterns, product preferences and network connections of individual consumers and thus target them more directly.

The third type of power described in the model is *network-based power*. This includes the power generated by consumers who distribute content (created by themselves, others or in collaboration) via their online social network and through this 'social word of mouth' influence the purchases of others. Labrecque et al. (2013) describes this as largely positive for the consumer, but they also acknowledge that the social obligations and dynamics that follow may carry some risks. Furthermore, as consumers increasingly lose control of what is public and what is private, marketers regain power by their ability to 'identify, reach, and influence more socially connected consumers' (p. 264). As such, this type of power illustrates not only the power of marketers over consumers but also that some consumers have disproportionate influence over others due to the extent of their networks and social connections.

Finally, the last type of consumer power described by Labrecque et al. (2013) is *crowd-based power*: 'the ability to pool, mobilize, and structure resources in ways that benefit both the individuals and the groups' (p. 264). As examples of this type of power the authors mention crowd-creation platforms (e.g. Wikipedia), crowd-funding, crowd-sourcing, crowd-selling and crowd-supporting in peer-to-peer problem-solving communities. These types of community-driven platforms disrupt the power of traditional companies, as they offer alternative ways for consumers to create new marketplaces. However, automated ranking systems may still generate new stratified social systems, which disadvantages some consumers over others.

As a whole, Labrecque et al.'s (2013) model shows not only how consumers may use digital technology to express their demands, access and produce information, influence their social networks and join to shape new markets altogether, but also how some of their actions may decrease their consumer power in relation to producers and marketers. Considering the particular position of children as consumers adds a number of additional layers and complexities. In relation to demand-based power, children, as well as adults, may benefit from access to the global market, where they can shape demand via the volume of their purchases. However, particularly for younger children, these will most often have to be negotiated with parents (Thaichon, 2017), and their potential demand-based power is thus more indirect than the one held by adults. On the other hand, children and young people may teach their parents about online shopping or use the information they obtain via the Internet to influence family purchase decisions (Kaur and Medury, 2011; Thaichon, 2017). This shows the link to the second type of power – information-based power – where children and young people may access information and educate themselves about available products. Depending on their age and reading comprehension, they may not always be able to do this by themselves. Age restrictions and digital literacy skills may furthermore limit their ability to produce content, and thus the extent to which they can influence others online is likely to increase with age. The paradox mentioned by Labrecque et al. (2013) in relation to adults, where increasing information about consumers may increase the power of marketers through profile marketing, has also been identified in relation to children (van Reijmersdal et al., 2017), with significant impact on positive brand associations and intended purchases.

The third type of power – network-based power – is also relevant to children, whose steadily increasing online interactions with their peers result in many of them having a large online network, which can be tapped into for social, political and commercial purposes. The extent to which children themselves can influence the actions of others through online networks will depend significantly on their age, digital literacy level or any legal/parental restrictions in place. Similarly, the extent to which they can exercise the last type of consumer power described by Labrecque et al. (2013) – crowd-based power – will be limited by the same age-based restrictions and digital skills, and therefore, their potential crowd-based power is also likely to grow with age. As is the case with adults, there are, however, important questions about how children navigate online crowds and whether the Internet enables existing inequalities between them to level or rather to be reproduced.

As the model and its application to children has shown, power operates at a number of levels in relation to children's consumption, some of which are related to parent–child dynamics, others to the nature of online peer groups, and others again to marketers. All four types of power seem to describe a notion of power which mostly considers the influence of different agents on each other's purchase decisions or, in the case of producers, production decisions (one-dimensional power). Here children may potentially exercise a certain extent of kid power but also, at the same time and to varying degrees, be influenced by the power of others. However, considering also two- and three-dimensional power, the question remains whether children, through their Internet and social media activity, may also extend the scope of decisions available to them and challenge dominant regimes of knowledge around children and consumption. Given the relative lack of literature on children as active and deliberate internet consumers and the dominance of risk narratives in the context of children's Internet consumption, this is questionable.

## Diversity of Children's Online Experiences

The Internet and social media have significant potential for expanding children and young people's power by enabling them to reach a larger group of people than previously possible, by giving them a platform to express social views and political or community concerns and by obtaining and sharing information which may influence family or peer purchases. This provides an avenue through which children can influence the decisions of others. It may also, as we have seen in relation to political and community activism, enable them to shape agenda-setting and, potentially and more long-term, change some of the dominant ways children and young people are conceived in society.

That being said, children are not equally positioned in relation to these affordances, and their potential to exercise power versus their risks of experiencing a lack of power is thus significantly diverse. One digital divide discussed in the literature is between high- and low-connectivity countries, with children in the Global South often citing problems of access to the Internet (Third et al., 2014). But as we have seen, access is only one element of digital inequality. Others relate to the particular devices (mobile phones vs computers) and settings (home vs cybercafes, alone vs in groups) available to children and young people, and their subsequent diverse experiences of being able to produce content. While mobile phones and cybercafes may provide less advantaged social groups with access to the Internet, mobile-based users have also been found to engage in 'less advantageous and beneficial uses of the Internet' (Mascheroni and Ólafsson, 2016: 1660). In addition, Livingstone and Bulger (2014) note that the lack of safety net and digital skills is important to understand the vulnerability and risk of children in the Global South:

> Providing children with opportunities tends to bring risks which societies seek to manage through a mix of regulation, education and parenting. In the global North, it is recognised that exposure to some risk can be the means of developing resilience, but in the global South it may be that such risks are too great, since safety nets are often lacking […] it is already clear, however, that children in the global South receive little if any digital literacy teaching that could enable them to meet the interpretative

challenges that are demanding even for those in the global North for whom such services were designed. (Livingstone and Bulger, 2014: 323)

Digital skills are a key aspect of children and young people's online experiences, and these may vary significantly, not only due to access, but also depending on the resources they have available to support them (Eynon and Geniets, 2016). In addition to these differences between countries, other differences may shape children and young people's experiences of using the Internet and consequently their potential power, including age, gender and other background characteristics.

In relation to age, we have seen that older children are more likely to use those features of the Internet and social media which allow them to connect to their friends, galvanise support for political and community causes, and produce content which may potentially influence the actions of others. However, the increased time they spend online and their growing participation in producing rather than merely consuming content may also make older children more susceptible to some of the negative and disempowering effects of social media interactions, such as cyberbullying, online abuse, exposure to harmful or upsetting content, and the negative effects of sexting.

Gender represents another characteristic around which children and young people's online experiences may be shaped. Girls have been found to be disproportionally affected by some types of disempowering experiences, for example, rumour spreading (Anderson, 2018) and pressure or coercion to send nude images of themselves (Jørgensen et al., 2019). The gendered risks of social media participation have also been identified by Nawaila et al. (2018), who note that not only are girls more likely to be exposed to the risks posed by the Internet, but in many countries they also receive much less instruction and support than boys in how to navigate the Internet safely making them doubly vulnerable. This further emphasises the importance of digital skills and the close link between offline and online inequalities and vulnerability (Livingstone and Bulger, 2014). It illustrates the key importance of considering children's diversity and the many factors which may intersect to decide whether the Internet and social media present them with opportunities to exercise power or, conversely, disempower them in relation to others. A further dimension of this question is the extent to which children's Internet and social media use may serve to alter their power in relation to adults.

## Intergenerational Issues

The emergence and spread of digital technology among children and young people have been argued to give adolescents a new kind of freedom from their parents (Ephraim, 2013) and provide them with a way to 'reclaim sociality' in societies increasingly defined by risks (boyd, 2014). As we have seen particularly in relation to political and community activism, the Internet and social media may also be used by young people to organise themselves and, through this, challenge existing structures and agendas to facilitate change. In this light, the Internet and social media could therefore be argued to have increased children's relative power in relation to parents and other adults. However, at the same time, adults often use a range of mechanisms to control and limit children's use of the Internet and social media, suggesting the opposite. In addition, mobile phones may function as an instrument of control, particularly when purchased by parents to monitor and regulate their children's use of time and space. While this illustrates the complexities of intergenerational relations in the context of the Internet and social media, it also seems to support the predominantly zero-sum conception of power. A possible alternative approach could be to consider and acknowledge the potential of co-learning and mediation for increasing the joint power of children and adults.

Studies have shown that in many countries, children use the Internet more than their parents (Livingstone et al., 2012; Ministry of Communications et al., 2017) and that children may consequently feel they know more about it than their parents (Ravalli and Paoloni, 2016). Although such patterns and perceptions vary across countries and change over time, at least in some settings they may thus be used to support the digital immigrant/native discourse, where children, rather than adults, are 'the experts'. However, as pointed out by Ní Bhroin and Rehder, digital expertise includes more than technical skills:

> This positioning raises an interesting dilemma in terms of how children, as experts, can access support from their parents, or other adults, who may have less experience with the specific technologies that they use. Although the children may be able to program games and devices and explore new applications that their parents have not had any experience with, they still lack a holistic understanding of the risks and opportunities that may be associated with their actions. (Ní Bhroin and Rehder, 2018: 6)

As suggested by this quote, some of the risks associated with children's online activities require an intergenerational approach which acknowledges the expertise of both children and adults and supports more involvement of parents in their children's online activities. It also requires adults to critically reflect on their own perceptions of what constitutes a 'good childhood' and how the Internet and social media might fit into it (boyd, 2014: 16).

Dias and Brito (2020) have summarised parental mediation styles in relation to children's Internet and social media use into two main categories: enabling and restricting. The former describes an approach where parents participate in their children's digital activities, support and teach them; the second, an approach where 'parents perceive the dangers of digital media as higher than the opportunities and rely on supervision, monitoring and even prohibitions' (p. 57). Not surprisingly, parental mediation strategies are linked to their general attitudes to the Internet (Nikken and Schols, 2015), but often restrictive and safeguarding approaches take priority over enabling strategies. The dominance of risk narratives in relation to children and young people's digital activities as well as the strategies used by adults to monitor or restrict their children's online activities further challenge the idea of children as powerful digital experts.

Acknowledging the potential of other, less restrictive approaches, several researchers have argued for a more active participation of parents in their children's Internet and social media activities. Ephraim (2013) has called for more involvement from parents in teaching their children how to become responsible users of social networks. Johansen (2019: 65) has argued that the lack of adult engagement with young children's online play is lamentable because it is 'precisely these types of practices that might lead to reflexive digital literacy'. O'Keeffe et al. (2011: 803) have encouraged parents to learn more about the social media sites their children are using in order to help their children develop into 'responsible, sensible, and respectful digital citizens'.

Seemingly supporting intergenerational co-learning approaches, Livingstone et al. (2012) found that the majority of children in their EU Kids Online survey thought their parents had 'got it about right' in relation to the interest they take in their children's Internet activities. About 15 per cent of the children would have liked their parents to take more of an interest in their Internet use, and half of the parents felt that they should do more in relation to their children's Internet use. In addition, Correa et al. (2015) have shown that mediation strategies may also be reversed. Children can be an important socialising factor in their parents' adoption or usage of digital media. This further illustrates the potential benefits of intergenerational co-learning and the more consensual notion of power whereby children and adults jointly develop and make use of their digital skills.

## Conclusion: Children's Use of the Internet and Social Media through a Power Lens

Analysing children and young people's online social, political and consumption/economic opportunities, as well as common associated risks, shows that the relationship between children's Internet and social media use and their power is highly diverse, multilayered and contextual.

Livingstone et al. have argued as follows:

> As the Internet becomes ever more embedded into children's lifeworld in a host of increasingly taken-for-granted ways, research is called to examine children's engagement with the world not only *on* but also, more importantly, *through* the Internet. In other words, the research agenda no longer concerns children's relationship with the Internet as a medium but, more profoundly, it concerns their relationship with the world as mediated by the Internet in particular and changing ways. (Livingstone et al., 2018: 1117)

This chapter has shown that while children's engagement with the world through the Internet has the potential to challenge some of the existing power dynamics between children and adults and between children themselves, digital kid power is still predominantly one-dimensional. That is, while children and young people may be able to influence the actions of others through their online activities, they are less likely to be able to change the 'rules of the game' or dominant perceptions of children and childhood as vulnerable and in need of protection in an increasingly risky world. This is illustrated by the multitude of digital interventions, campaigns and Internet safeguarding guidelines developed by adults without much input from children and young people themselves. As we have argued, there is significant potential for co-learning in the area of digital skills and development. This might not only help mitigate some of the potential risks involved in children's online activities but also open up for more opportunities. And from a power perspective, it suggests a more positive-sum intergenerational power sharing.

# Chapter 7

# CHILDREN'S COMMUNITY ACTION

In this chapter we shift our focus from the contributions that children make within the private realm of family and the public/private online sphere, to their participation within the more explicitly public realm of school and broader community. Children across the globe get involved in their schools, communities and societies, where they contribute and aim to make a difference through direct actions, participation in decision-making, awareness raising and challenging common assumptions about their capacities. In this chapter, we discuss three examples of children's diverse contributions and analyse the many levels upon which power may operate within them. Our first example is the involvement of children in school councils, which have a long tradition in many countries and have gained further prominence after the ratification of the UN Convention on the Rights of the Child (CRC). Our second example is the more recent mobilisation of children and young people through the climate strikes (Fridays for the Future), which gained momentum across the world in 2019. Finally, our third example is the activism by working children's movements in Latin America, Asia and Africa to improve the conditions of working children and destigmatise child labour. Through these three examples, we discuss different dimensions of power and analyse the extent to which the actions of children can or should be seen as manifestations of kid power. We trace some of the discourses and paradigms around childhood and children's involvement, which are common in commentary and responses to children's involvement in all three contexts. Finally, we challenge the zero-sum conception of power commonly used to describe children's involvement and activism, by considering various power differentials between children and adults and between children themselves and the many potential combinations through which the interests of children and adults may coincide.

## Case 1: Children's Involvement in School Councils

School councils are representative structures, where student councillors meet regularly to discuss areas of interest to the children at their school. The councils are often highlighted as a way to increase children and young people's engagement and active citizenship, and they are closely related to the broader focus on children's rights to participation, learning for democracy and 'pupil voice' (Maitles and Deuchar, 2006; Whitty and Wisby, 2007). In some countries, the term 'school council' is used to describe councils for parents (see e.g. Stelmach, 2016) or larger councils including teachers, parents and student representatives (Mayes, 2019). However, in this chapter we refer to school councils solely as those composed of primary or secondary school pupils. Much of the literature on this type of school councils stem from the United Kingdom and Europe, and the focus in this section will also primarily be on this part of the world, although some parallels will be drawn with literature from other regions.

School councils are compulsory in some countries (e.g. Wales and Norway) and considered optional in others. In England, school councils are not mandatory, but they are found in the majority of primary schools and often considered an integral element of school life (Burnitt and Gunter, 2013; Whitty and Wisby, 2007). Despite the widespread and sometimes long-standing establishment of school councils, research from England and other countries indicates that there is significant variation in their effectiveness and that much depends on the cultural context and the particular school in question. In a commentary on school councils in England, British newspaper reporter Tom Bennett (2012) noted that 'some schools support the use of student councils as laboratories of democracy, others still regard them as unwelcome guests at *the table of power*' (Bennett, 2012: 4, our emphasis). This association between school councils and power provides the basis for including them in this chapter, where we discuss who gets to have a say in the councils and whether the councils enable changes to practice, that is, what is the extent of their power?

### Who gets to have a say in school councils?

School councils are usually modelled on adult democratic participation processes, whereby children are elected on a regular basis to represent their peers (Cox and Robinson-Pant, 2005; Percy-Smith, 2010). However, the balance between election and selection may vary significantly, with children often describing what they perceive as an unfair s/election process, as, for example, illustrated by Stafford et al.:

> If it's in our school, it's always the same people that get picked for everything/people like [ ] and [ ] get picked to do lots of things/ I've never been picked [general agreement] […] People think once someone's done one thing they like them, and they'll pick them for loads

of other things … how do they know other people wouldn't be good at it? (Stafford et al., 2003: 369)

Stafford et al. (2003) further describe how the young people in their Scottish study perceived school councils as structures set up by adults, representing only a small selected group of children. This is an issue mirrored in other studies, which have found that the representative model combined with a s/election process that tends to favour certain types of students over others runs the risk of creating elites (Mager and Nowak, 2012) and only hearing the voices of 'academically able' and confident students (Hartas, 2011). Children themselves may reinforce this tendency by self-(de)selecting, based on their perceived relative standing in relation to other students and their ideas about criteria for participation in the school council. This is well illustrated by a quote from Cox and Robinson-Pant's (2005) study of three English primary schools.

| RORY: | Well in a way I'm quite glad [I'm not on the school council] because I'm dyslexic so I'm not … |
|---|---|
| INTERVIEWER: | Mm. Dyslexic? |
| RORY: | Yeah. |
| INTERVIEWER: | So do you think that would be a problem on the School Council? |
| RORY: | Well maybe because I'm not that good and stuff, so that … |

(cited in Cox and Robinson-Pant, 2005: 15)

Commenting on this quote, Cox and Robinson-Pant (2005: 15) argue that while school councils have created new ways in which children might influence the decisions about what happens in the school, they are also set against a new power relationship emerging between children. S/election processes and assumptions about particular criteria for involvement have been shown to risk disengagement or alienation of other students with the council and its decisions (Carvalho, 2012; Stafford et al., 2003). For example, in a study of over two thousand pupils in England, Whitty and Wisby (2007: 312) found that only 15 per cent of those whose school had a school council had been approached by a school councillor to talk about the work of the council and 23 per cent didn't know what changes were implemented by the council. Furthermore, Hartas (2011: 106) describes incidents of bullying of student councillors, due to the council being conceived as being 'formed by and for the "clever students, those who get good marks"'. She concludes that for the young people in her study, 'formal channels of participation did not offer acceptable avenues for them because they were seen as irrelevant and not fitting with their peer culture, reinforcing their invisibility at school'.

These points on school councils and the dynamics between student councillors and other children demonstrate two key issues relevant to the discussion of power. First, if considering the school council as a platform for exercising power through decision-making, student councillors have significantly more one-dimensional power than their peers, and any favouritism in the s/election process thus represents a reproduction of wider inequalities between children. However, if the school council is considered an 'irrelevant channel' for any desired changes, the power balance shifts and may potentially result in council members being disempowered in relation to their peers, for example, if their participation results in bullying. Both scenarios illustrate the importance of understanding children as a complex group, rather than a uniform category. Considering the councils in relation to the theories of power outlined in Chapter 1, the question also still remains as to whether the councils result in any significant changes based on the decisions made by council members, whether certain areas remain off-limits and how grievances about the extent of children's influence may be prevented.

### Changes to practice? Power as decision-making, non-decision-making and prevention of grievances

In a personal recollection of being involved in a student council in Brazil, Carvalho describes how the students on one occasion sought influence in the decisions of their school in relation to staffing:

> I remember having led a petition, signed by almost every student in our year, in order to keep a biology teacher in the school. We believed he had been the best biology teacher we had had in the last three years. We talked with the people responsible within the school but to no avail. We were not even informed of the reason why he was leaving, which made things more difficult. All we knew is that he was not leaving of his own accord. Whatever the reason, we were not able to influence the school and no response or argument was given as to why he had left. (Carvalho, 2012: 155)

This example clearly illustrates one of the limits to children's decision-making within school: their lack of first-dimensional power. It also shows that there are areas which children are seldom involved in, for example, strategic decisions about staffing. Other studies have similarly shown that the topics upon which children are allowed to have a say and make decisions on in school councils are often relatively narrow. For example, Burnitt and Gunter (2013) found that most school councils focused on everyday issues such as 'sufficient balls in the playground' and that those requiring more complex planning and implementation were rarely discussed. In a slightly dated but still relevant study, Alderson (2000) found that while 65 per cent of the students reported that the council was free to talk about any topic they liked, 20 per cent said that it only talked about topics decided by teachers. Furthermore, some of the teachers in her study said that 'school councils were not useful because pupils want to talk only about uniform and other *forbidden questions*' (Alderson, 2000: 132, our emphasis), although what might constitute 'forbidden' topics is variable, and depends on the extent of change sought by children.

Relating school councils to children's rights, Shier (2019: 2) argues that the rights of children to have a say on 'all matters affecting the child' should include issues of the curriculum and the quality of the teaching, but the fact that these are 'rarely if ever discussed in the official participation spaces in schools [...] raises questions about who is setting the agenda, on what terms and in whose interests'. This emphasises that school councils often lack non-decision-making/two-dimensional power, although in the particular context of the curriculum, teachers may also have limited power as these are often mandated from above. Furthermore, quotes from Bjerke's (2011) study of student participation in Norway, and Thornberg and Elvstrand's (2012) study of children's experiences of democracy, participation and trust in Swedish schools show how decision-making and non-decision-making power are closely interlinked in the context of school councils:

BOY A:    They have to listen more to the pupil's council. They have to be more open to other possibilities, like ... for example in the case of the school reform, they decided, before we got the opportunity to say anything at all, whether it was going to happen. They were not open to discussing what we had to say at all.

BOY B:    They did say that they would listen to us and that we should have the final word and all that, but they didn't care about it for a second. And that's bad. It would have been one thing if they said that they would decide, but when they say that we can participate in deciding and then do nothing about it, that's what's bad.

(Bjerke, 2011: 99)

INTERVIEWER:    Who makes the decisions about all these rules at school?

LINA:           The teachers and the principal, I think.

INTERVIEWER:    Okay, but what chance do you pupils have to join in making these decisions?

LINA:    A little bit in the pupil council, but we can't do much there either.

INTERVIEWER:    Why not?

SANDRA:    Because the teachers have already made up their minds.

LINA:    Yes. (From a group interview with two schoolgirls in fifth grade.)

(Thornberg and Elvstrand, 2012: 49)

As these quotes show, it may not always be completely clear when power is exercised as decision-making over areas of 'observable conflict' (Lukes, 2005) (one-dimensional power) and when it is exercised as control over the topics children are allowed to have a say in altogether (two-dimensional power). Furthermore, while the young people in Bjerke's study clearly challenged their lack of both one- and two- dimensional power, the students in Thornberg and Elvstrand's study were more ambivalent. In fact, many of them were positive about their own lack of power, because they trusted their teachers' decision-making over their own, as illustrated by some of their participants:

If the pupils decided the rules in school, they would make bad rules. There would be no rules against shouting in classroom, running in corridors, fighting, teasing and so on.

(a boy, second grade, quoted in Thornberg and
Elvstrand, 2012: 49)

In an interpretation closely resembling Lukes's third dimension of power, the authors interpret the children's views as a 'hidden curriculum' whereby children are constructed as not able to manage without adult rules and 'cannot participate in real decision making in school and classroom rules because of childish incompetence' (Thornberg and Elvstrand, 2012: 49). Devine's (2003) study of primary schools in the Republic of Ireland identifies a similar discourse which presents children as incapable of acting responsibly. However, Devine notes that this dominant discourse competes with an alternative notion of children being entitled to have their voices heard at school. Likewise, Thornberg and Elvstrand (2012: 51) identify a conflict between children wanting teachers to decide, due to them being more knowledgeable, and wanting to have more of a say in school. Furthermore, Thornberg and Elvstrand (2012: 49) argue that the previously described 'hidden curriculum' is based on perception rather than experience, because when 'the children actually decided things in schools the outcome was seldom as negative as the children think'.

These examples show how a third dimension of power/regime of truth may operate to convince children of their own limitations and thus 'prevent grievances from arising in the first place' (Lukes, 2005: 27). As Mayes (2019) has critically commented, in school councils it is not only 'decisions' that are being made but also particular 'subjects' such as the chairperson and 'structures' in the form of rules and conventions of the meetings. School councils are a commonly studied aspect of children's participation in schools, perhaps because they are relatively easily observed. However, they are also highly structured by existing power relationships between children and their teachers. Acknowledging that formal structures for participation, such as school councils, often do not achieve the perceived benefits and outcomes they set out to, Percy-Smith (2010: 110) has argued for a rethink of the 'spaces' for participation, including 'a wider array of social contexts wherein agency, identity and empowerment, rather than structures, define participation'. One such social context may be our second case, the recent global youth climate strikes.

## Case 2: Children Striking from School for the Climate

What has now become known as the 'Climate Strikes' or 'Fridays for the Future' (https://www.fridaysforfuture.org/) began with teenager Greta Thunberg's action outside of the Swedish parliament in August 2018. Her school strike rapidly grew into a movement of children and young people across the globe routinely striking from schools on Fridays (Jourdan and Wertin, 2020). Greta Thunberg herself has subsequently gained status as the voice of environmentally aware children and young people and has been invited to speak to the United Nations, the European parliament, Davos and other national parliaments and organisations. In 2019, she was nominated for the Nobel Prize.

While other (mostly adult) individuals and organisations have emphasised the importance of climate action, the mass movement of youth strikers has strongly illustrated the urgency felt by children and young people about this global issue. Commentators and young people alike have invoked the concept of power to describe the actions of the school strikers. For example, an editorial in the international medical journal the *Lancet* discussed the strikes using the title 'Power to the Children' (*The Lancet*, 2019), and when writing about her own participation in the strikes, a 17-year-old British student wrote in the *Guardian*, 'I am taking part in the school climate strike. It's the only power I have' (Smarth-Knight, 2019). However, considering the strikes with reference to our framework of power makes it relevant to explore in more detail the different dimensions of power which the climate strikes may operate at and the extent to which the school strikers have managed to exercise their power by changing the actions of others. The strikes are still too recent to have produced much academic research, and a systematic review of newspaper articles from across the globe would be too big an endeavour for this chapter. In our analysis of the strikes, we thus draw on selected news items, mainly from the United Kingdom and the limited existing academic literature.

### The power dimensions of climate strikes

We the young, have started to move. We are going to change the fate of humanity, whether you like it or not. United we will rise until we see climate justice. We demand the world's decision-makers take responsibility and solve this crisis.

(open letter, *The Guardian*, 1 March 2019)

As we discussed in Chapter 4, the children's aim of striking for the climate is not to usurp the power of adults to shape global policy on climate change. The young people who have been involved in the climate strikes have been relatively clear that they do not want to be in charge of making the decisions needed for climate change action, but instead call on adults to step up and do so (Lawton, 2019; Sengupta, 2019). As previously quoted UK student Rosie Smart expressed it in her piece, 'I'm not striking because I know how to tackle climate change, I'm striking because I want the people with the power to do something to start addressing it' (Smarth-Knight, 2019). Signalling the same idea, the Swedish magazine *The Local* described what they call an unofficial slogan for the movement: 'Dear adults, use your power!' (*The Local*, 2019). This suggests that the type of power sought by climate strikers is not so much in the form of decision-making (one-dimensional) power, but rather that they want to change the agenda and challenge what they see as adult non-decision-making (two-dimensional) power.

Throughout the strikes, the responses from adults have varied between complimenting the participating children for showing engagement and exercising citizenship to arguing that children should not be expressing their views by striking from school. Putting aside the dismissal and individual personal attacks on Greta Thunberg from right-wing voices (Buranyi, 2019), the main arguments against the strikes have been that children's place should be at school (rather than at a strike), that condoning strikes for the climate might lead to new strikes for all sorts of other issues, and that striking results in significant practical and safeguarding issues for schools (Adams, 2019; Doward,

2019). Earlier examples of such statements were made by education authorities after children in several UK cities took to the streets during school time to demonstrate against the invasion of Iraq by UK forces in 2003 (Cunningham and Lavalette, 2004). With respect to the current strikes, the Australian education minister was quoted for saying that 'students leaving school during school hours to protest is not something that we should encourage', and the then UK education secretary Damian Hinds for claiming that the disruption 'increased teachers' workloads and wasted lesson time' (Laville et al., 2019). While the latter was also reported to say that he was 'delighted' that pupils were taking a keen interest, he still added, 'I want children in school, and I want children learning to be the engineers, the climate scientists, the geographers of the future [...] And you've got a much better chance of that being in school than not being in school' (Busby, 2019). This emphasises some of the discourses around participation outlined in Chapter 2, which view school attendance almost as a prerequisite for children's activities.

However, parallel to this critical discourse, other adults have supported the school strikers and argued that in the light of the climate challenges facing our planet, any potential disruptions caused by the strikes must be seen as relatively insignificant (Laville, 2019). Coming together to support their children, a network of 'Parents for the Future' has emerged with branches across the world (https://www.parentsforfuture.org.uk). In an open letter to the leaders at the COP25 summit (December 2019) they write,

> Millions of children have led the way with the school-strikes in showing resolve to fight the pending catastrophe and now we, the parents, are also rising up to protect all our children and demand climate action. Together we will do whatever it takes to protect them. Addressing the climate crisis is not the responsibility of our children – it's our job as adults and parents to act to try to give our children the future that they deserve. (https://www.parentsforfuture.org.uk/plea)

As illustrated by these varied adult responses, the climate strikers challenge not only what they believe is wrong with the current climate policy but also one of the key mechanisms of adult authority and power – schools and the dominant Northern conception of 'the schooled child' (Wyness, 2018). In some ways there has been a disproportionate critical response from politicians and some head teachers to the climate strikes, given the very occasional levels of unauthorised absence from school. This suggests that they may symbolise something more fundamental, possibly the negotiation of and resistance to an existing regime of knowledge (three-dimensional power), which places children within a structured institutional and apolitical sphere. However, in addition it may be argued that the discourse of the strike sidesteps the first dimension of power (decision-making), and through this to some extent reproduces the image of the 'innocent' and 'passive' child who has no power in the context of climate change and is fully dependent on adults to make a change.

While there are quite naturally limits to what children and young people (and adults for that matter) can do without wider political backing, two points contradict this mainly passive notion of the child. One is, as acknowledged by some commentators, that children are 'tomorrow's voters' and that forward-looking politicians need to take into consideration the priorities of this segment of the population (*The Local*, 2019). The second point is that children themselves may (and many do) take a more active role by trying to change habits, exercise influence over their family's consumption and transport habits, and joining up with their peers, parents and schools to initiate climate actions and improve their local environments (Chawla, 2011; Kirby and Lirius, 2020). Where the strikes have often been presented in terms of children versus adults (mainly head teachers and policymakers), such initiatives present a more intergenerational approach to climate action, with adults and children actively working together to further a particular goal. Furthermore, any discussion of power in relation to the climate strikes needs to consider whether they have succeeded in changing the actions of others who would otherwise not have acted so. More private and local initiatives may form part of the evidence for that.

### The power of strikes – changing the actions of others

> I have been really frustrated and really angry about the fact I don't have a voice in politics and I don't have a voice in the climate conversation when my politicians are pretty much refusing to do anything … So I decided to strike and … suddenly us kids are being listened to and that's why we continue to strike and feel it's so important.
>
> (14-year-old Australian student, cited in Laville et al., 2019)

It would be premature to attempt to determine the effects of the school strikes and also difficult to separate their impact from those of other simultaneous developments, such as the actions of other groups of climate activists (e.g. Extinction Rebellion), international reports on climate change and the acceleration of climate-related natural disasters. However, the youth climate strikes seem to have had some success in promoting change by putting climate change firmly on the political agenda and making clear that the environment is a key priority of young people (and soon-to-be voters) across the globe. In several countries, parties running for election have put forward ambitious green policies and, in the United Kingdom, the first climate change debate in two years was attributed to the strikes, although attendance was relatively low (Laville, 2019; *The Lancet*, 2019). However, shaping the agenda may not be enough to constitute power and, as noted by several commentators, the challenge of the strikes will be to translate the movement into something which changes the actions of governments and decision-makers (Sengupta, 2019).

Due to the dominant discourse of children versus adult power in the context of climate strikes, their impact is generally discussed in relation to any observed changes in the actions of adults (e.g. policymakers). However, another level upon which the strikes may result in changes to action is through their effect on the young people themselves. In an article on the effects of a Climate Change Education Initiative and the Fridays for the Future strikes on secondary school students in southern Germany and Austria, Deisenrieder et al. (2020: 11) show the effect the strikes may have on the participating children and their immediate families. They found that while there were significant changes in behaviour for both students who had participated in the strikes and those who had participated only in the in-school learning initiative, the former group reported increased self-efficacy and had found that the strikes enhanced their feeling of 'getting into action and taking concrete actions'.

As previously noted, it is difficult to determine whether such actions would have happened also without the school strikes, as the school strikes are part of a more general global move towards climate action. Our third example, which discusses working children's movements in Latin America, Asia and Africa, similarly presents a case of children's activism coinciding with broader developments around children's rights and participation. However, similar to the strikes, these movements are also up against prevalent and dominant conceptions of children as predominantly passive and in need of protection.

## Case 3: Working Children's Movements

It is estimated that 152 million children across the world engage in child labour, of them 73 million in hazardous work (Alliance 8.7, 2017). Child labour is a complex phenomenon with many underlying factors (Fors, 2012) and links to both family structures and international trade patterns (Nieuwenhuys, 2009). International and national responses to child labour vary from abolitionist to more regulative approaches (Orkin, 2010) with large international organisations, such as the International Labour Organization (ILO) and the United Nations International Children's Emergency Fund (UNICEF) advocating for an elimination of child labour in all its forms (UNICEF: https://www.unicef.org/protection/57929_child_labour.html).

This section does not engage with the topic of child labour per se or the complex discussions over the most appropriate response. Our focus is the local and international mobilisation of working children through movements or unions, and the extent to which these can be seen as increasing the power of children.

Movements of working children have emerged in Latin America, Asia and Africa, first locally in the 1970s and 1980s and increasingly internationally since the mid-1990s (Liebel, 2003, 2012b). They draw heavily on the principles of children's rights to have a voice, be heard, recognised and participate in decisions of importance to their lives. They challenge the exclusion of children from political decision-making (Taft, 2019) and call for a more equal relationship between children and adults (Liebel, 2003). Furthermore, while all of the movements call for children's work to be socially recognised, some explicitly demand that children should have a right to work (Liebel, 2003) and argue that it should be the individual child's right to 'freely decide whether, where, how and for how long they would like to work' (Liebel, 2012b: 225). The movements thus

> see their members as active participants of their social world and want their right to work in dignity and to organize to fight exploitation recognized. They do not reject schooling, but believe that children also learn when at work. Schooling should be an option that is open to working children, which they can combine with work but which should not be compulsory or a tool to prevent them from working. Their position is far removed from the trade union model of child labour prohibition. (Nieuwenhuys, 2009: 295)

This section discusses the call of the working children's movements for more involvement in decision-making and their attempts to change dominant perceptions and actions of adults and the wider community towards working children in relation to the three dimensions of power and intergenerational relations.

### Dimensions of power of working children's movements

As discussed by Liebel (2012b) and Nieuwenhuys (2009), one of the key demands of working children is that they be consulted on decisions that affect them. However, in their article on the 'enforced silence' of working children's movements in relation to the ILO, Liebel and Invernizzi (2019) give examples of numerous meetings and conferences where working children were explicitly excluded from decision-making fora. They outline some of the 'ups and downs' of children's participation in international conferences on child labour but ultimately conclude,

> Until the present, ILO has refused to allow working children to participate in decisions affecting them and does not foresee any opportunity for children to participate in its institutional structures. (Liebel and Invernizzi, 2019: 143)

Furthermore, they argue that while the ILO occasionally call on children to engage in discussions, these discussions tend to follow prescribed questions and frameworks and allow only opinions which support the goal to ban child labour in every form. From a power perspective, this thus seems to suggest that in the international macropolitical context, the working children's movements lack both one-dimensional and two-dimensional power. In addition, and implicitly drawing on Foucault's notion of 'regimes of truth', Nieuwenhus (2009) argues that the international discourse on working children constitutes a powerful 'regime of truth about the superiority of Northern childhood' which presents work carried out by children in the North as unproblematic and in the South as exploitative. She notes,

> The imagery of the coloured Asian child as the icon of today's child labour issue should leave no doubts that this regime rests on racist prejudice preventing working children from building solidarity on the basis of shared global interests and experiences. (Nieuwenhus, 2009: 299)

Similarly, Taft (2019: 48–50) discusses how conceptions of working children in Peru are closely linked to colonial paradigms about children, and in particular poor indigenous children, as unruly, in need of discipline and whose misbehaviour is a result of 'bad, absent parents'. Both examples show how powerful 'regimes of truth' about working children intersect with deeply ingrained ideas about ethnicity, race and class, constituting a third dimension of power which works to prevent the children from taking part in political and social decisions about their own lives.

There is some indication that local movements of working children have managed, at least to some extent, to change perceptions and actions of policymakers and other relevant adults, which has in some cases enabled them to take part in decision-making. For example, Liebel (2003) quotes the Final Declaration of the Fifth Meeting of the African Movement of Working Children and Youth (2000):

In those places where we are organised, our 12 Rights have considerably progressed for us and for other Working Children and Youth. We can now learn to read and write, we benefit from better healthcare, we can express ourselves, we are respected by everyone as well as by the Judiciary, we are well treated and can work in safer environments, working in a manner in line with our capacities and can rest sometimes. (cited in Liebel et al., 2001: 355)

Liebel (2015) also describes the Bolivian Code for Children and Adolescents (2014) as the first law in the world to have come into existence with a decisive input from children. It was furthermore part of a general social transformation which goes against former patterns of exploitation and racism, illustrating the link between perceptions of child work and broader division in society.

In a report on children's participation and policy change in South Asia, Williams (2004) similarly describes some of the more regional and local policy influences of two Indian working children's unions: Bal Mazdoor Sangh, formed in New Delhi in 1991, and Bhima Sangha, set up in Karnataka in southern India in 1990. Both unions aim to improve the conditions of working children, raise awareness among the public and politicians, and advocate for their rights and recognition (Wyness, 2001). Williams describes the specific attempts of Bal Mazdoor Sangh to gain legal recognition from the Indian government and their success in getting political parties to include children's rights in their electoral manifestos for the election of 1999. The union has also taken action on individual cases by raising them with policymakers, the policy and the courts, but with varying levels of success. Similarly, Bhima Sangha was getting involved in individual cases through protests and demonstrations, but members have also become more directly involved in decision-making through their participation in village councils (with adults) and the setting up of a child's general assembly, which, according to a local Member of Parliament, began to make their views heard and priorities enacted upon at the district level.

As these examples show, the influence of working children's unions varies. Often they may not be recognised or included in formal agreements but may still lead to significant improvements in the daily life of the children, such as improved access to health care or better understanding from schools (Liebel, 2003) and changes in attitudes (Williams, 2004). The examples also show the close connection between the three dimensions of power and that, in the case of working children, involvement in decision-making often follows quite significant changes to the dominant 'regimes of truth' regarding childhood and working children, in particular. As noted by Liebel,

The resistance is probably so great not only because the children demand more participation and influence, but also because they explicitly present themselves as *working* children and insist that their work be recognized by society and that 'the right to work in dignity' should be an option for all children. With that they contradict a further essential element of the modern Western understanding of childhood, that which aims at a strict separation between childhood and work and would therefore abolish every form of child work. (Liebel, 2003: 275)

As previously discussed, this modern Western or Northern understanding of childhood is closely related to other dominant ideas about race, social structures and superiority, illustrating the relevance of considering the power of working children's unions in an intergenerational context and considering the complexity of both child and adult groups.

### Working children's unions and intergenerational relations

The literature on working children's unions show that while the unions are predominantly led by children, adults often play an important role in supporting them (including in the set-up) and many of the unions have close links to non-governmental organisations (NGOs) or individual adult advocates (Liebel, 2003; Taft, 2019; Williams, 2004). Movements may also have explicit aims of intergenerational equality, as described in Taft's (2019) book on the Peruvian working children's movement. She describes how the movement reconfigures child–adult relationships through their interactions and practices and provides a model for intergenerational politics, although she also notes some of the difficulties of maintaining equality and horizontalism within the everyday dynamics and social context of age-based power (Taft, 2019, 2015).

Another important rationale for considering intergenerational relations in the context of working children's movements is the acknowledgement that some of the challenges they face are shared with adults. For example, Crowley (2015) mentions that in her study of children's parliaments in Dalit villages in India, the interviewed children and female activists (many of whom were also parents of dependent children) shared 'a number of common concerns and interests, for example in relation to education; hygiene; water; transport; as well as sharing a subordinate position within a robustly patriarchal society' (p. 615). This shows how children and adults may come together around a number of dimensions, including gender. Acknowledging the intergenerational relevance of the structural issues of inequality and discrimination experienced by children and adults alike in many societies, Liebel (2003) points out that if there are strong 'adult' human rights organisations, this also helps the cause of the children, and that much depends on the political structures and social climate:

> The existence of social movements and initiatives that continually try hard to achieve respect for human rights and the realization of the UN Convention on the Rights of the Child is of equal importance. If this is the situation, then it is also more likely that the children's organizations will find support from adults and especially from NGOs. (Liebel, 2003: 279)

## Decision-Making, Agenda-Setting and Dominant Regimes of Truth

The three examples discussed in this chapter illustrate some of the very different ways in which children may organise themselves and attempt to exercise power in areas of relevance to their lives – from structured school councils within predominantly adult-centric school settings in the Global North, to global youth-led climate strikes, to movements of working children in the Global South. They reveal the diversity of children's interests and needs and consequently the areas they seek to influence. In this discussion we try to draw together some of the commonalities between them that are relevant to our overall discussion of power, inequalities and intergenerational relations: (1) the importance of moving beyond understandings of power as decision-making and considering the close links between decision-making, agenda-setting and dominant regimes of truth around what constitutes the 'right' childhood, (2) the diversity of children's experiences within each of the three examples and (3) the relevance of moving beyond child versus adult power discourses and considering intergenerational convergence of interests.

### *Three-dimensional power*

In the literature on children's participation in the United Kingdom, there tends to be a focus on their involvement in direct decision-making (Percy-Smith, 2010). However, as this chapter has shown, the extent to which children are able to make decisions regarding matters of importance to them (one-dimensional power) is often closely interlinked with non-decision-making on behalf of relevant adults (two-dimensional power) and dominant regimes of truth about the capabilities and responsibilities of children (three-dimensional power). For example, we have seen that school councils often focus on selected items and learning for democracy and citizenship (Cox and Robinson-Pant, 2008; Mager and Nowak, 2012) rather than involving council members in strategic decisions about their school, thus reproducing the notion of children as 'becomings' rather than 'beings' (Uprichard, 2008). The councils furthermore tend to follow a model of participation prescribed by adults and thus do not challenge existing hierarchies between teachers and children, or as we have argued between different groups of children.

In the example of climate strikes, we have seen that much of the focus has been on children and young people exercising their power by changing the adult agenda and challenging adult non-decision-making (two-dimensional power). However, at the same time, this discourse seems to side-step the power of children to make their own decisions and through this change their own actions and the actions of those around them (one-dimensional power). To some extent this reproduces a notion of children as 'powerless' as well as a zero-sum notion of power, which disregards the many ways in which children and adults can (and do) take joint action to improve their environment. Holmberg and Alvinius (2020) have speculated that the Western view of children as lacking political agency may be a reason that their power has been overlooked. They refer to research from the anti-apartheid movement which we discussed in Chapter 4, showing that 'Western-based activists framed children's participation in this protest movement in ways that victimised children' (Holmberg and Alvinius, 2020: 81). To some extent the discourses around the climate strikes seem to illustrate a similar trend, which victimises children of adult inaction, rather than see them as active members of their family and communities with capacity for instigating change.

Finally, the case of the working children's movement also shows us that the extent to which working children are allowed to make decisions on their own behalf is closely related to the ways they are perceived in society and that this, in turn, is influenced by dominant international ideas about race/ethnicity, class and inequality. Some of the examples we have shown illustrate not only how the children's movements have been instrumental in challenging deficit ideas about working children at the local level with consequent impact on agenda-setting and decision-making, but also how the powerful international regime of truth of the 'superior Northern childhood' continues to limit their power internationally.

### Childhood diversity and inequality

As a consequence of the common child versus adult discourse in discussions of child participation and power, the diversity of children's experiences of exercising power is often ignored. In the case of the school councils, Whitty and Wisby (2007) have warned against concepts such as 'pupil power' as the term may ignore the classed, raced and gendered dimensions of power. Students who are actively involved in school councils tend to represent advantaged backgrounds (Whitty and Wisby, 2007; Wyness, 2009). This may lead to a reproduction of power relationships at school, but also a reversal, if those involved in councils are targeted for bullying. Within any activities, and perhaps particularly the ones set up by adults, selection and representation are key, and internal power dynamics between children thus need to be acknowledged and addressed.

Our two other examples provide less information about inequalities between children. Given the recentness of the climate strikes, not much information exists about the background of the participating children. A comparative report of climate strikes in 13 European cities (Wahlström et al., 2019) found that the strikes were dominated by female participants (66.4 per cent, a fact which the authors attribute to Greta Thunberg's strong personal role model) and that there was an overrepresentation of students with a well-educated family background. However, no similar data has been found for the strikes in countries outside Europe, making it difficult to make any firm conclusions on the international profile of the climate strikers. Children involved in the working children's movements are, quite inevitably, from a particular segment of the society but may still represent a variety of ethnicities and communities (Taft, 2019). As noted by Williams (2004) in the Indian context, it is difficult to determine whether a particular gender or caste dominates the meetings without direct observations, but she does provide some evidence that the unions follow democratic principles in their selection of representatives.

### The potential of intergenerational alliances

The notion of children having a say and taking initiative to change the actions of adults does not always sit well within dominant ideas of child–adult relations, which, as we have previously discussed, are often described in zero-sum terms. Whitty and Wisby (2007: 315) have noted that 'more radical conceptions of pupil power would seem to be in direct conflict with conventional notions of teacher professionalism'. Such perceived tensions between 'adult professionalism' and 'child voice' quite clearly limit the power of school councils. The inability of councils to make any significant decision without the involvement of adults has led Burnitt and Gunter (2013: 61) to argue that schools operate 'pseudo-democracies'. However, another interpretation might be that the framing of child and adult interests as opposed to one another serves to conceal areas where teacher and child agendas converge in opposition to more top-down political agendas (Fielding, 2007). For example, the increasing policy focus on performativity and standardisation seen in England and other countries may limit the scope of action of both teachers and children.

In the context of the climate strikes, the wider discourse and the terminology used to describe them also often present children and adults, particularly those in a position of power, as opposing categories (Holmberg and Alvinius, 2020). The increasing adult involvement in the strikes, as well as the young people's invitation of adults to join the strikes (Thunberg and 46 Activists, 2019), however, blurs some of this distinction and challenges the dominant zero-sum notion of power. As intergenerational alliances within climate change action suggest, obvious convergence of interests exists between children and adults, and more focus on the way children and adults can and do work together to improve their environment would both enable an increase of their joint power and acknowledge that children are not only 'victims' of adult inaction but also active and capable actors themselves.

Finally, intergenerational relations have been seen to feature as an important element in the working children's movements, both because adults have often been instrumental in the setting up and support of the movements and because the involved children and their adult community members may share many of the same challenges. Taft (2019: 8) describes the Peruvian working children's movement as an explicit attempt to generate more equal and horizontal intergenerational relationships – 'relationships rooted in a belief in children's fundamental equality with adults and in practices of non-hierarchical collaboration with adults'. Illustrating the powerful effect of dominant 'regimes of truth' about children's capacities, she notes that some adults express reservations when she presents her work on intergenerational power-sharing. However, she also mentions that 'many other adults, and certainly most children and youth who I talk to about this work, are excited about the prospect of at least discussing the (il)legitimacy of profoundly unequal power relations between children and adults' (Taft, 2019: 9). As this illustrates, intergenerational dynamics in the context of working children's movements, as well as in our two other examples of school councils and climate strikes, are complex, negotiated and challenged. By inviting readers to consider the potential for children's equality and intergenerational horizontalism, Taft (2019: 86) asks questions relevant not only to her particular area of interest but also more generally to our discussion of the different dimensions of kid power: 'Why is thinking about children as equals so unsettling for many adults?' and 'How would the social and political institutions that structure adult–child interactions be different if we recognized children's equality?'

# Chapter 8

# THE POWER OF CHILDREN'S PARTICIPATION AND INVOLVEMENT IN RESEARCH

In the last three decades, children's role within social research has changed significantly. Based on developments within children's rights and the 'new social studies of childhood', researchers have increasingly shifted from conducting research *on* children to research *with* children (Barker and Weller, 2003). This has involved recruiting children as research participants (Christensen and James, 2017; Wyness, 2019) and also sometimes for more active research roles, for example, as co- or peer researchers (Bradbury-Jones and Taylor, 2015; Doná, 2006). In the now well-established body of literature on research with and by children, *power* and the related notion of *empowerment* figure as key concepts. Three key themes dominate discussions. The first relates to power differences between children and adults in the research encounter and the need to minimize them through appropriate research methodologies and practices. The second describes power as something which can be 'handed over' to children in the research process and which has significant impact on the outcomes of the research. The third emphasises the empowering effect that involvement in research may have on the children who are involved. Where the first two predominantly focus on the research benefits of involving children as participants or active researchers, the last thus emphasises the positive impacts this may have for the children themselves.

Within all three themes, references to theoretical understandings of power and empowerment and in-depth analysis of how the two concepts may be operationalised in the context of children's participation in research are rare. The literature on children's participation includes a few explicit discussions and references to power theory, particularly with reference to Foucault and Giddens (Bradbury-Jones, 2014; Devine, 2003, 2002; Gallagher, 2008b; Meehan, 2016; Morgan and Sengedorj, 2015). However, discussions of empowerment from a theoretical perspective, and considerations of whether short-term gains from participating in a particular project may translate into wider and more long-term experiences of empowerment, are relatively absent.

While the literature includes a wealth of well-constructed and important studies, which discuss and seek to challenge the power dynamics between children and adults within research, conclusions about children's subsequent level of power and empowerment therefore often remain partial.

This chapter critically discusses the extent to which children's participation and involvement in research can be argued to change children's level of power and empowerment. Drawing on our theoretical framework we argue that, while there has indeed been a considerable empirical and epistemological shift within research towards children's knowledge, participation and involvement, the extent to which this has translated into more power for children over the research agenda and outcomes, and empowerment more broadly, is debatable. We outline some of the contradicting discourses around children's power in research, particularly the ever-present tensions between 'voice' and 'protection', and discuss the different dimensions of power in relation to children and research. Following the general line of argument in the book, and recent developments within childhood studies, we furthermore emphasise the need for paying closer attention to child inequalities and children's diverse experiences within research activities, as well as considering intergenerational research relations and commonalities in a less dichotomous manner.

## Unequal Power Relations between Children and Adults in the Research Encounter

The disparities in power and status between adults and children have been described as the biggest challenge for childhood researchers, and power differentials have been the topic of much attention and discussion in research with children (O'Kane, 2008). Parallel to the increasing acknowledgement of children as competent social actors, with experiences, understandings and ideas of their own (Christensen and James, 2008; Kellett et al., 2004; Prout, 2005; Wyness, 2015), and the growing attention to these within research, child/adult power differences have come to be seen as increasingly problematic and in need of altering. Arguments for increasing children's power in the context of research have focused on two main rationales: (1) a moral/ethical rationale, which focuses on children's rights to have a say in matters concerning their own lives and the consequent need to involve them as equal (as far as possible) research partners (Harcourt and Einarsdottir, 2011) – also described as 'the empowerment rationale' (Mannion, 2007: 408) – and (2) an 'enlightenment rationale' (ibid.) which acknowledges that power relations between children and adults, if left unaddressed, will hinder the researcher's ability to access and understand children's worlds (Davis, Watson and Cunningham-Burley,

2017), and that research involving children will obtain better insights into their experiences.

Several researchers have discussed the most appropriate methods to approach and minimize the child/adult imbalance of power. They have described how they have given children a say in the methods applied (Meehan, 2016) and allowed them to decide to what extent they want to participate in different research activities (Dalli and Te One, 2012). Considering specific methods, group interviews are generally considered as advantageous in research with children, as the presence of peers is seen to give children more confidence and alter the child/adult power imbalance in the interview situation (Hill, 1997). In addition, child-centred methods (such as drawings, mapping, photography) and participatory research have been described as particularly useful for shifting power relations (Einarsdóttir, 2007) as they give children and young people more control over the research process (Ansell et al., 2012). For example, O'Kane (2008) notes that her use of participatory techniques assisted in transforming the power relations between adults and children, because they enabled the children to set the agenda.

While participatory and child-centred methods have grown increasingly popular, critics have warned that the way they are employed needs to be carefully considered and that there is a risk that they, similar to the child-centred pedagogies we discussed in Chapter 3, become another way for adults to regulate and control children. It has been acknowledged that methods which adult researchers consider child-friendly may not always be felt as such by the children (Barker and Weller, 2003) and that children may not always feel able to say no to participation in research, particularly if their recruitment was facilitated by adults (Morgan and Sengedorj, 2015). Mannion (2007: 410) has furthermore noted that 'there is plenty of evidence to suggest that what children say can be easily scripted by adults with their own agendas', and therefore, he argues that adults may fail to discover and understand children and young people's views, in spite of their best efforts to do so.

However, illustrating the complexities of power within the research context, Holt (2004) has reminded us that power relations are shifting, dynamic and context specific, and that we should not consider 'adults' as a definite category and always in a position of power. Discussing some of the ways in which children may control their interactions with adults, she notes that when it comes to games and discussions children are often their own gatekeepers and can, in effect, deny adults participation. In their study of researchers reflecting on involving children, Dalli and Te One (2012) also describe how children may express power in subtle ways. For example, one of the researchers interviewed mentioned that the children she studied took away her pencil to stop her recording data. Furthermore, and as Holt (2004) argues, it is problematic to emphasise age as the only defining characteristic in the research encounter, when in fact other aspects of both the children and the researcher's identity (e.g. appearance, gender, sexuality, 'race', 'class' and bodily performance) may influence their interactions. Rather than making assumptions about the respective levels of power of children and adults in the research context, Christensen and Prout (2002) have therefore argued that researchers should work from a starting point on 'ethical symmetry', which means that they do not in advance develop specific methods or ethical practices based on their assumption of children's capabilities. Similarly, others have argued for the importance of making research 'participant-friendly' to all members of the specific group they work with, rather than attempting to make it specifically 'child-friendly' (Fraser, 2004; Punch, 2002). This involves not only a critical consideration of methods and research design but also a reflexive and sensitive approach to the researcher's own position.

To adapt or 'engineer' their own position in relation to the children they work with, researchers have attempted to establish themselves as an 'other adult' or 'non-authoritative adult' in the field (Christensen, 2004; Eder and Corsaro, 1999) or adopt the 'least-adult role' by 'undertaking a responsive, interactive, fully involved participant observer role with the children in as least an adult manner as possible' (Mandell, 1988: 36). Trust and relationships have been described as key to deal with adult/child power differences in research relationships, and consequently it has been acknowledged that it is time consuming to do good research with children (Spyrou, 2011). However, researchers have also repeatedly described situations beyond their control, where power relations between children and other adults are acted out, for example, adults interrupting interviews (Ansell et al., 2012), parents adding to children's views in data collection (Barker and Weller, 2003) or in schools, where students were compelled to participate (Robinson and Kellett, 2004).

As this shows, the researcher's scope for fostering equal research relationship with children and young people depends significantly on the way children and adults interact within the particular space of the research (e.g. a school or at home) and beyond. For example, in her fieldwork in two schools in Spain and England, Jørgensen (2015, 2011) found significant differences in the way that children and young people interacted with their teachers, and this in turn set the scene for her own interactions with the children. In both settings, she asked the students to call her by her first name and carefully considered how to dress in order to obtain the role of a non-authoritative adult. However, this was much more 'radical' in one of the contexts, England, where students usually call their teachers by last name and wear uniforms, than in the other, Spain, where they generally wear their own clothes and approach their teachers using their first name. She consequently found it much easier to 'blend in' with the students in Spain. As this illustrates, dividing practices between children and adults manifest themselves in different ways across countries and necessarily create different contexts for researchers, who wish to challenge them by attempting to fit in between.

'Power' in childhood research is, as this theme illustrates, most often described through the lens of child–adult relations and as something that adult researchers can attempt to manage by being reflexive about their own role and by letting children themselves decide whether they want to participate, what they want to share with the researcher and the methods that they prefer or engage best with. This notion reflects a conceptualisation of power which seems limited to its one-dimensional sense, as decision-making power. The framework within which research with children takes place, however, often limits the choices that children are actually given and able to make decisions on – their two-dimensional power. This may be due to structural and practical limitations, such as funder requirements (Franks, 2011), adult-centric institutional (school) settings (Flewitt et al., 2018; Kim, 2017) or ethical requirements which prioritise protection over self-determination (Lomax, 2012). In addition, and as noted by Langhout and Thomas (2010: 61), 'dominant narratives in many societies hold that children are not able to participate in making important decisions that affect them'. Such narratives represent a third dimension of power in the form of a particular 'regime of truth' about children, which conceives them as primarily vulnerable and authorises adult control. Any conclusions about children's increased power as a result of their increasing involvement in decision-making, which do not at the same time take into account their role in agenda-setting and dominant narratives about childhood, thus remain partial, as they almost exclusively focus on the first dimension of power. Our second theme somewhat begins to approach this partiality by discussing how researchers can 'hand over' agenda-setting power to children by involving them as co- or peer-researchers. However, as we will also discuss, this theme comes with theoretical problems of its own.

## 'Handing Over' Power to Children

Recruiting children to take on the role of co- or peer-researchers is a practice which is often described as a way to address or minimise the previously mentioned power imbalances between children and adults (Casas et al., 2013; Jacquez et al., 2013). The co-/peer-researcher role can include them taking part in research advisory or steering groups, as consultants and advisors on research topics or design (Doná, 2006; Hooper and Gunn, 2014), as initiators and developers of their own research (Kellett et al., 2010), as data collectors (Murray, 2006) and/or as taking part in data analysis and dissemination

(Jørgensen, 2019). Motivations for involving children as co-/peer-researchers follow relatively similar rationales to the ones that form the basis for recruiting them as research participants: namely, that it should be their rights to have a say in matters of importance to them and that it improves research findings. However, the involvement of children in more active and advisory roles is also often argued to add an additional dimension to the research and strengthen children's power within it.

One of the reasons for this is that co-/peer-researchers have been found to be able to strike up a better rapport with other child participants due to their shared experiences and common language (Fleming et al., 2009; Taylor et al., 2012; Thomson et al., 2015). As peers, they may be able to reach out to children who do not wish to speak to adults (McLaughlin, 2005) and level out power differences in interview situations. Co-/peer-researchers are also given a certain control over research decisions and priorities, and this may help them challenge some of the adult-centric elements of research. Finally, child co-/peer-researchers may have significant impact on the dissemination of research, which may bridge gaps between children and adults (Gaillard et al., 2018). However, in addition to these benefits, researchers have also acknowledged some of the potential challenges of peer interviews, including the relative inexperience of co-/peer-interviewers of interview techniques, the potential distress caused by interviewing people in similar situations and the possibility that they may deliberately or unintentionally exclude the participation of other children (Bradbury-Jones, 2014; Devotta et al., 2016; Lomax, 2012; Lushey and Munro, 2015). Thus, as acknowledged by Alderson (2001) and Clavering and McLaughlin (2010), working with child researchers does not in itself resolve problems of power, and much depends on their level of training, communication, institutional structures and the particular relationships between the co-/peer-researchers and the children they research. Furthermore, the literature has illustrated some important ethical dilemmas with regards to the balance between the power of co-/peer-researchers over researcher decisions, on the one hand, and protection and safeguarding obligations of the adult researcher, on the other.

Lomax (2015) discusses some of these dilemmas, particularly in relation to confidentiality, anonymity and representation. While research ethics protocols generally stipulate that research participants should be kept anonymous, she argues that this may prove practically impossible in participatory research. Furthermore, child co-/peer-researchers may prefer to have their contributions recognised, and thus challenge common research conventions. She also discusses several examples of where she, as the adult researcher, disagreed with the child co-researchers about what to include in a film produced as part of the research. In one of these, the children wished to include images of their pets in the film, but Lomax herself was reluctant to do so, as she felt that this seemed to 'fix' a particular view of childhood, which might risk reproducing unequal power relations rather than challenging them. She thus argues that decision-making with regards to dissemination needs to be carefully balanced with the (adult) researchers' responsibility to co-researchers.

Lomax's research serves as a very useful reminder of the many different levels upon which power operates in the context of research and shows that children and adults may have different ideas about the most appropriate ways of representing children's views. In addition, working with co-/peer-researchers may raise other ethical dilemmas around consent, safety and gatekeeping (Bradbury-Jones, 2014). Considering these, researchers have argued that the ultimate responsibility for the research needs to lie with the adult researchers, rather than the co-/peer-researchers (Bradbury-Jones and Taylor, 2015) and that it is not always feasible or ethical to give children full control of a project (Burton et al., 2010). Willumsen et al. (2014) have questioned whether the term 'co-researcher' can be applied to children at all, as it signals too much responsibility over the research process and outcomes and may force children into making ethical and moral decisions for which they are not prepared. Similarly, Broström notes that in most cases, it may be an exaggeration to use the phrase 'co-/peer–researcher' about the role that children perform:

> As described, we can arrange situations where they inform us about their thoughts, they can collect data via digital photos and when they interview each other. However, when doing this, they are not co-researchers. They have not been involved in the formulation of research goals or the planning of the research process. They do not design methods themselves; we ask them to use research methods constructed by the researchers. Although we ask them question[s] about how to interpret photos and other results, they are really not a part of the process of analysis. Nevertheless, they are not only objects. They are invited into the research process. We listen to them. We take them seriously. They act as subjects. They are conscious of our research goals and they agree to help us. I guess this is what is possible (at this historical moment). So, they are not really co-researchers, but active and (more than less) conscious research supporters. (Broström, 2012: 265)

Considering children as research supporters, rather than co-/peer-researchers, has important implications for any conclusions about their power. One is the previously noted acknowledgement that children's power seldom reaches beyond its first dimension (where they are able to make decisions about particular and often selected issues), another that both researchers and funders are often uncomfortable with the prospects of letting children having a say in more significant decisions, for example, around ethics. This illustrates that both second and third dimensions of power generally stay in the hands of adults. The debate also reveals a tendency to consider power (or related terms such as control and responsibility) as something which is the possession of one group (adults) and can be 'handed over' (or not) by adults to children in the research process. This particular approach has been criticised for its zero-sum, hierarchical and unidirectional connotations (Cox and Robinson-Pant, 2008; Lomax, 2012) and for conceiving of power as a 'property'. As noted by Holland et al.,

> In many of the discussions surrounding the limitations and possibilities of conducting participatory research, there is a tendency to theorize agency and power almost as attributes that children can 'have' and that are enabled, promoted or 'given' by the 'adult researcher'. (Holland et al., 2010: 362)

Instead, they argue with reference to Foucault (1995) and Gallagher (2008a, 2008b) that power is 'not something that exists "out there" but always in relation as a social and discursive phenomenon' (Holland et al., 2010: 362). This reflects well the framework of power we draw on in this book, which considers power as a relation rather than a property. It acknowledges that power differences will not be altered by 'handing over power' over particular decisions alone. They also need to be reflected in changes to the roles and relationship inherent in the process of agenda-setting and dominant discourses.

Holland et al. (2010) and others (Gallagher, 2008b) have furthermore challenged the tendency to see power in child–adult relations as inherently negative and noted that depending on the context, power relations may be both productive and repressive. This reflects the distinction between interest and domination in relation to power that we discussed in Chapter 1. O'Brien and Moules discuss two contrasting views of power, the first a negative view, which is

> about being able to control others or being controlled by them. Power is therefore a zero-sum concept in which we, as researchers, would have more power and the young people would have less. If this view were taken then adults would need to give up power, as power can only be gained by taking it from another. (O'Brien and Moules, 2007: 397)

If power is viewed positively, however, they argue that a whole different perspective emerges – one which focuses much more on 'having the ability or capacity to act'. In the research context, this means that it becomes more about changing adult perceptions of children and child–adult relationships to facilitate joint action than adults handing over and giving up on their power. This approach is illustrated by Kellett's (2010) argument that 'genuine participation' needs to involve power sharing, which enables children to lead on some of the issues which directly affect their lives, but also that children need the support of adults to carry out their research and disseminating it via platforms they might find difficult to access (e.g. government agencies). Considering that children are also, at least to some extent, affected by the dominant discourses around their own capacities (Devine, 2003), any changes to kid power also necessarily involves changing children's perceptions of their own capacity to act. This last point is, as we will discuss below, often conceptualised as 'empowerment'.

## Empowerment through Research Participation and Involvement

Empowerment is a commonly used concept in the literature on children's participation in research, where it is often equated with other concepts such as 'participation' and 'voice'. Consequently, discussions of empowerment tend to focus on the process of the research and the methods used to elicit children's voices. For example, in their discussion of 'fun' and child-centred research methods, Barker and Weller (2003) mention photography as an empowering method, as children can use the cameras in their own time and place, without the adult researchers being present. Dockett and Perry (2005: 507) also describe the use of interactive methods, such as conversational interviews, oral and written journals, drawings, reflections and digital photographs, as having 'been successfully introduced in order to empower four- and five-year-old children to express what they see as important as they start school'. Similarly, Leitch et al. (2007: 467) argue that giving a group of 11–14-year-old students the responsibility of a camcorder for the taping of lessons empowered them and created a more egalitarian research project.

In addition to these methodological 'tools' for empowerment, some researchers have considered the wider empowering implications of children having a voice within more participatory projects. Examples of this approach, which focuses on children's voice within research projects more generally, include Morgan and Sengedorj's (2015) study of Mongolian and Zambian children's perspectives on educational research. They argue that 'hearing the "voice" of children and including children in the research process is viewed as a means of empowering a group whose perspectives are often overlooked due to ideas around "competence"' (Morgan and Sengedorj, 2015: 321). Hawkins

(2015: 467) explicitly states that the aim of her participatory action research project in preschool settings in Australia was to 'empower and enable all participants', and she conceptualises this as all participants being 'afforded a valued voice, debate and discussion would be encouraged, action agreed upon collaboratively would be promoted and each participant would be represented in every stage of the project'. Expressing a similar idea, Casas et al. (2013: 204) state that their work with children to design and assess questionnaires were 'useful as a vehicle for the child's voice to be listened to and we therefore consider it to have been an empowering process'. Finally, Kellett has discussed the process of empowering young people as active researchers and by having their voices heard in several research projects (Kellett, 2005, 2010; Kellett et al. 2010).

These examples seem to illustrate a common perception of children as relatively disempowered before joining the research, and that giving them a 'voice' through particular methods or participation in general almost automatically empowers them. However, from a theoretical perspective this reflects a somewhat partial understanding of empowerment. As described in Chapter 1, empowerment is a concept derived from community psychology studies and includes both an individual and a collective level of analysis. Initial conceptualisations of empowerment and Lawson and Kearns's (2010) specific framework open up for both individual and collective understandings, and furthermore consider empowerment in both processes and outcomes of research. However, the way the concept has been applied to children's involvement in research has predominantly been as internal to the individual children (Ansell, 2014: 23–24) rather than to them as a group. In addition, and as shown by our examples, empowerment of children is often understood in relation to the process of participation and having a voice, rather than any particular outcomes.

It may be argued that process and outcomes are interlinked, and that participation in itself can be transformative (Tisdall, 2012). Kellett (2010: 197), for example, has argued that participation 'leads to a virtuous circle of increased confidence and raised self-esteem resulting in more active participation by children in other aspects affecting their lives' and thus can be considered empowering. Others have described 'empowerment indicators', such as increased confidence and self-esteem (Bailey et al., 2015; Clark, 2004; Fleming et al., 2009), social skills and other more specific skills (e.g. project management, communication and presentation skills) (Alderson, 2001; Bradbury-Jones and Taylor, 2015; Burton et al., 2010; Coppock, 2011; Gaillard et al., 2018; Kellett, 2010). However, specific examples of how these empowerment indicators have helped the children achieve any outcomes outside the limited space of the research project are rare.

This is not to say that participation in research does not lead to empowerment or that children's involvement in research does not give them skills that they can use to achieve desired outcomes beyond the research. However, along with others, we find it important to challenge the sometimes taken-for-granted equation of participation and voice with empowerment. As noted by Wickenden and Kembhavi-Tam (2014: 401), 'researchers should be cautious in claiming the power or essential "goodness" of participation per se and wary in interpreting and representing what children say and in claiming its authenticity or potential to empower'. In addition, and as we have previously discussed, participatory research with children takes place within a broader context of power relations, which limits not only the extent of children's empowerment within any given project (Schäfer and Yarwood, 2008) but also their likelihood of translating increased confidence and skills into more lasting empowerment outcomes for themselves or other children outside the project. Finally, and similar to what we have previously noted in relation to dominant conceptualisations of power within childhood research, the focus on empowerment through methods and research participation seems to indicate that empowerment is something that adults 'do' for children. As noted by Tisdall (2013: 185), such 'power-transfers' are bound to fail as 'one cannot empower others (they must empower themselves)' and because the institutionalisation of power means that power relations remain the same. This furthermore supports our previously made argument that dominant narratives around children's participation and involvement in research primarily focus on one-dimensional power (decision-making) and to some extent two-dimension power (agenda-setting). Rarely do we see practice which is able to challenge three-dimensional power, here understood as institutional and dominant discourses around childhood and children's place in research and more broadly.

## Diversity of Children's Experiences

As we have seen in the above discussion, the literature on power and children's participation in research predominantly focuses on differences in power between children and adults. This is based on the notion that children are jointly and subordinately placed within a particular generational order due to their age (Alanen, 2001). Their child-specific experiences and their position as 'insiders' and 'experts in their own lives' are the main rationale for them as research participants or co-/peer-researchers. However, recognizing children as 'experts in their own lives' does not necessarily make them experts in other children's lives (Tisdall, 2012) or representatives of all children (Coppock, 2011). Furthermore, children's social experiences, and consequently their experiences of being involved in research, will differ significantly because of factors such as gender, ethnicity, disability and socio-economic inequalities. In recognition of this, researchers are increasingly criticising the idea of a universal 'child voice' and calling for more attention to 'the ways in which children may drive and shape research and the ways this may be unequally experienced by individual children during the research process' (Lomax, 2012: 114). The dangers of a vocal and articulate few monopolising or 'hijacking' the research agenda have been described as a concern (Kellett, 2010; Kellett et al., 2010), as has the under-representation of alternative child voices (e.g. of minority ethnic children and disabled children) in research (Clavering and McLaughlin, 2010; Gray and Winter, 2011).

Two key areas are of importance in relation to children's diverse levels of power in research. The first is the question of selection. Similar to our previous discussion of school councils (Chapter 7), selection for participation in research is often highly managed, particularly when doing research in schools. Adult-driven selection of particular students over others may therefore risk becoming a 'marker of childhood inequity and inequality' (Kim, 2016: 235). The second relates to the dynamics between the children involved in the research, where power imbalances may arise within the group (Murray, 2006) or in relations between peer researchers and child participants. On the first point, Ansell et al. (2012) have warned that local inequalities between children may impact who gets a say in participatory activities and consequently the knowledge produced. In their study of the impact of AIDS on young people's lives in Southern Africa, they describe well how some of the children and young people who participated in group activities attempted to copy from one another, but also how their answers were often moderated by social norms. On the second point, Schaefer and Yarwood (2008) provide some interesting examples of how power is shifted and negotiated in interviews where young people interview each other. However, they also show how the common emphasis on unequal power relations between adult researchers and young research participants led to a negation of the multiple power relations between young people. As noted by Willumsen et al. (2014), such power dynamics may not always be noticed when children themselves collect the data, and consequently, the researcher may not know whose voices are heard and whose are omitted.

As these examples illustrate, power differences between children are of key importance to the understanding of kid power within research. Considering them in relation to Lukes's three dimensions of power requires a careful consideration of (1) which children get to have a say in research decisions, that is, who are selected for participation and who decides within the participating group; (2) who decides what is up for discussion, and what are the internal dynamics which shape non-decision-making among children; and finally

(3) what are the dominant regimes of truth that decide about children's role, and who controls these? This last question may show up differences not only between child and adult perceptions but also between children themselves. Furthermore, as the third dimension works by convincing people (both children and adults) of its legitimacy, it is most likely the one that is hardest to challenge and, as we will argue in the last section, one which requires increased acknowledgement of intergenerational relations.

## Intergenerational Generation of Power

This chapter has already extensively discussed power differences between children and adults and the way researchers have tried to limit or alter them by developing particular methods, being reflexive about their own roles and sometimes also involving children as co-/peer-researchers. While acknowledging that power differences may be more pronounced in childhood research due to age differences and 'socially sanctioned adult responsibilities towards children' (Spyrou, 2011), we have seen that the dichotomous perception of children and adults has also led to a lack of attention to power differences between children. This has resulted in a somewhat partial understanding of kid power in the context of research. Another outcome of the dominant focus on children as a distinctive and separate group has been a lack of attention to potential similarities between children and adults as research participants and co-/peer-researchers, and the scope for a more intergenerational understanding of power. The dichotomous division of children and adults is increasingly challenged within childhood research (Wyness, 2013a), and it has been argued that the idea of studying children in their own right is problematic not only because they, as a group, are very diverse but also because much of the variation between them 'reflect[s] characteristics that they share with adults' (Hammersley, 2017).

Illustrating this, Jørgensen's (2019) comparative review of children's and adult service-users' involvement in research found that many of the same challenges were prevalent in research with both groups, including, for example, issues of tokenistic and 'tick box' involvement (Howe et al., 2017; Ocloo and Matthews, 2016; Supple et al., 2015), devaluation of the input of the involved children and adults, and researchers being reluctant to 'hand over control' of the research (Brett et al., 2014). This illustrates that child/adult power differences may not be the only imbalances at play in research involving children, and that some of these may derive from more general power dynamics between the scientific research community and the public (Green, 2016). In addition, the tension between participatory approaches and the more rigid approaches of funders is common in research with both children and adults and reflects a more general challenge of conflicting research paradigms and regimes of truth. Drawing on the experiences of university organisations, which have specifically been set up to facilitate adult service-user involvement, Jørgensen's review ends with a recommendation that similar organisations could also usefully and more consistently be developed to support children and adults in how best to work in research partnership.

In addition to this primarily methodological rationale for an increased consideration of intergenerational experiences, there are also other more empirical reasons. While children do have experiences of their own, many of them are also shared or to some extent shaped by adults. As noted by Crivello et al. (2009) in relation to the 'Young Lives' study of children growing up in the context of poverty in Ethiopia, Peru, Vietnam and Andhra Pradesh (India), involving caregivers and other adults in the project acknowledged the influence and decision-making power that adults often have over children, and respected both their views and those of children. In addition, new research 'spaces', such as the Internet and online platforms, may require even greater attention to intergenerational perceptions and power dynamics, as we saw in Chapter 6.

## Conclusion

Children's involvement in research can to some extent be seen as having become the 'new norm'. However, even though social studies of children have gone largely from being about children (from other people's perspectives) to being with children, it is questionable whether this has simultaneously led to increased power for children, at least if conceived in conventional zero-sum terms. This is not to say that research with and by children does not have valid or positive outcomes, but rather that claims to power changes or empowerment of children via research should be much more clearly conceptualised and analysed in relation to theories of power. In addition, power has within childhood studies increasingly come to be seen as a process of self-transformation (Ansell, 2014). This, we would argue, reflects a tendency to conflate power with individual empowerment, rather than fully acknowledge the many dimensions and complexities of power in the context of children's participation and involvement in research.

In his discussion of ethics in research with children and young people, Gallagher (2009: 25) poses a number of important questions in relation to power, namely, whether power is always a source of oppression or could also be seen as a productive, enabling force, whether power can take different forms, how to understand situations where children exercise power over adults or each other, and whether empowerment should be seen as a process or a product. In this chapter we have attempted to answer some of these questions. We have argued that power can indeed be a productive, enabling force, especially if we include the potential of intergenerational relations to challenge dominant narratives about the capacities and capabilities of research participants (children as well as adults). We have discussed the different dimensions of power and argued for the importance of not automatically equating power and empowerment with voice and participation or narrowly conceiving of power as decision-making. We have furthermore shown that power is inherently complex and that both children and adults should be acknowledged as diverse groups, allowing for the possibility that power may not only be exercised over children, but also that they themselves may exercise power over adults or one another. Finally, we have argued that power is not a product which can be owned by a group or an individual but needs to be acknowledged as a relation, which may shift depending on the time, location and particular space (Mannion, 2007). Considering the traditional definition of power as 'the capacity of an actor to get other actors to do something which they would otherwise not have done' (Dahl, 1968) furthermore distinguishes it significantly from empowerment, which is more focused on an individual's or a collective's 'mastery' (Zimmerman, 1995). Nevertheless, important questions remain with regard to how any increase or decrease in both power and empowerment can be measured, particularly when taking into consideration the many different layers upon which the two concepts may operate in the context of research.

# CONCLUSION: A MODEL FOR KID POWER – IMPLICATIONS AND THINKING FORWARD

In this book, we have set out to explore the notion of kid power, both as it is understood more conventionally and as we believe it should more fully be analysed and recognized. In Section 1, we concentrated on the former. We argued, in Chapters 2–4, that a conventional conception of kid power which emphasises the rise of children's power at the expense of adults, offers a limited understanding of the power dynamics between adults and children. Furthermore, kid power is, in many ways, complicated by the growing attention to adult 'responsibility' within policy and practices. Chapter 2 discussed the rights agenda, which has placed a much higher premium on adults' 'caretaker role' in relation to children. It described a set of global expectations that adults and institutions oversee and monitor children's welfare and well-being, as well as provide limited channels through which children have some involvement in the latter. However, adults have a regulatory role and implicit responsibility, leading to more complex configurations of generational power than the conventional idea of adults having overt power over children. Furthermore, while the UN Convention on the Rights of the Child challenges the view that adults retain power over children in terms of viewing children as property, in the majority of countries parents still retain the capacity to physically chastise their children. In addition, children's rights are often conceptualised rather unidimensionally and discursively, as them 'having a voice', leaving other dimensions and more material contributions less explored.

Chapter 3 focused on the role of teachers controlling and regulating children's educational and cognitive development at a distance. Child-centred education is increasingly becoming a norm globally, albeit there is large variation as to how it is perceived and practiced. Child-centred education represents a departure from earlier forms of teacher-centred pedagogy and opens up spaces, especially for young children, to express themselves. However, as we have argued, this should not be confused with a redistribution of power to children, as adults continue to construct spaces through which education and development are merged, underwriting children's emotional, cognitive and educational growth. While the rise of children's rights and the dominance of child-centredness in education among elementary school teachers have thus undoubtedly changed the way that we view and engage with children, they have not significantly increased the power of children, at least not beyond the first dimension. In Chapter 4, we followed this argument up with a critical discussion of the thesis that adults have lost power, arguing that not only does that present a simplistic analysis of the many dimensions of power, it also overlooks both inter- and intragenerational complexities.

Chapter 4, and to some extent Chapter 3, also discussed how the binary relationship between adults and children is disrupted through the introduction of tripartite relations between children, their parents and the state. In political and legal terms, the child becomes a third party, and adult 'power over' children is replaced by new constructs of child welfare and normalized judgements on parental responsibility. In a Foucauldian sense, the sovereign power of parents has been displaced by the concept of responsibility (Foucault 1977). Power is exercised at a distance by various institutional actors including the school and social services, who generate and reproduce discourses or regimes of knowledge on acceptable forms of parental engagement with children. This is likely to be experienced differently by parents of different backgrounds, emphasising inequalities and power dynamics between adults.

In Section 2 of the book we moved away from the zero-sum and binary conception of generational power and argued that kid power is intergenerational, multidimensional and intragenerational. As part of this, kid power was described as incorporating not only the *voices* but also the *practices* of different groups of children as they engaged with the adults around them. We explored intergenerational relations within four different fields inhabited by children and adults: (1) the family, (2) the virtual realm, (3) community action and (4) research. In challenging conventional notions of kid power, we confronted the idea that generational power, and more broadly intergenerational relations within these fields, can be viewed simply in terms of adults having 'power over' children (or the opposite). Three key areas emerged from our analysis which help us sketch out a framework for thinking about an alternative conception of kid power as intergenerational, intragenerational and multidimensional: children's interstitial role as mediators and representatives, the acknowledgements of intragenerational differences and both material and discursive elements of power and, finally, the ubiquity of intergenerational dialogue.

## Mediation and Representation

Section 2 discussed various examples of children's interstitial role within families and between families and communities in terms of mediation. Mediation shifts the focus away from the binary nature of power relations within families. As we argued in Chapter 5, children mediate spaces and in the process disrupt 'power' conceptions of the 'dominant' adult and the 'subordinate' child. Children's mediation can also be seen in terms of representation, where a small group of children represent the interests of others in a range of different forums. Representation challenges the idea of adults as protectors of children's 'best interests' by suggesting that children themselves can construct an agenda which represents their own interests and pursue it with adults. Both concepts thus create a 'thirdspace' (Bhabha, 2004) that breaks down the binary power of adults and suggests more positive-sum notions of power. In Chapter 5, we referred to the role that children play in mediating between different family households as a consequence of divorce, and we discussed the social and, on occasion, economic responsibilities that children take on in the context of migration and child-headed households. Mediating means greater involvement of children in family life and signifies a role different from the dependency role attributed to them within dominant regimes of truth regarding childhood.

The more collective and political examples of children's participation and organisation described in Chapter 7 similarly represent a challenge to dominant notions of children as apolitical and economically dependent. However, they also illustrate a sliding scale of challenge to adult power, with the first example, school councils, rarely going beyond one-dimensional power and the second and third, the climate strikes and the working children's movements, showing more promise for challenging also two- and three-dimensional power. The participatory rights of school councillors are carefully regulated, and there is little sense that school councillors are able to challenge or refine school agendas. Furthermore, participation in school councils is part of the dominant global construct of the schooled child, where school attendance and engagement are viewed as preconditions of children's formal participation (Thomson and Holdsworth, 2003). Children are incorporated within the structure and culture of mass compulsory schooling, and agendas are shaped around formal knowledge, distributed developmentally and chronologically by adult teachers. Any power accrued to school councillors is thus limited and one-dimensional, a rehearsal for more significant political and economic action once they leave school.

The climate strikes and the working children's unions both represent a departure from the 'schooled child', albeit to different degrees. The unions actively promote the idea of work as a central activity of children and emphasise that children should have a right to learn alongside a right to work (African Movement of Working Children and Youth, 2016). Unlike the school council, where children's interests are articulated through carefully choreographed institutional structures, the representation of children's interests through the working children's unions is driven by grounded economic and social necessity. Along with the adults who support them, they challenge two- and three-dimensional power as they aim to change the agenda and dominant conceptions of working children.

As Chapters 5 and 6 showed, children's active support for their families and their political and community actions position them in a mediate space between their family and the community or between the 'schooled child' and other constructs of children. In Chapters 4 and 6, this idea of mediate spaces was extended to our analysis of children's online activities. The virtual realm by definition occupies a third space, as the blurred boundaries between private and public access create a semi-public space, where children and adults have limited control over the information available to and about them. Children's occupancy of online private/public spaces, often without the panoptical powers of parents, puts them in a position to influence their peers and on occasion the adults around them, and could to some extent be interpreted as 'digital kid power'. However, while digital technology has brought about significant changes to children's lives, it has also opened up additional areas of intergenerational power negotiation and mediation and furthermore put a spotlight on the significant digital divides that shape their varied and unequal experiences.

## Inequalities and Material Challenges to Adult Power

Throughout the book we have made it clear that intergenerational power is complicated by intragenerational factors and inequalities, both between adults and between children. In Section 1, we referred to the displacement of power across the adult population with states and professionals intervening and delegating responsibilities to parents, with disproportionate impact on those of low-income or minority backgrounds. However, in Section 2 of the book we focused rather more on disaggregating the child population and exploring the impact of adult power on different groups of children. While the key dimension of inequality described in the book has been generational, additional characteristics of children, such as their age, gender and ethnicity, as well as where they live, have been described throughout the book as impacting their material and discursive levels of power.

An intersectional approach provides an 'analytical framework for understanding how hierarchies of race, class, gender, disability, sexuality and age (re)produce structural inequalities for certain groups' (Konstatoni and Emejulu, 2017: 9). In the context of this book, we have seen that complex configurations of relations within the population of children have generated new identities that both mitigate and exacerbate the extent to which children are dominated by adults. We have also seen that power, understood as the ability to change the actions of others, is distributed unevenly among children.

Inequalities between children were identified in several chapters. For example, in Chapters 6 and 7, we showed how 'social media–savvy' children and young people have been able to mobilise and shape the agenda on gun control and climate strikes and challenge adult policymakers to take action. However, we also saw that children's varied access to the Internet constitutes a significant digital divide both across and within countries. This, in turn, impacts children's opportunities to participate in online communities, access learning and influence the actions of others. Furthermore, there is some evidence that children involved in other activities, such as school councils, are predominantly from middle-class majority families, and that there is a lack of representation of minority ethnic and disabled children within research. Institutionalised expressions of rights and participation such as school councils, which emphasise discursive relations with powerful adults, are furthermore likely to connect more closely with the lifeworlds of more affluent children from liberal democratic countries. Finally, age is a key category across all settings, with younger children less likely to exercise power in the form of participation and decision-making in formal or informal activities than older ones.

If we compare the different modes of community action discussed in Chapter 7, we furthermore see a significantly different perception of the type of contributions by children. Whereas school councils are predominantly *discursive*, the climate strikes and the working children's unions are inherently *material*, as they involve the physical mobilisation of thousands of children's bodies globally on to the streets. Contrary to the positive embracing of school councils, both climate strikes and working children's unions have received a more mixed or negative response. This links in important ways with our argument in Chapter 2 – that children's participatory rights are predominantly understood in terms of *discursive* forms of participation, rather than more *material* forms such as those of working children or children heading households.

Material expressions of participatory rights fit less neatly into the dominant and Northern-centric discourse of childhood, which, as we have argued throughout the book, constitutes an important third dimension of power. It serves to negate the many ways in which children (particularly those living in adverse social circumstances) mediate between their families and the surrounding society and contribute materially to change the actions or perceptions of others around them.

## Intergenerational Dialogue

Much of our analysis has focused on the limited capacity of children to challenge adult agendas and dominant adult discourses about their capacities and roles. However, the chapters in Section 2 also included many examples of children working *with* adults, for example, by mediating or, as discussed in Chapter 7, exploring alternative political agendas. While there is now a substantial body of research within childhood studies on children's agency, there is little research on children investigating or discussing adult power. Where children have been in a position to comment on adults, and by implication the power they wield, they seem to favour 'trusted' adults retaining their power. In some cases, children have commented on a generational power vacuum, where parents and political leaders have abdicated their responsibilities. We discussed this in Chapter 4, when we referred to the role that children in exceptional cases played in advancing the political interests of the anti-apartheid movement in South Africa in the 1970s and 1980s. In other cases, such as the climate strikes, politicians have been berated by teenagers for their neglect of climate change and cajoled by the same young people into taking more responsibility for the environment. However, there is very little attempt among the children to assume power over adults, and the claims made by most children are modest in intergenerational terms. Instead, they confirm the extent of adult power by articulating the social, moral and political responsibilities of world leaders and national politicians towards the environment.

What is interesting and potentially transformative in generational terms and from a power perspective is not so much the message or their claims but the fact they are in a position to be able to articulate their interests and that they have a receptive audience with some political clout. There is also a constituency of adult support, largely generated through social media, which promotes their voices and reports on their demands, thus representing forms of intergenerational dialogue and collaboration (Fielding, 2007).

Other examples of potential intergenerational dialogue were suggested in Chapter 6, where we discussed children's online activities, particularly in relation to their friends, political engagement and consumption. We showed that 'digital kid power' is primarily one-dimensional, as children are still restricted, both in economic terms and by a dominant global safeguarding agenda which attempts to regulate their use of the Internet and social media. However, the Internet also brings with it a significant potential for intergenerational co-learning and dialogue. For example, children may help parents strengthen their practical digital skills, and parents and children may work together to find ways to respond to a rapidly changing online world and develop critical digital literacy. This provides an example of a context where children and parents may thus potentially begin to share power in a more positive-sum sense.

Finally, Chapter 8 illustrated how the most self-conscious and reflexive adult group discussed in the book, childhood researchers, have attempted to radically alter generational power relations in favour of children and generate more intergenerational dialogue. The chapter discussed some of the possibilities and pitfalls of child-led research and the difficulties of 'handing over power' to children. While intergenerational power relations are under-theorised within the field of childhood studies, the agentic child who is individually empowered through the research process has become the 'ideal' model of childhood to which researchers aspire when conducting empirical research. In Chapter 2 we explored different typologies of participation, ordered in hierarchical terms, starting with adult initiated modes through to child-initiated forms of participation. The aspiration here is for research with children to move towards 'higher' forms of participation. As acknowledged by Hart (1992), this might mean activities where children and adults work together. However, at the same time, questions relating to protection and safeguarding are intrinsic features of both contemporary childhoods and research ethics guidelines and ultimately dominate intergenerational relations within research.

As with all fields that we have discussed within the book, the state plays a significant role in shaping the agenda within which children and adults engage with one another. Within the research field, particularly the imperative to protect and nurture children constrains their engagements. For example, the extent to which children under 16 are allowed to participate in research is governed by parents and guardians consenting to their participation (BERA, 2018). There is little sense in which child respondents have equal access to research agendas and there is no simple transfer of power. Nevertheless, there is some potential for children and researchers to demonstrate a limited form of intergenerational dialogue and collaboration, what Fielding (2007: 109) defines as children's 'engagement with adults on the basis of mutuality, reciprocal learning and joint responsibility'.

In this final summary of key themes running throughout the book, we have sought to emphasise the importance of acknowledging kid power as an intergenerational construct, generated in situations where children work with adults and mediate between different adult actors in their lives. Through this, we have distanced ourselves from dominant zero-sum conceptions of adult/child power, which tend to be limited to a one-dimensional analysis of children's participation in decision-making. We have highlighted that children's opportunities of exercising power, in all three dimensions, are shaped, not only by their age, but also by the way generation intersects with other socio-economic characteristics. Throughout the book, we have provided examples of how a Northern construct of childhood constitutes a third dimension of power, which tends to favour children's discursive participation over their more material contributions, and which perceives children as predominantly dependent and vulnerable. However, exploring children's activities more broadly and considering their material contributions and mediation, we have sought to offer an alternative, more positive-sum and multidimensional model of kid power.

# POSTSCRIPT: COVID-19

A large part of this book was written during the Covid-19 pandemic. We briefly discussed the implications the virus may have had for intergenerational relations and the concept of kid power in the 'postscript' of the first print of the book. We are now writing in March 2023 and want to reflect on these implications in what we might refer to as a post-Covid phase. Covid-19 is still a significant cause of death in many countries, and it has a variable and shifting impact globally. At the time of writing, China, for example, is still struggling with the Omicron variant (Editorial 2023). Nevertheless, the introduction of national vaccination programmes in 2021 has significantly mitigated the effect of the virus across populations globally, and many countries have returned to pre-Covid practices.

Fairly early on in the pandemic, evidence confirmed that younger children were less likely to be seriously affected from Covid-19 than adults (UKRI, 2020). Generation thus became a key variable in the analysis of the immediate health effects of Covid-19. However, the political and social effects of the virus affected both children and adults, and much still remains to be learned about the more long-term impacts of Covid-19 on children's mental health and wellbeing as a result of lockdowns and restrictions on social interactions (Lemkow-Tovias et al 2022).

Across many countries, the onset of the pandemic in the first few months of 2020 resulted in a sudden and absolute rise of overt state action with the imposition of national and regional lockdowns. This continued throughout most of 2020 and 2021, with many countries experiencing several periods of lockdowns. Levels and forms of enforcement of these restrictions varied across different countries. Power was nevertheless crude, top down and one dimensional with the state justifying the restrictions on people's physical movements in terms of restricting the spread of the virus. Lockdowns placed similar physical restrictions on children and adults, and social distancing became a familiar reference point for both adults and children when negotiating common and routine interactions outside of households. Interactions amongst children were discouraged as parents, and in some instances, teachers extended their safeguarding responsibilities to protecting children from the virus. State power was also clearly apparent in the way that physical restrictions were lifted or reimposed, depending on the virulence of Covid-19, with more routine social interactions outside of the household allowed or limited.

While it is still too early to establish precisely how the pandemic will affect the themes we have discussed in the book in the long term, we are able to speculate on some of the implications, at least in the immediate post-Covid period. For example, in Chapter 3 we argued that child-centredness in school settings illustrates a more Foucauldian notion of power, where social interactions rival more traditional curriculums and teacher-centred pedagogy in regulating children's schooling and development. However, child-centredness also has a significant spatial dimension, and as schools adopted social distancing requirements, the extent to which children were able to work in groups and interact flexibly was restricted. Covid-19 thus necessarily changed the way children and adults used classroom spaces, with teaching styles reverting to more teacher-centred pedagogies, and consequently, more overt expressions of power. The extent to which some of these changes may prevail remains to be seen.

Disadvantaged and poor communities have been disproportionally affected by the pandemic, both directly as a result of greater exposure to the virus, higher rates of co-morbidities and disparate access to care (Quantin and Tubert-Bitter, 2022), and indirectly, for example in relation to loss of employment and income (World Bank 2023). Existing and growing inequalities have also presented in relation to other areas of life for children and adults. For example, as we have discussed in Chapter 6, digital technology became an even more compelling and often necessary social frame of reference for adults and children during the pandemic, as physical restrictions were introduced. However, communities varied significantly in their access and use of technology, leaving some significantly disadvantaged in terms of social interactions, education and access to the community (Sharp and Skipp 2022).

The pandemic also had major impact on other groups of children discussed in this book. In Chapter 5, we discussed the mediating role of children with significant household responsibilities, particularly older children in child-headed households or in contexts of migration. We also discussed the work of young carers in affluent world settings, who, as a result of the pandemic, struggled to reach out to adults and agencies outside of their households in order to mediate between their parents and siblings and the outside world (Blake-Holmes 2020). Children in these three categories are more likely to be poor and have limited access to virtual support. This, in turn, has implications for their capacity to continue with their formal education through home schooling. Vulnerable children have experienced more difficulties in maintaining crucial friendships in the absence of regular face-to-face contact with peers at school (Wyness 2023).

Finally, considering power in other areas, such as children's community action and research, there is some evidence to suggest that Covid-19 compromised children's participation at community level. Recent research in Nordic countries, for example, has highlighted set-backs for children in developing spaces and communication structures to influence decision-making processes (Loberg 2023) Furthermore, the pandemic made the intergenerational collaborative possibilities in social research with children impossible in the short term, as social interactions were restricted.

While the full-scale implication of the pandemic are still unclear, what may potentially join these different areas is the recognition that child and adult levels of power are interconnected and multidimensional but also significantly complex and shifting. The pandemic has thrown a spotlight on inequalities and challenges faced by particular groups of children and adults. It has emphasised the need for a world where power and resources are redistributed in intragenerational terms as much as in intergenerational terms, and where we will have to look at children's participation not only discursively but also materially.

# REFERENCES

Adams, R., 2019. Headteachers in a bind as pupils prepare to go on UK climate strike. *The Guardian*, 14 February, https://www.theguardian.com/environment/2019/feb/14/uk-pupils-climate-change-strike-headteachers-unions-schools (accessed 27 August 2020).

African Union, 1990. *African Charter on the Rights and Welfare of the Child*. African Union, Addis Ababa.

African Movement of Working Children and Youth (AMWCY), 2016. http://www.english.maejt.org/ (accessed 20 February 2019).

Alanen, L., 2001. Childhood as a Generational Condition: Children's Daily Lives in a Central Finland Town, in: Alanen, L., and Mayall, B. (eds), *Conceptualizing Child-Adult Relations*, Future of Childhood Series. Routledge, London, pp. 129–43.

———, 2009. Generational Order, in: Qvortrup, J., Corsaro, W. A., and Honig, M.-S. (eds), *The Palgrave Handbook of Childhood Studies*. Palgrave Macmillan, Basingstoke, Hampshire, pp. 159–74.

Alderson, P., 1994. Researching Children's Rights to Integrity, in: Mayall, B. (ed.), *Children's Childhoods: Observed and Experienced*. Falmer Press, London.

———, 2000. School students' views on school councils and daily life at school. *Children & Society* 14 (2), 121–34.

———, 2001. Research by children. *International Journal of Social Research Methodology* 4 (2), 139–53.

Alexander, R. J., 2001. *Culture and Pedagogy: International Comparisons in Primary Education*. Blackwell, Malden, MA.

Alexander, R. J., Rose, J., and Woodhead, C., 1992. *Curriculum Organisation and Classroom Practice in Primary Schools: A Discussion Paper (The Three Wise Men's Report)*. DfE, London.

Alim, S., 2016. Cyberbullying in the world of teenagers and social media: A literature review. *International Journal of Cyber Behavior, Psychology and Learning* 6 (2), 68–95.

Allan, J., and Jørgensen, C. R., 2020. Inclusion, social capital and space within an English secondary free school. *Children's Geographies*, https://doi.org/10.1080/14733285.2020.1807463.

Alliance 8.7, 2017 *Global Estimates of Child Labour – Results and Trends*, 2012–2016 Executive Summary. ILO, Geneva, Switzerland.

Alter, C., 2018. The school shooting generation has had enough. *Time*, 22 March, https://time.com/longform/never-again-movement/ (accessed 27 August 2020).

An, S., and Kang, H., 2014. Advertising or games? Advergames on the internet gaming sites targeting children. *International Journal of Advertising* 33 (3), 509–32.

Anderson, M., 2018. *A Majority of Teens Have Experienced Some Form of Cyberbullying*. Pew Research Centre.

Anderson, M., and Jingjing J., 2018. *Teens' Social Media Habits and Experiences*. Pew Research Centre.

Andersson, N., Cockcroft, A., and Shea, B., 2008. Gender-based violence and HIV: Relevance for HIV prevention in hyperendemic countries of southern Africa. *AIDS* 22 (4), 73–86.

Ansell, N., 2014. Challenging empowerment: AIDS-affected southern African children and the need for a multi-level relational approach. *Journal of Health Psychology* 19 (1), 22–33.

Ansell, N., Robson, E., Hajdu, F., and van Blerk, L., 2012. Learning from young people about their lives: Using participatory methods to research the impacts of AIDS in southern Africa. *Children's Geographies* 10 (2), 169–86.

Appleton, J. V., Terlektsi, E., and Coombes, L., 2015. Implementing the Strengthening Families approach to child protection conferences. *British Journal of Social Work* 45 (5), 1395–414.

Archard, D., 2015. *Children: Rights and childhood*, 3rd ed. Routledge, Abingdon, Oxon.

Arnstein, S. R., 1969. A ladder of citizen participation. *Journal of the American Institute of Planners* 35 (4), 216–24.

Avert, n.d. *Children, HIV and Aids*. https://www.avert.org/professionals/hiv-social-issues/key-affected-populations/children#to (accessed 27 August 2020).

Ay Çeviker, Ş., Keskin, H. K., and Akıllı, M., 2019. Examining the effects of negotiation and peer mediation on students' conflict resolution and problem-solving skills. *International Journal of Instruction* 12 (3), 717–30.

Bachrach, P., and Baratz, M. S., 1962. Two faces of power. *American Political Science Review* 56 (4) (December 1962), 947–52.

———, 1970. *Power and Poverty: Theory and Practice*, Oxford University Press, Baltimore, MD.

Bailey, S., Boddy, K., Briscoe, S., and Morris, C., 2015. Involving disabled children and young people as partners in research: A systematic review. *Child: Care, Health and Development* 41 (1), 505–14.

Baldwin, H. J., Freeman, B., and Kelly, B., 2018. Like and share: Associations between social media engagement and dietary choices in children. *Public Health Nutrition* 21 (17), 3210–15.

Ball, S., 2003. *Class Strategies and the Education Market: The Middle Classes and Social Advantage*, RoutledgeFalmer, London.

Banks, C., 2007. The discourse of children's rights in Bangladesh: International norms and local definitions. *International Journal of Children's Rights* 15 (3–4), 391–414.

Barker, J., and Weller, S., 2003. 'Is it fun?' Developing children centred research methods. *International Journal of Sociology and Social Policy* 23(1–2), 33–58.

Barn, R., and Das, C., 2016. Family group conferences and cultural competence in social work. *British Journal of Social Work* 46 (4), 942–59.

Bauer, E., 2016. Practising kinship care: Children as language brokers in migrant families. *Childhood* 23 (1), 22–36.

BBC News, 2020. *Scotland Becomes the First Part of the UK to Ban Smacking*, 7t November, https://www.bbc.co.uk/news/uk-scotland-54825151 (accessed 10 November 2020).

Bennett, T., 2012. School councils: Shut up, we're listening. *The Guardian*, 12 March, https://www.theguardian.com/education/2012/mar/12/school-councils-number-lip-service (accessed 27 August 2020).

BERA, 2018. *Ethical Guidelines for Educational Research*, 4th ed., https://www.bera.ac.uk/publication/ethical-guidelines-for-educational-research-2018 (accessed 12 March 2021).

Bergström, K., Jonsson, L., and Shanahan, H., 2010. Children as co-researchers voicing their preferences in foods and eating: methodological reflections. *International Journal of Consumer Studies* 34 (2), 183–89.

Bernstein, B., 1971. A Critique of the Concept of Compensatory Education, in: Bernstein, B. (ed.), *Class, Codes and Control: Theoretical Studies towards a Sociology of Language*. Routledge and Kegan Paul, London, pp. 190–201.

Bessell, S., 2009. Children's participation in decision-making in the Philippines: Understanding the attitudes of policy-makers and service providers. *Childhood* 16 (3), 299–316.

Bevelander, K. E., Anschütz, D. J., Creemers, D. H. M., Kleinjan, M., and Engels, R. C. M. E., 2013. The role of explicit and implicit self-esteem in peer modeling of palatable food intake: A study on social media interaction among youngsters. *PLoS ONE* 8 (8), 72481.

Bhabha, H. K., 2004. *The Location of Culture*, Routledge Classics. Routledge, London.

Birch, J., Parnell, R., Patsarika, M., and Šorn, M., 2017. Participating together: Dialogic space for children and architects in the design process. *Children's Geographies* 15 (2), 224–36.

Bjerke, H., 2011. 'It's the way they do it': Expressions of agency in child–adult relations at home and school. *Children & Society* 25 (2), 93–103.

Blagbrough, J., 2008. Child domestic labour: A modern form of slavery. *Children & Society* 22 (3), 179–90.

Blake-Holmes, K., 2020. *Understanding the Needs of Young Carers in the Context of Covid-19 Global Pandemic*. University of East Anglia, Norwich.

Bodovski, K., 2010. Parental practices and educational achievement: Social class, race, and habitus. *British Journal of Sociology of Education* 31, 139–156.

Boerman, S. C., and van Reijmersdal, E. A., 2020. Disclosing influencer marketing on YouTube to children: The moderating role of para-social relationship. *Frontiers in Psychology* 10, 1–15.

Bono, K. E., Sy, S. R., and Kopp, C. B., 2016. School readiness among low-income black children: Family characteristics, parenting, and social support. *Early Child Development and Care* 186 (3), 419–35.

Bourdieu, P., and Passeron, J. C., 1977. *Reproduction in Education, Society and Culture*. Sage, London.

Bourdillon, M. F. C., and Boyden, J. (Eds.), 2014. *Growing Up in Poverty: Findings from Young Lives*, Palgrave Studies on Children and Development. Palgrave Macmillan, Houndmills, Basingstoke, Hampshire.

boyd, danah, 2014. *It's Complicated: The Social Lives of Networked Teens*. Yale University Press, New Haven, CT.

Boyden, J., 1997. Childhood and Policy Makers: A Comparative Perspective on the Globalization of Childhood, in: James, A., and Prout, A. (eds), *Constructing and Reconstructing Childhood: Contemporary Issues in the Sociological Study of Childhood*. Falmer Press, London, pp. 190–216.

Bradbury-Jones, C., 2014. *Children as Co-researchers: The Need for Protection*, Protecting Children and Young People Series. Dunedin, Edinburgh.

Bradbury-Jones, C., and Taylor, J., 2015. Engaging with children as co-researchers: Challenges, counter-challenges and solutions. *International Journal of Social Research Methodology* 18 (2), 161–73.

Brett, J., Staniszewska, S., Mockford, C., Herron-Marx, S., Hughes, J., Tysall, C., and Suleman, R., 2014. Mapping the impact of patient and public involvement on health and social care research: A systematic review. *Health Expectations* 17 (5), 637–50.

Bridger, E., 2016. Functions and failures of transnational activism: Discourses of children's resistance and repression in global anti-apartheid networks. *Journal of World History* 26 (4), 865–87.

Broström, S., 2012. Children's participation in research. *International Journal of Early Years Education* 20 (3), 257–69, https://doi.org/10.1080/09669760.2012.715407.

Buckingham, D., 2007. Childhood in the age of global media. *Children's Geographies* 5 (1–2), 43–54.

Bundy, C., 1987. Street sociology and pavement politics: Aspects of youth and student resistance in Cape Town, 1985. *Journal of Southern African Studies* 13 (3), 303–30.

Buranyi, S., 2019. Greta Thunberg's enemies are right to be scared. Her new political allies should be too. *The Guardian*, 30 September, https://www.theguardian.com/commentisfree/2019/sep/30/greta-thunberg-enemies-inaction-climate-crisis (accessed 27 August 2020).

Burford, G., Pennell, J., and Edwards, M., 2011. Family team meetings as principled advocacy. *Journal of Public Child Welfare* 5 (2–3), 318–44.

Burman, E., 2007. *Deconstructing Developmental Psychology*, 2nd ed. Routledge, London.

Burnitt, M., and Gunter, H., 2013. Primary school councils: Organization, composition and head teacher perceptions and values. *Management in Education* 27 (2), 56–62.

Burr, R., 2002. Global and local approaches to children's rights in Vietnam. *Childhood* 9 (1), 49–61.

Burton, D., Smith, M., and Woods, K., 2010. Working with teachers to promote children's participation through pupil-led research. *Educational Psychology in Practice* 26 (2), 91–104.

Burton, P., Leoschut, L., and Phyter, J., 2016. *South African Kids Online: A Glimpse into Children's Internet Use and Online Activities*. Centre for Justice and Crime Prevention, Cape Town.

Busby, E. (2019) Climate strike: Give detentions to children who skip school to protest environmental catastrophe, headteachers' union leader says, *The Independent*, Friday, 15 March 2019.

Cairns, K., 2018. Relational foodwork: Young people and food insecurity. *Children & Society* 32 (3), 174–84.

Canty, J., Stubbe, M., Steers, D., and Collings, S., 2016. The trouble with bullying – deconstructing the conventional definition of bullying for a child-centred investigation into children's use of social media. *Children & Society* 30 (1), 48–58.

Carvalho, R. D., 2012. Student participation in Brazil – the case of the 'grêmio estudantil'. *Management in Education* 26 (3), 155–57.

Casas, F., González, M., Navarro, D., and Aligué, M., 2013. Children as advisers of their researchers: Assuming a different status for children. *Child Indicators Research* 6 (2), 193–212.

Chant, S., 2006. Revisiting the 'feminisation of poverty' and the UNDP gender indices: What case for a gendered poverty index? New Series Working Paper (18). LSE Gender Institute, London School of Economics and Political Science, London.

Chawla, L., 2011. Young voices on climate change. *Children, Youth and Environments* 21 (1), 185–211.

Child Trends, 2015. *Family Structure: Indicators on Children and Youth*.

Children's Commissioner, 2018. *Life in 'likes': Children's Commissioner Report into Social Media Use among 8–12 Year Olds*. Children's Commissioner, London.

Christensen, P., 2004. Children's participation in ethnographic research: Issues of power and representation. *Children and Society* 18, 165–76.

Christensen, P., and James, A., 2008. Introduction – Researching Children and Childhood Cultures of Communication, in: Christensen, P., and James, A. (eds), *Research with Children: Perspectives and Practices*. Routledge, London, pp. 1–9.

Christensen, P., and Prout, A., 2002. Working with ethical symmetry in social research with children. *Childhood* 9 (4), 477–97.

Christensen, P. M., and James, A., 2017. Introduction: Researching children and childhood: Cultures of Communication, in: Christensen, P. M., and James, A. (ds.), *Research with Children: Perspectives and Practices*. Routledge, London, pp. 1–11.

Clark, E., 2004. Action learning with young carers. *Action Learning: Research and Practice* 1 (1), 109–16.

Clarke, M., 2018. Global South: What does it mean and why use the term? University of Victoria, Global South Political Commentaries, https://onlineacademiccommunity. uvic.ca/globalsouthpolitics/2018/08/08/global-south-what-does-it-mean-and-why-use-the-term/ (accessed 27 August 2020).

Clavering, E. K., and McLaughlin, J., 2010. Children's participation in health research: From objects to agents? *Child: Care, Health and Development* 36 (5), 603–11.

Cleland, A., and Tisdall, E. K. M., 2005. The challenge of antisocial behaviour: New relationships between the state, children and parents. *International Journal of Law, Policy and the Family* 19 (3), 395–420.

Coates, A. E., Hardman, C. A., Halford, J. C. G., Christiansen, P., and Boyland, E. J., 2019. Food and beverage cues featured in YouTube videos of social media influencers popular with children: An exploratory study. *Frontiers in Psychology* 10. https://doi.org/10.3389/fpsyg.2019.02142.

Cook, D. T., 2013. Taking exception with the child consumer. *Childhood* 20 (4), 423–28.

Cook, D. T., Frønes, I., Rizzini, I., Qvortrup, J., Nieuwenhuys, O., and Morrow, V., 2018. Past, present and futures of childhood studies: A conversation with former editors of Childhood. *Childhood* 25 (1), 6–18.

Coppock, V., 2011. Children as peer researchers: Reflections on a journey of mutual discovery: Children as peer researchers. *Children & Society* 25 (6), 435–46.

Cornock, M., 2007. Fraser guidelines or Gillick competence? *Journal of Children's and Young People's Nursing* 1 (3), 142.

Correa, T., Straubhaar, J. D., Chen, W., and Spence, J., 2015. Brokering new technologies: The role of children in their parents' usage of the internet. *New Media & Society* 17 (4), 483–500.

Corsaro, W. A., 2017. *The Sociology of Childhood*. Sage, London.

Coughlan, S., 2020. 'Digital poverty' in schools where few have laptops. BBC News, 24 April, https://www.bbc.co.uk/news/education-52399589 (accessed 12 May 2020).

Courtois, C., and Verdegem, P., 2016. With a little help from my friends: An analysis of the role of social support in digital inequalities. *New Media & Society* 18 (8), 1508–27.

Cox, S., and Robinson-Pant, A., 2005. Challenging perceptions of school councils in the primary school. *Education 3–13* 33 (2), 14–19.

———, 2008. Power, participation and decision making in the primary classroom: Children as action researchers. *Educational Action Research* 16 (4), 457–68.

Crafter, S., Cline, T., de Abreu, G., and O'Dell, L., 2017. Young peoples' reflections on what teachers think about family obligations that conflict with school: A focus on the non-normative roles of young caring and language brokering. *Childhood* 24 (4), 517–30.

Crenshaw, K., 1991. Mapping the margins: Intersectionality, identity politics, and violence against women of color. *Stanford Law Review* 43 (6), 1241–99. https://doi.org/10.2307/1229039.

Crivello, G., Camfield, L., and Woodhead, M., 2009. How can children tell us about their wellbeing? Exploring the potential of participatory research approaches within young lives. *Social Indicators Research* 90 (1), 51–72.

Crowley, A., 2015. Is anyone listening? The impact of children's participation on public policy. *International Journal of Children's Rights* 23 (3), 602–21.

Cunningham, S., and Lavalette, M., 2004. 'Active citizens' or 'irresponsible truants'? School student strikes against the war. *Critical Social Policy* 24 (2), 255–69.

Dahl, R., 1968. Power. *International Encyclopaedia of the Social Sciences* 7, 405–15.

Dahl, R. A., 1957. The concept of power. *Behavioral Science* 2 (3), 201–15.

———, 2005. *Who Governs? Democracy and Power in an American City*, 2nd ed. Yale University Press, New Haven, CT. London.

Dahlberg, G., Moss, P., and Pence, A., 2013. *Beyond Quality in Early Childhood Education and Care*, Routledge, London.

Dalli, C., and Te One, S., 2012. Involving children in educational research: Researcher reflections on challenges. *International Journal of Early Years Education* 20 (3), 224–33.

Davies, H., 2015. Shared parenting or shared care? Learning from children's experiences of a post-divorce shared care arrangement. *Children & Society* 29 (1), 1–14.

Davis, J., Watson, N., and Cunningham-Burley, S., 2017. Disabled Children, Ethnography and Unspoken Understandings: The Collaborative Construction of Diverse Identities, in: Christensen, P. M., and James, A. (eds), *Research with Children: Perspectives and Practices*, 3rd ed., Routledge, New York, pp. 54–70.

Davis, K., 1991. Critical Sociology and Gender Relations, in: Davis, K., Leijenaar, M., and Oldersma, J. (eds), *The Gender of Power*. Sage, London, pp. 65–86.

DCSF, 2004. *Children Act England and Wales*. HMSO, London.

De Grave, K., 2015. Children's Rights from a Gender Studies Perspective: Gender, Intersectionality and Ethics of Care, in: Vandenhole, W., Desmet, E., Reynaert, D., and Lembrechts, S. (eds), *Routledge International Handbook of Children's Rights Studies*. Routledge, Milton Park, Abingdon, Oxon, pp. 147–63.

Deisenrieder, V., Kubisch, S., Keller, L., and Stötter, J., 2020. Bridging the action gap by democratizing climate change education – the case of k.i.d.Z.21 in the context of Fridays for Future. *Sustainability* 12 (5), 1748.

Devine, D., 2002. Children's citizenship and the structuring of adult–child relations in the primary school. *Childhood* 9(3), 303–20.

———, 2003. *Children, Power and Schooling: How Childhood is Structured in the Primary School.* Trentham, Stoke on Trent.

Devotta, K., Woodhall-Melnik, J., Pedersen, C., Wendaferew, A., Dowbor, T. P., Guilcher, S. J., Hamilton-Wright, S., Ferentzy, P., Hwang, S. W., and Matheson, F. I., 2016. Enriching qualitative research by engaging peer interviewers: A case study. *Qualitative Research* 16 (6), 661–80.

Dewey, J., 2014. *Democracy and Education: An Introduction to the Philosophy of Education.* Collier MacMillan, London.

Dewey, J., and Archambault, R. D., 1964. *On Education: Selected Writings.* University of Chicago Press, Chicago.

Dias, P., and Brito, R., 2020. How families with young children are solving the dilemma between privacy and protection by building trust – a portrait from Portugal. *Journal of Children and Media* 14 (1), 56–73.

Dingwall, R., Eekelaar, J., and Murray, T., 1995. *The Protection of Children: State Intervention and Family Life*, 2nd ed. Avebury, Aldershot.

Dockett, S., and Perry, B., 2005. Researching with children: Insights from the Starting School Research Project. *Early Child Development and Care* 175 (6), 507–21.

Dodel, M., Kweksilber, C., Aguirre, F., and Méndez, I., 2018. *Niños, niñas y adolescentes conectados: Informe Kids Online Uruguay*, UNICEF/Global Kids Online.

Doherty, C., and Dooley, K., 2018. Responsibilising parents: The nudge towards shadow tutoring. *British Journal of Sociology of Education* 39 (4), 551–66.

Doná, G., 2006. Children as research advisors: Contributions to a 'methodology of participation' in researching children in difficult circumstances. *International Journal of Migration, Health and Social Care* 2 (2), 22–34.

Donzelot, J., 1979. *The Policing of Families*, 1st American ed. Pantheon Books, New York.

Doward, J., 2019. Pupils' climate change strike threat poses dilemma for heads. *The Guardian*, 10 February, https://www.theguardian.com/education/2019/feb/10/pupil-strike-climate-change-puts-schools-on-spot (accessed 30 June 2020)

Dowding, K., 2012. Why should we care about the definition of power? *Journal of Political Power* 5 (1), 119–35.

du Bois-Reymond, M., Büchner, P., and Krüger, H.-H., 1993. Modern family as everyday negotiation: Continuities and discontinuities in parent-child relationships. *Childhood* 1 (2), 87–99.

Dumais, S. A., Kessinger, R. J., and Ghosh, B., 2012. Concerted cultivation and teachers' evaluations of students: Exploring the intersection of race and parents' educational attainment. *Sociological Perspectives* 55 (1), 17–42.

Dunn, J., 2015. Insiders' perspectives: A children's rights approach to involving children in advising on adult-initiated research. *International Journal of Early Years Education* 23 (4), 394–408.

Eder, D., and Corsaro, W., 1999. Ethnographic studies of children and youth: Theoretical and ethical issues. *Journal of Contemporary Ethnography* 28, 520–31.

Edwards, C. P., 2002. Three approaches from Europe: Waldorf, Montessori, and Reggio Emilia. *Early Childhood Research & Practice* 4 (1), 78–90.

Educational International ECE Task Force, 2010. *Early Childhood Education: A Global Scenario*. Education International, Brussels.

Editorial, 2023. The Covid-19 pandemic in 2023: far from over. *The Lancet* 401, 79.

Einarsdóttir, J., 2007. Research with children: Methodological and ethical challenges. *European Early Childhood Education Research Journal* 15 (2), 197–211.

Ephraim, P. E., 2013. African youths and the dangers of social networking: A culture-centered approach to using social media. *Ethics and Information Technology* 15 (4), 275–84.

Esser, F., Baader, M., Betz, T., and Hungerland, B., 2016. Reconceptualising Agency and Childhood: An Introduction, in: Esser, F., Baader, M. S., Betz, T., and Hungerland, B. (eds), *Reconceptualising Agency and Childhood: New Perspectives in Childhood Studies*, Routledge Research in Education. Routledge, Abingdon, Oxon, pp. 1–16.

Estrada, E., 2013. Changing household dynamics: Children's American generational resources in street vending markets. *Childhood* 20 (1), 51–65.

European Commission, 2015. *Evaluation of Legislation, Policy and Practice on Child Participation in the European Union (EU)*. European Commission, Brussels.

European Union, 2000. *Charter of Fundamental Rights of the European Union*.

Eurostat, 2020. *EU SILC Survey*.

Eynon, R., and Geniets, A., 2016. The digital skills paradox: How do digitally excluded youth develop skills to use the internet? *Learning, Media and Technology* 41 (3), 463–79.

Farson, R. (1978) *Birthrights*, New York: Penguin.

Fielding, M., 2007. Beyond 'Voice': New roles, relations, and contexts in researching with young people. *Discourse: Studies in the Cultural Politics of Education* 28 (3), 301–10.

Fischer, C., Harvey, E. A., and Driscoll, P., 2009. Parent-centered parenting values among Latino immigrant mothers. *Journal of Family Studies* 15 (3), 296–308.

Fishman, S. M., and McCarthy, L. P., 1998. *John Dewey and the Challenge of Classroom Practice*, The Practitioner Inquiry Series. Teachers College Press, New York; National Council of Teachers of English, Urbana, IL.

Fleming, J., Goodman Chong, H., and Skinner, A., 2009. Experiences of peer evaluation of the Leicester Teenage Pregnancy Prevention Strategy. *Children & Society* 23(4), 279–90.

Flewitt, R., Jones, P., Potter, J., Domingo, M., Collins, P., Munday, E., and Stenning, K., 2018. 'I enjoyed it because … you could do whatever you wanted and be creative': Three principles for participatory research and pedagogy. *International Journal of Research & Method in Education* 41(4), 372–86.

Floberg, D., 2020. US students are being asked to work remotely. But 22% of homes don't have internet. Bloomberg, 23 March, https://www.bloomberg.com/news/articles/2020-03-26/covid-19-school-closures-reveal-disparity-in-access-to-internet (accessed 20 May 2020).

Fors, H. C., 2012. Child labour: A review of recent theory and evidence with policy implications. *Journal of Economic Surveys* 26(4), 570–93.

Foucault, M., 1977. *Discipline and Punish: The Birth of the Prison*, Penguin, London.

———, 1980. Truth and Power, in: *Power/Knowledge: Selected Interviews and Other Writings, 1972–1977*. Pantheon Books, New York, pp. 78–108.

———, 1982. The subject and power. *Critical Inquiry* 8 (4), 777–95.

———, 1991. *Discipline and Punish: The Birth of the Prison*, repr., Penguin Social Sciences. Penguin Books, London.

———, 1995. *Discipline and Punish: The Birth of the Prison*, 2nd Vintage Books ed. Vintage Books, New York.

Fowler, R. C., 2017. Reframing the debate about the relationship between learning and development: An effort to resolve dilemmas and reestablish dialogue in a fractured field. *Early Childhood Education Journal* 45(2), 155–62.

Franklin, A., and Franklin, B., 1996. Growing Pains: The Developing Children's Rights Movement in the UK, in: Pilcher, J., and Wagg, S. (eds), *Thatcher's Children? Politics, Childhood and Society in the 1980s and 1990s*. Falmer Press, London, pp. 95–114.

Franks, M., 2011. Pockets of participation: Revisiting child-centred participation research *Children & Society* 25(1), 15–25.

Fransson, J. R., 2020. *Socialrådgiver: Det går stik imod min faglighed, når jeg tager børnechecken fra udsatte familier*. Altinget, 13 August, https://www.altinget.dk/uddannelse/artikel/socialraadgiver-det-gaar-stik-imod-min-faglighed-naar-jeg-tager-boernechecken-fra-udsatte-familier (accessed 26 August 2020).

Fraser, S., 2004. Situating Empirical Research, in: Fraser, S., et al. (eds), *Doing Research with Children and Young People*. Sage, London, pp. 15–26.

Frye, M., 1983. *The Politics of Reality: Essays in Feminist Theory*, The Crossing Press Feminist Series. Crossing Press, Trumansburg, NY.

Gaillard, S., Malik, S., Preston, J., Escalera, B. N., Dicks, P., Touil, N., Mardirossian, S., Claverol-Torres, J., and Kassaï, B., 2018. Involving children and young people in clinical research through the forum of a European Young Persons' Advisory Group: Needs and challenges. *Fundamental & Clinical Pharmacology* 32 (4), 357–62.

Gainsborough, J., and Lean, L., 2008. Convention on the Rights of the Child and juvenile justice. *The Link* 7 (1), 1–5.

Gallagher, M., 2008a. Foucault, power and participation. *International Journal of Children's Rights* 16(3), 395–406.

———, 2008b. 'Power is not an evil': Rethinking power in participatory methods. *Children's Geographies* 6(2), 137–50.

———, 2009. Ethics, in: Tisdall, E., Davis, J., and Gallagher, M. (eds), *Researching with Children and Young People: Research Design, Methods and Analysis*. Sage, London, pp. 23–42.

Germann, S. E., 2006. An exploratory study of quality of life and coping strategies of orphans living in child-headed households in an urban high HIV-prevalent community in Zimbabwe, Southern Africa. *Vulnerable Children and Youth Studies* 1(2), 149–58.

Ghirotto, L., and Mazzoni, V., 2013. Being part, being involved: The adult's role and child participation in an early childhood learning context. *International Journal of Early Years Education* 21 (4), 300–8.

Giardello, P., and McNulty, J., 2009. Back to the Future of Early Childhood – Same but Different, in: Bignold, W., and Gayton, L. (eds), Global Issues and Comparative Education, Learning Matters, Exeter.

Giesinger, J., 2019. Children, rights, and powers. *International Journal of Children's Rights* 27 (2), 251–65.

Gilbert, N., Parton, N., and Skivenes, M., 2011. Changing Patterns of Response and Emerging Orientations, in: Gilbert, N., Parton, N., and Skivenes, M. (eds), *Child Protection Systems: International Trends and Orientations*, International Policy Exchange Series. Oxford University Press, New York, pp. 243–58.

Giroux, H. A., 2001. *Stealing Innocence: Youth, Corporate Power, and the Politics of Culture.* Paperback ed. Palgrave, New York.

Global Initiative to End All Corporal Punishment of Children (GIEACPC), 2018. *Ending Legalised Violence against Children by 2030.* https://resourcecentre.savethechildren.net/node/13139/pdf/pathfinders-report-2018-singles.pdf (accessed 14 June 2020).

Golden, D., and Erdreich, L., 2020. Keeping mum: The mediation of military conflict in the everyday mothering of middle-class Israeli Palestinian and Jewish women. *Childhood* 27 (3), 369–82, https://doi.org/10.1177/0907568220906213.

Goldson, B., and Children's Society (Great Britain), 2002. *Vulnerable Inside: Children in Secure and Penal Settings.* Children's Society, London.

Goodman, A., Gregg, P., Chowdry, H., and Joseph Rowntree Foundation, 2010. *Poorer Children's Educational Attainment: How Important Are Attitudes and Behaviour?* Joseph Rowntree Foundation, York.

Gray, C., and Winter, E., 2011. Hearing voices: Participatory research with preschool children with and without disabilities. *European Early Childhood Education Research Journal* 19(3), 309–20.

Green, G., 2016. Power to the people: To what extent has public involvement in applied health research achieved this? *Research Involvement and Engagement* 2(1). https://doi.org/10.1186/s40900-016-0042-y.

Greene, S., and Nixon, E., 2020. *Children as Agents in Their Worlds: A Psychological–Relational Perspective*, Routledge, Abingdon, Oxon.

Guttmann, 2020. *Spending on Advertising to Children Worldwide from 2012 to 2021.* Statista. https://www.statista.com/statistics/750865/kids-advertising-spending-worldwide/ (accessed 14 June 2020).

Haley, J. F., and Bradbury, J., 2015. Child-headed households under watchful adult eyes: Support or surveillance? *Childhood* 22(3), 394–408.

Hammarberg, T., 1990. The UN Convention on the Rights of the Child – and how to make it work. *Human Rights Quarterly* 12(1), 97–105.

Hammersley, M., 2017. Childhood studies: A sustainable paradigm? *Childhood* 24 (1), 113–27.

Hancock, R., and Gillen, J., 2007. Safe places in domestic spaces: Two-year-olds at play in their homes. *Children's Geographies* 5(4), 337–51.

Hanson, K., Abebe, T., Aitken, S. C., Balagopalan, S., and Punch, S., 2018. 'Global/local' research on children and childhood in a 'global society'. *Childhood* 25 (3), 272–96.

Harcourt, D., and Einarsdottir, J., 2011. Introducing children's perspectives and participation in research. *European Early Childhood Education Research Journal* 19 (3), 301–7.

Harms, S., Jack, S., Ssebunnya, J., and Kizza, R., 2010. The orphaning experience: Descriptions from Ugandan youth who have lost parents to HIV/AIDS. *Child and Adolescent Psychiatry and Mental Health* 4(1), 1–10.

Harris, J. L., Speers, S. E., Schwartz, M. B., and Brownell, K. D., 2012. US food company branded advergames on the internet: Children's exposure and effects on snack consumption. *Journal of Children and Media* 6 (1), 51–68.

Hart, R. A., 1992. *Children's Participation: From Tokenism to Citizenships*. UNICEF International Child Development Centre, Florence, Italy.

———, 1997. *Children's Participation: The Theory and Practice of Involving Young Citizens in Community Development and Environmental Care*. Earthscan, London.

———, 2002. *Children's Participation: The Theory and Practice of Involving Young Citizens in Community Development and Environmental Care*, UNICEF, New York.

Hartas, D., 2011. Young people's participation: Is disaffection another way of having a voice? *Educational Psychology in Practice* 27 (2), 103–15.

Haugaard, M., 2017. Power-to, power-over, resistance and domination: An editorial. *Journal of Political Power* 10 (3), 271–73.

Haugaard, M., 2012. Rethinking the four dimensions of power: Domination and empowerment. *Journal of Political Power* 5 (1), 33–54.

Haugaard, M. (ed.), 2002. *Power: A reader*. Manchester University Press, Manchester.

Haugen, G. M. D., 2010. Children's perspectives on everyday experiences of shared residence: Time, emotions and agency dilemmas. *Children & Society* 24 (2), 112–22.

Hawkins, K., 2015. The complexities of participatory action research and the problems of power, identity and influence. *Educational Action Research* 23 (4), 464–78.

Heimer, M., Näsman, E., and Palme, J., 2018. Vulnerable children's rights to participation, protection, and provision: The process of defining the problem in Swedish child and family welfare. *Child & Family Social Work* 23 (2), 316–23.

Hendrick, H., 2015. Constructions and reconstructions of British childhood: An interpretative survey, 1800 to the present, in: James, A., and Prout, A. (eds), *Constructing and Reconstructing Childhood: Contemporary Issues in the Sociological Study of Childhood*, 3rd ed., Routledge, London, pp. 29–54.

Hetherington, E. M., 2003. Social support and the adjustment of children in divorced and remarried families. *Childhood* 10 (2), 217–36.

Hill, M., 1997. Participatory research with children. *Child & Family Social Work* 2 (3), 171–83.

———, 2006. Children's voices on ways of having a voice: Children's and young people's perspectives on methods used in research and consultation. *Childhood* 13 (1), 69–89.

Hill, M., Davis, J., Prout, A., and Tisdall, K., 2004. Moving the participation agenda forward. *Children & Society* 18 (2), 77–96.

Hinton, R., 2008. Children's participation and good governance: Limitations of the theoretical literature. *International Journal of Children's Rights* 16 (3), 285–300.

Hogan, D. M., Halpenny, A. M., and Greene, S., 2003. Change and continuity after parental separation: Children's experiences of family transitions in Ireland. *Childhood* 10 (2), 163–80.

Hojnoski, R. L., and Missall, K. N., 2006. Addressing school readiness: Expanding school psychology in early education. *School Psychology Review* 35 (4), 602–14.

Holland, S., Renold, E., Ross, N. J., and Hillman, A., 2010. Power, agency and participatory agendas: A critical exploration of young people's engagement in participative qualitative research. *Childhood* 17 (3), 360–75.

Holland, S., Scourfield, J., O'Neill, S., and Pithouse, A., 2005. Democratising the family and the state? The case of family group conferences in child welfare. *Journal of Social Policy* 34 (1), 59–78.

Hollingsworth, K., 2007. Responsibility and rights: Children and their parents in the youth justice system. *International Journal of Law, Policy and the Family* 21 (2), 190–219.

Holmberg, A., and Alvinius, A., 2020. Children's protest in relation to the climate emergency: A qualitative study on a new form of resistance promoting political and social change. *Childhood* 27 (1), 78–92.

Holmes, J., 2011. Cyberkids or divided generations? Characterising young people's internet use in the UK with generic, continuum or typological models. *New Media & Society* 13 (7), 1104–22.

Holt, J., 1975. *Escape from Childhood*. Penguin, Harmondsworth.

Holt, L., 2004. The 'voices' of children: De-centring empowering research. *Children's Geographies* 2 (1), 13–27.

Honwana, A., 2000. Innocents et Coupables: les Enfants-Soldats Comme Acteurs Tactiques. *Politique Africaine* 80, 58–78.

Hood-Williams, J., 1990. Patriarchy for Children: On the Stability of Power Relations in Children's Lives, in: Chisholm, L., Büchner, P., Krüger, H.-H., and Brown, P. (eds), *Childhood, Youth, and Social Change: A Comparative Perspective*. Falmer Press, London, pp. 111–22.

Hooper, C.-A., and Gunn, R., 2014. Recognition as a framework for ethical participatory research: Developing a methodology with looked after young people. *International Journal of Social Research Methodology* 17 (5), 475–88.

Horgan, D., 2017. Child participatory research methods: Attempts to go 'deeper'. *Childhood* 24 (2), 245–59.

Houri, A. K., and Miller, F. G., 2020. A systematic review of universal screeners used to evaluate social-emotional and behavioral aspects of kindergarten readiness. *Early Education and Development* 31 (5), 653–75.

Howe, A., Mathie, E., Munday, D., Cowe, M., Goodman, C., Keenan, J., Kendall, S., Poland, F., Staniszewska, S., and Wilson, P., 2017. Learning to work together – lessons from a reflective analysis of a research project on public involvement. *Research Involvement and Engagement* 3 (1), https://doi.org/10.1186/s40900-016-0051-x.

Howe, R. B., and Covell, K., 2005. Denying Children's Rights, in: *Empowering Children: Children's Rights Education as a Pathway to Citizenship*. University of Toronto Press, Toronto, pp. 3–18.

Howse, P., 2014. Internet gap hits poorer children, campaigners claim. BBC News, 14 January, https://www.bbc.co.uk/news/education-25729973 (accessed 27 August 2020).

Human Rights Watch, 2005. U.S.: Supreme Court ends child executions. https://www.hrw.org/news/2005/02/28/us-supreme-court-ends-child-executions (accessed 25 August 2020).

ILO, 1999. *Convention 182*. Geneva, Switzerland.

———, 2017. *Global Estimates of Child Labour*. Geneva, Switzerland.

Imoh, A. T.-D., 2014. Realising Children's Rights in Africa: An Introduction, in: Imoh, A. T.-D., and Ansell, N. (eds), *Children's Lives in an Era of Children's Rights: The Progress of the Convention on the Rights of the Child in Africa*, Routledge Research in Human Rights Law. Routledge, Abingdon, Oxon.

Jacquez, F., Vaughn, L. M., and Wagner, E., 2013. Youth as partners, participants or passive recipients: A review of children and adolescents in community-based participatory research (CBPR). *American Journal of Community Psychology* 51 (1–2), 176–89.

James, A., 2011. Agency, in: Qvortrup, J., Corsaro, W. A., Honig, M.-S. (eds), *The Palgrave Handbook of Childhood Studies*. Palgrave Macmillan, Houndmills, Basingstoke, Hampshire, pp. 34–45.

James, A., Jenks, C., and Prout, A., 1998. *Theorizing Childhood*, repr. Polity Press, Cambridge.

Johansen, S. L., 2019. Small Children's Use of Digital Media(s) – Consuming or Creating?, in: Sparrman, A. (ed.), *Making Culture: Children's and Young People's Leisure Cultures*. Kulturanalys Norden, Göteborg.

John, M., 1995. Children's Rights in a Free Market Culture, in: Stephens, S. (Ed.), *Children and the Politics of Culture*, Princeton Studies in Culture/Power/History. Princeton University Press, Princeton, NJ, pp. 105–139.

———, 2003. *Children's Rights and Power: Charging Up for a New Century*, Children in Charge Series. Jessica Kingsley, London.

Jolobe, Z., 2019. *International Mediation in the South African Transition: Brokering Power in Intractable Conflicts*, Routledge Contemporary South Africa. Routledge, New York.

Jørgensen, C. R., 2011. 'Schooling and Life Projects – Experiences and Perspectives of Migrant and Minority Ethnic Youth in England and Spain'. PhD thesis, University of Warwick.

———, 2015. Three advantages of cross-national comparative ethnography – methodological reflections from a study of migrants and minority ethnic youth in English and Spanish schools. *Ethnography and Education* 10 (1), 1–16.

———, 2019. Children's involvement in research – A review and comparison with service user involvement in health and social care. *Social Sciences* 8 (5), 149.

Jørgensen, C. R., Dobson, G., and Perry, T., 2020. Migrant children with special educational needs in European schools – a review of current issues and approaches. *European Journal of Special Needs Education*. https://doi.org/10.1080/08856257.2020.1762988.

Jørgensen, C. R., Weckesser, A., Turner, J., and Wade, A., 2019. Young people's views on sexting education and support needs: Findings and recommendations from a UK-based study. *Sex Education* 19 (1), 25–40.

Jourdan, D., and Wertin, J., 2020. Intergenerational rights to a sustainable future: Insights for climate justice and tourism. *Journal of Sustainable Tourism* 28 (8), 1245–54.

Kaur, A., and Medury, Y., 2011. Impact of the internet on teenagers' influence on family purchases. *Young Consumers* 12 (1), 27–38.

Kellett, M., 2005. *Children as Active Researchers: A New Research Paradigm for the 21st Century?* NCRM Methods Review Papers NCRM/003, ESRC National Centre for Research Methods.

———, 2010. Small shoes, big steps! Empowering children as active researchers. *American Journal of Community Psychology* 46 (1–2), 195–203.

Kellett, M., et al., 2010. WeCan2: Exploring the implications of young people with learning disabilities engaging in their own research. *European Journal of Special Needs Education* 25(1), 31–44.

Kellett, M., Robinson, C., and Burr, R., 2004. Images of Childhood, in: Fraser, S., et al. (ed.), *Doing Research with Children and Young People*. Sage, London, pp. 27–42.

Kelly, J. B., 2003. Changing perspectives on children's adjustment following divorce: A view from the United States. *Childhood* 10 (2), 237–54.

Kendrick, M., and Kakuru, D., 2012. Funds of knowledge in child-headed households: A Ugandan case study. *Childhood* 19 (3), 397–413.

Kim, C.-Y., 2016. Why research 'by' children? Rethinking the assumptions underlying the facilitation of children as researchers. *Children and Society* 30, 230–40.

———, 2017. Participation or pedagogy? Ambiguities and tensions surrounding the facilitation of children as researchers. *Childhood* 24 (1), 84–98.

Kim, S., and Yi, S.-H., 2010. Is privacy at risk when commercial websites target primary school children? A case study in Korea: Commercial websites target children's privacy? *Children & Society* 24 (6), 449–60.

Kirby, L., and Lirius, A., 2020. *Old Enough to Save the Planet*, Magic Cat, London.

Kitzinger, J., 2015. Who Are You Kidding? Children, Power and the Struggle against Sexual Abuse, in: James, A., and Prout, A. (eds), *Constructing and Reconstructing Childhood: Contemporary Issues in the Sociological Study of Childhood*. Routledge, London, 3rd ed., pp. 165–89.

Klocker, N., 2007. An Example of 'Thin' Agency: Child Domestic Workers in Tanzania, in: Panelli, R., Punch, S., and Robson, E. (eds), *Global Perspectives on Rural Childhood and Youth: Young Rural Lives*, Routledge Studies in Human Geography. Routledge, New York, pp. 83–94.

Klusener, E., 2019. *Protests in the Age of Social Media: How Was the March For Our Lives Movement Shaped by Social Media?* University of Manchester. https://sites.manchester.ac.uk/global-social-challenges/2019/06/06/protests-in-the-age-of-social-media-how-was-the-march-for-our-lives-movement-shaped-by-social-media/.

Konstantoni, K., and Emejulu, A., 2017. When intersectionality met childhood studies: The dilemmas of a travelling concept. *Children's Geographies* 15 (1), 6–22.

Križ, K., and Skivenes, M., 2017. Child welfare workers' perceptions of children's participation: A comparative study of England, Norway and the USA (California): Children's participation. *Child & Family Social Work* 22, 11–22.

Labrecque, L. I., vor dem Esche, J., Mathwick, C., Novak, T. P., and Hofacker, C. F., 2013. Consumer power: Evolution in the digital age. *Journal of Interactive Marketing* 27 (4), 257–69.

Langford, R., 2010. Critiquing child-centred pedagogy to bring children and early childhood educators into the centre of a democratic pedagogy. *Contemporary Issues in Early Childhood* 11(1), 113–27.

Langhout, R. D., and Thomas, E., 2010. Imagining participatory action research in collaboration with children: An introduction. *American Journal of Community Psychology* 46 (1–2), 60–66.

Lansdown, G., 2010. The Realisation of Children's Participation Rights, in: Percy-Smith, B., and Thomas, N. (eds), *A Handbook of Children and Young People's Participation: Perspectives from Theory and Practice*. Routledge, London, pp. 11–23.

———, 2011. *Every Child's Right to Be Heard: A Resource Guide on the UN Committee on the Rights of the Child General Comment No 12*. Save the Children.

Lareau, A., 2011. *Unequal Childhoods: Class, Race, and family Life*, 2nd ed. University of California Press, Berkeley.

Lasch, C., 1995. *Haven in a Heartless World: Family Besieged*. Norton, New York.

Lau, G., and Cheng, D., 2010. Learning through play in the early childhood classroom: Myth or Reality? *Hong Kong Journal of Early Childhood* 9 (2), 27–43.

Laville, S., 2019. MPs debate climate after school strike – but only a handful turn up. *The Guardian*, 28 February, https://www.theguardian.com/politics/2019/feb/28/mps-debate-climate-after-school-strike-but-only-a-handful-turn-up (accessed 30 June 2020).

Laville, S., Taylor, M., and Hurst, D., 2019. 'It's our time to rise up': Youth climate strikes held in 100 countries. *The Guardian*, 15 March, https://www.theguardian.com/environment/2019/mar/15/its-our-time-to-rise-up-youth-climate-strikes-held-in-100-countries (accessed 24 April 2019).

Lawlor, M.-A., and Prothero, A., 2011. Pester power – a battle of wills between children and their parents. *Journal of Marketing Management* 27 (5–6), 561–81.

Lawson, L., and Kearns, A., 2010. 'Community empowerment' in the context of the Glasgow housing stock transfer. *Urban Studies* 47 (7), 1459–78.

———, 2016. 'Power to the (young) people'? Children and young people's empowerment in the relocation process associated with urban re-structuring. *International Journal of Housing Policy* 16 (3), 376–403.

Lawton, G., 2019. The children striking over climate change speak to New Scientist. *New Scientist*, 15 February. https://www.newscientist.com/article/2194067-the-children-striking-over-climate-change-speak-to-new-scientist/ (accessed 19 June 2019).

Leitch, R., Gardner, J., Mitchell, S., Lundy, L., Odena, O., Galanouli, D., and Clough, P., 2007. Consulting pupils in Assessment for Learning classrooms: The twists and turns of working with students as co-researchers. *Educational Action Research* 15 (3), 459–78.

Lemkow–Tovías, G., Lemkow, L., Cash-Gibson, L., Teixidó-Compañó, E., and Benach, J., 2023. Impact of COVID-19 inequalities on children: An intersectional analysis. *Sociology of Health & Illness* 45 (145), 145–62. https://doi.org/10.1111/1467-9566.13557.

Lessel, S., 2020. For højt skolefravær koster mindst 200 familier børnechecken. Altinget, 07 August, https://www.altinget.dk/uddannelse/artikel/for-hoejt-skolefravaer-koster-mindst-200-familier-boernechecken (accessed 27 August 2020).

Lewis, J., 2006. Introduction: Children in the Context of Changing Families and Welfare States, in: Lewis, J. (ed.), *Children, Changing Families and Welfare States*. Edward Elgar, Cheltenham, pp. 1–26.

Liebel, M., 2003. Working children as social subjects: The contribution of working children's organizations to social transformations. *Childhood* 10 (3), 265–85.

———, 2012a. *Children's Rights from Below: Cross-Cultural Perspectives*. Palgrave, Basingstoke.

———, 2012b. Do Children Have a Right to Work? Working Children's Movements in the Struggle for Social Justice, in: Hanson, K., and Nieuwenhuys, O. (eds), *Reconceptualizing Children's Rights in International Development*. Cambridge University Press, Cambridge, pp. 225–49.

———, 2015. Protecting the rights of working children instead of banning child labour. *International Journal of Children's Rights* 23 (3), 529–47.

———, 2018. Welfare or agency? Children's interests as foundation of children's rights. *International Journal of Children's Rights* 26 (4), 597–625.

Liebel, M., and Invernizzi, A., 2019. The movements of working children and the International Labour Organization: A lesson on enforced silence. *Children & Society* 33 (2), 142–53.

Liebel, M., Overwien, B., and Recknagel, A. (eds), 2001. *Working Children's Protagonism: Social Movements and Empowerment in Latin America, Africa, and India*. Internationale Beiträge zu Kindheit, Jugend, Arbeit und Bildung. IKO-Verlag für Interkulturelle Kommunikation, Frankfurt am Main.

Lightburn, A., 1992. Participant Observation in Special Needs Adoptive Families, in: Gilgun, J. F., Daly, K. J., and Handel, G. (eds), *Qualitative Methods in Family Research*. Sage, Newbury Park, CA.

Livingstone, S., 2013. Children's Internet Culture: Power, Change and Vulnerability in Twenty-First Century Childhood, in: Lemish, D. (ed.), *The Routledge International Handbook of Children, Adolescents and Media*. Routledge, London, pp. 111–19.

Livingstone, S., and Bulger, M., 2014. A global research agenda for children's rights in the digital age. *Journal of Children and Media* 8 (4), 317–35.

Livingstone, S., Haddon, L., and Ólafsson, K., 2012. *Final Report, EU Kids Online II*. EU Kids Online Network.

Livingstone, S., Haddon, L., Anke, G., and Ólafsson, K., 2011. *Risks and Safety on the Internet: The Perspective of European Children: Full Findings and Policy Implications from the EU Kids Online Survey of 9–16 Year Olds and Their Parents in 25 Countries*. EU Kids Online, Deliverable D4. EU Kids Online Network, London, UK.

Livingstone, S., and Helsper, E., 2007. Gradations in digital inclusion: Children, young people and the digital divide. *New Media & Society* 9 (4), 671–96.

Livingstone, S., Mascheroni, G., and Staksrud, E., 2018. European research on children's internet use: Assessing the past and anticipating the future. *New Media & Society* 20 (3), 1103–22.

Loberg, M., 2023. New report about children's participation and influence during Covid-19. Nordic Welfare Centre.

Logar, S., Anzelm, D., Lazic, D., and Vujacic, V., 2016. *Global Kids Online Montenegro Opportunities, Risks and Safety*. Global Kids Online/UNICEF.

———, 2012. Contested voices? Methodological tensions in creative visual research with children. *International Journal of Social Research Methodology* 15 (2), 105–17.

Lomax, H., 2015. Seen and heard? Ethics and agency in participatory visual research with children, young people and families. *Families, Relationships and Societies* 4 (3), 493–502.

Luet, K. M., 2017. Disengaging parents in urban schooling. *Educational Policy* 31 (5), 674–702.

Lukes, S., 2005. *Power: A Radical View*, 2nd ed. Palgrave Macmillan, Houndmills, Basingstoke, Hampshire.

Lundy, L., 2007. 'Voice' is not enough: Conceptualising Article 12 of the United Nations Convention on the Rights of the Child. *British Educational Research Journal* 33 (6), 927–42.

Lushey, C. J., and Munro, E. R., 2015. Participatory peer research methodology: An effective method for obtaining young people's perspectives on transitions from care to adulthood? *Qualitative Social Work: Research and Practice* 14 (4), 522–37.

Maes, S. D., De Mol, J., and Buysse, A., 2012. Children's experiences and meaning construction on parental divorce: A focus group study. *Childhood* 19 (2), 266–79.

Mager, U., and Nowak, P., 2012. Effects of student participation in decision making at school: A systematic review and synthesis of empirical research. *Educational Research Review* 7 (1), 38–61.

Maitles, H., and Deuchar, R., 2006. 'We don't learn democracy, we live it!': Consulting the pupil voice in Scottish schools. *Education, Citizenship and Social Justice* 1 (3), 249–66.

Mandell, N., 1988. The least-adult role in studying children. *Journal of Contemporary Ethnography* 16, 433–67.

Mannion, G., 2007. Going spatial, going relational: Why 'listening to children' and children's participation needs reframing. *Discourse: Studies in the Cultural Politics of Education* 28 (3), 405–20.

Marschall, A., 2014. Who cares for whom? Revisiting the concept of care in the everyday life of post-divorce families. *Childhood* 21 (4), 517–31.

Mascheroni, G., and Ólafsson, K., 2014. *Net Children Go Mobile: Risks and Opportunities*. Educatt, Milan.

———, 2016. The mobile internet: Access, use, opportunities and divides among European children. *New Media & Society* 18 (8), 1657–79.

Matshalaga, N. R., and Powell, 2002. Mass orphanhood in the era of HIV/AIDS. *BMJ* 324 (7331), 185–86.

Mayall, B., 2002. *Towards a Sociology for Childhood: Thinking from Children's Lives*. Open University Press, Buckingham.

Mayes, E., 2019. Reconceptualizing the presence of students on school governance councils: The a/effects of spatial positioning. *Policy Futures in Education* 17 (4), 503–19.

McLanahan, S. S., and Carlson, M. J., 2001. Poverty and Gender in Affluent Nations, in: *International Encyclopedia of the Social & Behavioral Sciences*. Elsevier, pp. 11894–900.

McLaughlin, H., 2005. Involving young service users as co-researchers: Possibilities, benefits and costs. *British Journal of Social Work* 36 (8), 1395–410.

———, 2016. *Empowerment: A Critique*, Routledge Key Themes in Health and Society. Routledge, Abingdon, Oxon.

Mead, G. H., 1934. *Mind, Society and Self from the Standpoint of a Social Behaviourist*, Chicago University Press, Chicago.

Meehan, C., 2016. Every child mattered in England: But what matters to children? *Early Child Development and Care* 186 (3), 382–402.

Ministry of Communications, Global Kids online, UNICEF, 2017. *Risks and Opportunities Related to Children's Online Practices – Ghana Country Report*.

Montgomery, H., 2010. The Rights of the Child: Rightfully Mine, in: Kassem, D., Murphy, L., and Taylor, E. (eds), *Key Issues in Childhood and Youth Studies*. Routledge, Abingdon, Oxon, pp. 149–158.

Morgan, J., and Sengedorj, T., 2015. 'If you were the researcher what would you research?': Understanding children's perspectives on educational research in Mongolia and Zambia. *International Journal of Research & Method in Education* 38 (2), 200–18.

Morlock, E., 2018. Social media has made school children more fashion conscious than ever – and parents are footing the bill. *The Conversation*, 05 September, https://theconversation.com/social-media-has-made-school-children-more-fashion-conscious-than-ever-and-parents-are-footing-the-bill-102417 (accessed 19 April 2019).

Morss, J., 1996. *Growing Critical: Alternatives to Developmental Psychology*. Routledge, London.

Moss, P., and Petrie, P., 2002. *From Children's Services to Children's Spaces: Public Policy, Children and Childhood*, RoutledgeFalmer, London.

Mount, F., 1992. *The Subversive Family: An Alternative History of Love and Marriage*. Maxwell Macmillan International, New York.

Moxnes, K., 2003. Risk factors in divorce: Perceptions by the children involved. *Childhood* 10 (2), 131–46.

Murray, C., 2010. Children's rights in Rwanda: A hierarchical or parallel model of implementation? *International Journal of Children's Rights* 18 (3), 387–403.

Murray, C., 2006. Peer led focus groups and young people. *Children and Society* 20, 273–96.

Myagmar, A., 2010. Child-centred approach: How is it perceived by preschool educators in Mongolia? *US-China Education Review* 7 (6), 63–77.

Nawaila, M. B., Kanbul, S., and Ozdamli, F., 2018. A review on the rights of children in the digital age. *Children and Youth Services Review* 94, 390–409.

Ndebele, M., 1995. Recovering Childhood: Children in South African Reconstruction, in: Stephens, S. (ed.), *Children and the Politics of Culture*, Princeton Studies in Culture/Power/History. Princeton University Press, Princeton, NJ.

Neale, B., and Flowerdew, J., 2007. New structures, new agency: The dynamics of child–parent relationships after divorce. *International Journal of Children's Rights* 15 (1), 25–42.

Newcomb, A., 2018. How Parkland's social media-savvy teens took back the internet – and the gun control debate. NBC News, 22 February. https://www.nbcnews.com/tech/tech-news/how-parkland-students-are-using-social-media-keep-gun-control-n850251 (accessed 14 May 2019).

Ní Bhroin, N., and Rehder, M. M., 2018. *Digital Natives or Naïve Experts? Exploring How Norwegian Children (Aged 9–15) Understand the Internet*, EU Kids Online.

Nicholls, A. J., and Cullen, P., 2004. The child–parent purchase relationship: 'Pester power', human rights and retail ethics. *Journal of Retailing and Consumer Services* 11(2), 75–86.

Nieuwenhuys, O., 2009. From Child Labour to Working Children's Movements, in: Qvortrup, J., Corsaro, W., and Honig, M.-S. (eds), *The Palgrave Handbook of Childhood Studies*. Palgrave Macmillan, Basingstoke, pp. 289–300.

Nieuwenhuys, O., 1994. *Children's Lifeworlds: Gender, Welfare, and Labour in the Developing World*. Routledge, London.

Nikken, P., and Schols, M., 2015. How and why parents guide the media use of young children. *Journal of Child and Family Studies* 24 (11), 3423–35.

NSPCC, 2021. Online safety during coronavirus, https://learning.nspcc.org.uk/news/2020/may/online-safety-during-coronavirus (accessed 12 March 2021).

Oakley, A., 1994. Women and Children First and Last: Parallels and Differences between Children's and Women's Studies, in: Mayall, B. (ed.), *Children's Childhoods: Observed and Experienced*. Falmer Press, London, pp. 13–32.

O'Brien, N., and Moules, T., 2007. So round the spiral again: A reflective participatory research project with children and young people. *Educational Action Research* 15 (3), 385–402.

Ocloo, J., and Matthews, R., 2016. From tokenism to empowerment: progressing patient and public involvement in healthcare improvement. *BMJ Quality & Safety* 25 (8), 626–32.

Ofcom, 2020. *Children and Parents: Media Use and Attitudes Report 2019*. Ofcom.

Office for National Statistics, 2015. *Families and Households 2014.*

O'Kane, C., 2008. The Development of Participatory Techniques: Facilitating Children's Views about Decisions Which Affect Them, in: Christensen, P., and James, A. (eds), *Research with Children: Perspectives and Practices*. Routledge, London, pp. 222–38.

O'Keeffe, G. S., Clarke-Pearson, K., and Council on Communications and Media, 2011. The impact of social media on children, adolescents, and families. *Pediatrics* 127(4), 800–4.

Open Letter, 2019. Climate crisis and a betrayed generation. *The Guardian*, 1 March, https://www.theguardian.com/environment/2019/mar/01/youth-climate-change-strikers-open-letter-to-world-leaders (accessed 30 June 2020).

Orellana, M. F., 2001. The work kids do: Mexican and Central American immigrant children's contributions to households and schools in California. *Harvard Educational Review* 71 (3), 366–90.

———, 2009. *Translating Childhoods: Immigrant Youth, Language, and Culture*. Rutgers University Press, New Brunswick, NJ.

Orkin, K., 2010. In the child's best interests? Legislation on children's work in Ethiopia. *Journal of International Development* 22 (8), 1102–14.

Oswell, D., 2013. *The Agency of Children: From Family to Global Human Rights*. Cambridge University Press, New York.

Pak, J., 2014. Malaysia's love for the cane is questioned. BBC News Kuala Lumpur, 5 April 2014, https://www.bbc.com/news/magazine-26883902 (accessed 17 October 2017).

Palmer, S., 2016. Why the iPad is a far bigger threat to our children than anyone realises: Ten years ago, psychologist Sue Palmer predicted the toxic effects of social media. Now she sees a worrying new danger. *Daily Mail*, 27 January, http://www.dailymail.co.uk/femail/article-3420064/Why-iPad-far-bigger-threat-children-realises-Ten-years-ago-psychologist-SUE-PALMER-predicted-toxic-effects-social-media-sees-worrying-new-danger.html (accessed 30 June 2020).

Pansardi, P., 2012. *Power to* and *power over:* Two distinct concepts of power? *Journal of Political Power* 5 (1), 73–89.

Parsons, T., 1951. *The Social System.* London: Routledge and Kegan Paul, London.

Parsons, T., and Bales, R. F., 1956. *Family Socialisation and Interaction Process.* Free Press, New York.

Parton, N., 2011. Child protection and safeguarding in England: Changing and competing conceptions of risk and their implications for social work. *British Journal of Social Work* 41 (5), 854–75.

Partovi, M., and Wyness, M., 2020. Breaking the silence: Working with pupil voice in Iranian primary schools. *Educational Review*, 1–17. https://doi.org/10.1080/00131911.2020.1713051.

Payne, R., 2012. Agents of support: Intra-generational relationships and the role of agency in the support networks of child-headed households in Zambia. *Children's Geographies* 10 (3), 293–306.

Pells, K., 2012. 'Rights are everything we don't have': Clashing conceptions of vulnerability and agency in the daily lives of Rwandan children and youth. *Children's Geographies* 10 (4), 427–40.

Percy-Smith, B., 2010. Councils, consultations and community: Rethinking the spaces for children and young people's participation. *Children's Geographies* 8 (2), 107–22.

Perry-Hazan, L., 2016. Children's participation in national policymaking: 'You're so adorable, adorable, adorable! I'm speechless; so much fun!' *Children and Youth Services Review* 67, 105–13.

Phillips, C., 2011. *Child-Headed Households a Feasible Way Forward, or an Infringement of Children's Right to Alternative Care?* ERIC Clearinghouse.

Piaget, J., 1932. *The Language and Thought of the Child.* Routledge and Kegan Paul, London.

Popadić, D., Pavlović, Z., Petrović, D., and Kuzmanović, D., 2016. *Global Kids Online SERBIA Balancing between Opportunities and Risks: Results from the Pilot Study.* Global Kids Online/UNICEF, University of Belgrade.

Postman, N., 1982. *The Disappearance of Childhood.* Knopf Doubleday, Westminster.

Power, S., Rhys, M., Taylor, C., and Waldron, S., 2019. How child-centred education favours some learners more than others. *Review of Education* 7 (3), 570–92.

Prensky, M., 2001. Digital natives, digital immigrants. *On the Horizon* 9 (5), 1–6.

Prensky, M., 2005. Listen to the natives. *Educational Leadership* 63 (4), 8–13.

Prout, A., 2005. *The Future of Childhood: Towards an Interdisciplinary Study of Children.* RoutledgeFalmer, London.

Prout, A., and James, A., 1997. *Constructing and Reconstruction Childhood,* 2nd ed. RoutledgeFalmer, London.

Punch, S., 2002. Research with children – the same or different from research with adults? *Childhood* 9 (3), 321–41.

———, 2016a. Exploring Children's Agency across Majority and Minority World Contexts, in: Esser, F., Baader, M., Betz, T., and Hungerland, B. (eds), *Reconceptualising Agency and Childhood: New Perspectives in Childhood Studies,* Routledge Research in Education. Routledge, Abingdon, Oxon, pp. 183–96.

———, 2016b. Cross-world and cross-disciplinary dialogue: A more integrated, global approach to childhood studies. *Global Studies of Childhood,* 6 (3): 352–64.

Quantin, C., and Tubert-Bitter, P., 2022. COVID-19 and social inequalities: A complex and dynamic interaction. *The Lancet* 7.

Quennerstedt, A., 2010. Children, but not really humans? Critical reflections on the hampering effect of the '3 p's'. *International Journal of Children's Rights* 18 (4), 619–35.

Qvortrup, J., 1994. Childhood Matters: An Introduction, in: Qvortrup, J., Bardy, M., Sgritta, G., and Wintersberger, H. (eds), *Childhood Matters: Social Theory, Practice and Politics, Public Policy and Social Welfare*. Avebury, Aldershot.

Rahman-Jones, I., 2018. Florida shooting: How teenagers started a political campaign in 30 days. *BBC Newsbeat*, 19 March, https://www.bbc.co.uk/news/newsbeat-43392821 (accessed 30 June 2020).

Rajabi-Ardeshiri, M., 2009. The rights of the child in the Islamic context: The challenges of the local and the global. *International Journal of Children's Rights* 17 (3), 475–89.

Raley, R. K., and Sweeney, M. M., 2020. Divorce, repartnering, and stepfamilies: A decade in review. *Journal of Marriage and Family* 82 (1), 81–99.

Rappaport, J., 1981. In praise of paradox: A social policy of empowerment over prevention. *American Journal of Community Psychology* 9 (1), 1–25.

Ravalli, M. J., and Paoloni, P. C., 2016. *Argentina – Research Study on the Perceptions and Habits of Children and Adolescents on the Use of Technologies, the Internet and Social Media*. Global Kids Online/UNICEF.

Regeringen, 2018. *Ét Danmark uden parallelsamfund: ingen ghettoer i 2030*. Økonomi- og Indenrigsministeriet.

Reig Alcaraz, M., Siles González, J., and Solano Ruiz, C., 2014. Attitudes towards female genital mutilation: An integrative review. *International Nursing Review* 61 (1), 25–34.

Reynaert, D., Bouverne-de-Bie, M., and Vandevelde, S., 2009. A review of children's rights literature since the adoption of the United Nations Convention on the Rights of the Child. *Childhood* 16 (4), 518–34.

Richards, D., Caldwell, P. H., and Go, H., 2015. Impact of social media on the health of children and young people: Social media and the health of young people. *Journal of Paediatrics and Child Health* 51 (12), 1152–57.

Ridge, T., 2017. The 'go-between': Low-income children negotiating relationships of money and care with their separated parents. *Children & Society* 31 (2), 87–97.

Riesman, D., 1950. *The Lonely Crowd*. Yale University Press, New Haven, CT.

Robinson, C., and Kellett, M., 2004. Power, in: Fraser, S. (ed.), *Doing Research with Children and Young People*. Sage, London, pp. 81–96.

Rodrick, S., 2020. How one Swedish teenager armed with a homemade sign ignited a crusade and became the leader of a movement. *Rolling Stone*, 26 March, https://www.rollingstone.com/politics/politics-features/greta-thunberg-climate-crisis-cover-965949/ (accessed 30 June 2020).

Rosen, D. M., 2007. Child soldiers, international humanitarian law, and the globalization of childhood. *American Anthropologist* 109 (2), 296–306.

Rowland, A., Gerry, F., and Stanton, M., 2017. Physical punishment of children. *International Journal of Children's Rights* 25 (1), 165–95.

Ryan, S., 2005. Freedom to Choose: Examining Children's Experiences in Choice Time, in: Yelland, N. (ed.), *Critical Issues in Early Childhood Education*. Open University Press, Maidenhead, pp. 99–114.

Sadowski, C., and McIntosh, J. E., 2016. On laughter and loss: Children's views of shared time, parenting and security post-separation. *Childhood* 23 (1), 69–86.

Salamon, E., 2018. March for Our Lives awakens the spirit of student and media activism of the 1960s. *The Conversation*, 24 March, https://theconversation.com/march-for-our-lives-awakens-the-spirit-of-student-and-media-activism-of-the-1960s-93713 (accessed 30 June 2020).

Salmivalli, C., Kärnä, A., and Poskiparta, E., 2011. Counteracting bullying in Finland: The KiVa program and its effects on different forms of being bullied. *International Journal of Behavioral Development* 35 (5), 405–11.

Sandberg, K., 2015. The Convention on the Rights of the Child and the vulnerability of children. *Nordic Journal of International Law* 84 (2), 221–47.

Sarangapani, P. M., 2003. Childhood and schooling in an Indian village. *Childhood* 10 (4), 403–18.

Saunders, B. J., 2013. Ending the physical punishment of children by parents in the English-speaking world: The impact of language, tradition and law. *International Journal of Children's Rights* 21 (2), 278–304.

Schabas, W., 1996. Reservations to the Convention on the Rights of the Child. *Human Rights Quarterly* 2, 472–91.

Schäfer, N., and Yarwood, R., 2008. Involving young people as researchers: Uncovering multiple power relations among youths. *Children's Geographies* 6 (2), 121–35.

Seabrook, J., 1998. Children of the market. *Race & Class* 39 (4), 37–48.

Seiter, E., 1993. *Sold Separately: Children and Parents in Consumer Culture*, Rutgers Series in Communications, media, and Culture. Rutgers University Press, New Brunswick, NJ.

Selwyn, N., 2009. The digital native – myth and reality. *Aslib Proceedings* 61 (4), 364–79.

Selwyn, N., 2001. *Children, Computers and the Discursive Construction of the Information Society.* Presented at the European Sociological Association Conference, Helsinki.

Sengupta, S., 2019. Protesting climate change, young people take to streets in a global strike. *New York Times*, 20 September, https://www.nytimes.com/2019/09/20/climate/global-climate-strike.html (accessed 30 June 2020).

Shah, A. 2010. Children as consumers, *Global Issues*, http://www.globalissues.org/article/237/children-as-consumers (accessed 27 August 2020).

Sharp, C., and Skipp, A., 2022. *Four Things We Learned about the Impact of Covid-19 on Mainstream Schools and Special Education Settings in 2020.* National Foundation for Educational Research, Slough.

Sharp, R., Green, A., and Lewis, J., 1975. *Education and Social Control: A Study in Progressive Primary Education.* Taylor and Francis, Milton.

Shier, H., 2001. Pathways to participation: Openings, opportunities and obligations. *Children & Society* 15 (2), 107–17.

———, 2019. Student Voice and Children's Rights: Power, Empowerment, and 'Protagonismo', in: Peters, M. A. (ed.), *Encyclopedia of Teacher Education*. Springer, Singapore, pp. 1–6.

Sime, D., and Fox, R., 2015. Home abroad: Eastern European children's family and peer relationships after migration. *Childhood* 22 (3), 377–93.

Skelton, T., 2007. Children, young people, UNICEF and participation. *Children's Geographies* 5 (1–2), 165–81.

Skinner, D., Tsheko, N., Mtero-Munyati, S., Segwabe, M., Chibatamoto, P., Mfecane, S., Chandiwana, B., Nkomo, N., Tlou, S., and Chitiyo, G., 2006. Towards a definition of orphaned and vulnerable children. *AIDS and Behavior* 10 (6), 619–26.

Sleijpen, M., Mooren, T., Kleber, R. J., and Boeije, H. R., 2017. Lives on hold: A qualitative study of young refugees' resilience strategies. *Childhood* 24 (3), 348–65.

Slicker, G., and Hustedt, J. T., 2019. Children's school readiness in socioeconomically diverse pre-K classrooms. *Early Child Development and Care* 190, 2366–79.

Smahel, D., Machackova, H., Mascheroni, G., Dedkova, L., Staksrud, E., Ólafsson, K., Livingstone, S., and Hasebrink, U., 2020. *EU Kids Online 2020 Survey Results from 19 Countries.* EUKids Online.

Smarth-Knight, R., 2019. I am taking part in the school climate strike. It's the only power I have. *The Guardian*, 15 February, https://www.theguardian.com/commentisfree/2019/feb/15/school-climate-strike-classroom-climate-change (accessed 30 June 2020).

Smith, A., 2007. Children as social actors: An introduction. *International Journal of Children's Rights* 15 (1), 1–4.

Smith, H. A., and Haslett, S. J., 2017. Children's rights in education research: From aims to outcomes. *Cambridge Journal of Education* 47(3), 413–38.

Sohn, S., Rees, P., Wildridge, B., Kalk, N. J., and Carter, B., 2019. Prevalence of problematic smartphone usage and associated mental health outcomes amongst children and young people: A systematic review, meta-analysis and GRADE of the evidence. *BMC Psychiatry* 19, 356.

Spyrou, S., 2011. The limits of children's voices: From authenticity to critical, reflexive representation. *Childhood* 18 (2), 151–65.

Spyrou, S., Arce, M.C., Eßer, F., Rosen, R., and Twum-Danso Imoh, A., 2018. Emerging scholars of childhood studies. *Childhood* 25 (4), 422–42.

Sriprakash, A., 2010. Child-centred education and the promise of democratic learning: Pedagogic messages in rural Indian primary schools. *International Journal of Educational Development* 30 (3), 297–304.

Stafford, A., Laybourn, A., Hill, M., and Walker, M., 2003. Having a say? Children and young people talk about consultation. *Children & Society* 17 (5), 361–73.

Stats SA, 2018. *General Household Survey*, South Africa.

Stelmach, B., 2016. Parents' participation on school councils analysed through Arnstein's ladder of participation. *School Leadership & Management* 36 (3), 271–91.

Steinbach, A., Kuhnt, A., and Knüll, M., 2016. The prevalence of single-parent families and stepfamilies in Europe: Can the Hajnal line help us to describe regional patterns? *History of the Family* 21 (4): 578–95.

Stewart, A., 2001. *Theories of Power and Domination: The Politics of Empowerment in Late Modernity*. Sage, London.

Sugrue, C., 1997. *Complexities of Teaching: Child-Centred Perspectives*, New Prospects Series. Falmer Press, London.

Supple, D., Roberts, A., Hudson, V., Masefield, S., Fitch, N., Rahmen, M., Flood, B., de Boer, W., Powell, P., and Wagers, S., 2015. From tokenism to meaningful engagement: Best practices in patient involvement in an EU project. *Research Involvement and Engagement* 1(1), 5.

Taft, J. K., 2015. 'Adults talk too much': Intergenerational dialogue and power in the Peruvian movement of working children. *Childhood* 22 (4), 460–73.

———, 2019. *The Kids Are in Charge: Youth Activism and Political Power*, Critical Perspectives on Youth. New York University Press, New York.

Taylor, J., Rahilly, T., Hunter, H., 2012. *Children Who Go Missing from Care: A Participatory Project with Young People as Peer Interviewers*. NSPCC; Quarriers.

Thaichon, P., 2017. Consumer socialization process: The role of age in children's online shopping behavior. *Journal of Retailing and Consumer Services* 34, 38–47.

*The Economist*, 2013. Cookie Monster crumbles. https://www.economist.com/international/2013/11/23/cookie-monster-crumbles (accessed 30 June 2020).

*The Lancet*, 2019. Power to the children. 03 March, https://www.thelancet.com/pdfs/journals/lanplh/PIIS2542-5196%2819%2930048-8.pdf (accessed 30 June 2020).

*The Local*, 2019. How Greta Thunberg's school strike became a global climate movement, 14 March, https://www.thelocal.se/20190314/how-greta-thunbergs-school-strike-became-a-global-climate-movement (accessed 30 June 2020).

Third, A., Bellerose, D., Dawkins, U., Keltie, E., and Pihl, K., 2014. *Children's Rights in the Digital Age: A Download from Children around the World*. Young and Well Cooperative Research Centre, Melbourne.

Thomson, J., Lanchin, S., and Moxon, D., 2015. *Be Real with Me: Using Peer Research to Explore the Journeys of Young People Who Run Away from Home or Care*. Railway Children, London.

Thomson, P., and Holdsworth, R., 2003. Theorizing change in the educational 'field': Re-readings of 'student participation' projects. *International Journal of Leadership in Education* 6 (4), 371–91.

Thornberg, R., and Elvstrand, H., 2012. Children's experiences of democracy, participation, and trust in school. *International Journal of Educational Research* 53, 44–54.

Thorne, B., 1987. Re-visioning women and social change: Where are the children? *Gender & Society* 1 (1), 85–109.

Thornton, L., and Brunton, P., 2015. *Understanding the Reggio Approach: Early Years Education in Practice*, 3rd ed. Routledge, London.

Thunberg and 46 Activists, 2019. Young people have led the climate strikes. Now we need adults to join us too. *The Guardian*, 23 May, https://www.theguardian.com/commentisfree/2019/may/23/greta-thunberg-young-people-climate-strikes-20-september (accessed 30 June 2020).

Tisdall , E. K. M., 2012. The challenge and challenging of childhood studies? Learning from disability studies and research with disabled children. *Children & Society* 26 (3), 181–91.

———, 2013. The transformation of participation? Exploring the potential of 'transformative participation' for theory and practice around children and young people's participation. *Global Studies of Childhood* 3 (2), 183–93.

Tisdall, E. K. M., and Bell, R., 2006. Included in Governance: Children's Participation in 'Public' Decision-Making, in: Tisdall, E. K. M., Davis, J., Hill, M., and Prout, A. (eds), *Children, Young People and Social Inclusion: Participation for What?* Policy Press, Bristol, pp. 105–20.

Tisdall, K., 2010. Governance and Participation, in: Percy-Smith, B., and Thomas, N. (eds), *A Handbook of Children and Young People's Participation: Perspectives from Theory and Practice*. Routledge, London.

Tsegaye, S., 2009. *Orphanhood in Africa: Old Problems and New Faces*, African Child Policy Forum, Addis Ababa.

Twum-Danso, A., 2010. The Construction of Childhood and the Socialisation of Children in Ghana: Implications for the Implementation of Article 12 of the CRC, in: Percy-Smith, B., and Thomas, N. (eds), *A Handbook of Children and Young People's Participation Perspectives from Theory and Practice*. Routledge, London, pp. 133–40.

UKRI, 2020. *Coronavirus in Children: Are Children Immune from Covid-19?* United Kingdom Research and Innovation. https://coronavirusexplained.ukri.org/en/article/und0008/ (accessed 26 August 2020).

UN Women, 2000. The feminization of poverty – fact sheet no. 1. https://www.un.org/womenwatch/daw/followup/session/presskit/fs1.htm (accessed 25 August 2020).

Underhill, G., 2015. The trials of child headed families. *Mail & Guardian*, https://mg.co.za/article/2015-01-30-00-the-trials-of-child-headed-families (accessed 30 June 2020).

United Nations (UN), 2015. *Millennium Development Goals Report 2014*, United Nations, Geneva.

UNESCO, 2015. *EFA Global Monitoring Report 2015.*

UNICEF, 1989. *The United Nations Convention on the Rights of the Child.*

────── (ed.), 2017. *Children in a Digital World: The State of the World's Children.* UNICEF, New York.

──────, 2020. *COVID-19 and Its Implications for Protecting Children Online.* UNICEF, New York.

Uprichard, E., 2008. Children as 'being and becomings': Children, childhood and temporality, *Children & Society*, 22, 303–13.

Utas, M., 2005. Victimcy, girlfriending, soldiering: Tactic agency in a young woman's social navigation of the Liberian war zone. *Anthropological Quarterly* 78 (2), 403–30.

Valentine, K. 2011. Accounting for agency. *Children & Society* 25 (3), 347–58.

van Reijmersdal, E. A., Rozendaal, E., Smink, N., van Noort, G., and Buijzen, M., 2017. Processes and effects of targeted online advertising among children. *International Journal of Advertising* 36 (3), 396–414.

Vincent, C., Ball, S., Rollock, N., and Gillborn, D., 2013. Three generations of racism: Black middle-class children and schooling. *British Journal of Sociology of Education* 34 (5–6), 929–46.

Vincent, C., and Maxwell, C., 2016. Parenting priorities and pressures: Furthering understanding of 'concerted cultivation'. *Discourse: Studies in the Cultural Politics of Education* 37 (2), 269–81.

Vis, S. A., Strandbu, A., Holtan, A., and Thomas, N., 2011. Participation and health – a research review of child participation in planning and decision-making: Child participation in planning and decision-making. *Child & Family Social Work* 16 (3), 325–35.

Viviers, A., and Lombard, A., 2013. The ethics of children's participation: Fundamental to children's rights realization in Africa. *International Social Work* 56 (1), 7–21.

Wahlström, M., et al., 2019. *Protest for a Future: Composition, Mobilization and Motives of the Participants in Fridays For Future Climate Protests on 15 March, 2019 in 13 European Cities,* retrieved from eprints.keele.ac.uk/6571/ (accessed 25 November 2020).

Walkerdine, V., 1984. Developmental Psychology and the Child-Centred Pedagogy: The Insertion of Piaget into Early Education, in: Henriques, J., Holloway, W., Urwin, C., Venn, C., and Walkerdine, V. (eds), *Changing the Subject: Psychology, Social Regulation and Subjectivity.* Methuen, London, pp. 153–201.

──────, 1993. Beyond developmentalism? *Theory & Psychology* 3 (4), 451–69.

Wallerstein, J. S., Lewis, J., and Blakeslee, S., 2014. *The Unexpected Legacy of Divorce: A 25 Year Landmark Study,* 1st Hachette trade ed. Hachette, New York.

Walters, R., and Woodward, R., 2007. Punishing 'poor parents': 'respect', 'responsibility' and parenting orders in Scotland. *Youth Justice* 7 (1), 5–20.

Weber, M., 1978. *Economy and Society.* California University Press, Berkeley.

Wells, K., 2009. Policy and Practice, in: *Childhood in a Global Perspective.* Polity, Cambridge, pp. 26–46.

White, S. C., and Choudhury, S. A., 2007. The politics of child participation in international development: The dilemma of agency, *European Journal of Development Research* 19 (4), 529–50.

Whitman, J. Q., 2003. The two Western cultures of privacy: Dignity versus liberty. *SSRN Electronic Journal.* https://doi.org/10.2139/ssrn.476041.

Whitty, G., and Wisby, E., 2007. Whose voice? An exploration of the current policy interest in pupil involvement in school decision-making. *International Studies in Sociology of Education* 17 (3), 303–19.

Wickenden, M., and Kembhavi-Tam, G., 2014. Ask us too! Doing participatory research with disabled children in the global south. *Childhood* 21 (3), 400–17.

Widding, U., 2018. Parental determinism in the Swedish strategy for parenting support. *Social Policy and Society* 17 (3), 481–90.

Williams, E., 2004. *Children's Participation and Policy Change in South Asia* (CHIP report no. 6). Childhood Poverty Research and Policy Centre, Save the Children UK, London.

Willumsen, E., Hugaas, J. V., and Studsrød, I., 2014. The child as co-researcher – moral and epistemological issues in childhood research. *Ethics and Social Welfare* 8 (4), 332–49.

Woodhead, M., 2009. Child Development and the Development of Childhood, in: Qvortrup, J., Corsaro, W. A., and Honig, M.-S. (eds), *The Palgrave Handbook of Childhood Studies*. Palgrave Macmillan, Basingstoke, Hampshire, pp. 46–61.

World Bank, 2023. *Global Economic Prospects, January 2023*. World Bank, Washington, DC https://doi.org/10.1586/978-1-4648-1906-3.

Wyness, M. G., 2001. Children, childhood and political participation: Case studies of young people's councils. *International Journal of Children's Rights* 9, 193–212. https://doi.org/10.1163/15718180120494937.

———, 2009. Children representing children: Participation and the problem of diversity in UK youth councils. *Childhood* 16 (4), 535–52.

———, 2013a. Children's participation and intergenerational dialogue: Bringing adults back into the analysis. *Childhood* 20 (4), 429–42.

———, 2013b. Global standards and deficit childhoods: The contested meaning of children's participation. *Children's Geographies* 11 (3), 340–53.

———, 2015. *Childhood*, Key Concepts Series. Polity Press, Cambridge, UK.

———, 2018. *Childhood, Culture & Society: In a Global Context*. Sage, Los Angeles.

———, 2018. Children's Participation: Definitions, Disputes and Narratives, in: Baraldi, C., and Cockburn, T. (eds), *Theorising Childhood: Citizenship, Rights and Participation, Studies in Childhood and Youth*. Palgrave Macmillan, Switzerland, pp. 53–72.

———, 2019. Introduction, in: Wyness, M. G. (ed.), *Childhood and Society*, Palgrave Macmillan, Basingstoke, pp. 1–4.

———, 2020. The responsible parent and networks of support: A case study of school engagement in a challenging environment. *British Educational Research Journal* 46, 161–76. https://doi.org/10.1002/berj.3573.

———, 2023. The uneven distribution of children's rights: schooling, caring and living rights. *International Journal of Children's Rights*. Advanced article.

Xia, X., Hackett, R. K., and Webster, L., 2020. Chinese parental involvement and children's school readiness: The moderating role of parenting style. *Early Education and Development* 31 (2), 289–307.

Xie, S., and Li, H., 2018. Does tiger parenting work in contemporary China? Exploring the relationships between parenting profiles and preschoolers' school readiness in a Chinese context. *Early Child Development and Care* 188 (12), 1826–42.

Yamashita, H., and Davies, L., 2012. *School Councils, School Improvement*. School Councils UK, London.

Yang, Y., 2013. A qualitative study of teachers' involvement in children's play. *Literacy Information and Computer Education Journal* 4 (4), 1244–51.

Zimmerman, M. A., 1995. Psychological empowerment: Issues and illustrations. *American Journal of Community Psychology* 23 (5), 581–99.

# INDEX